BE LESS

DICKISH

the definitive self-help book about men

DAVID COATES

COREY KILPACK

ISBN 9798514435616

CONTENTS

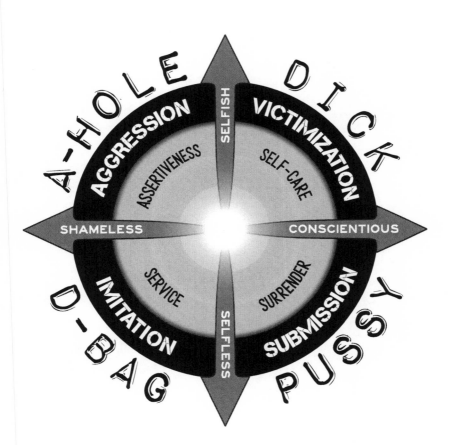

PREFACE

by Corey Kilpack

Why do dudes do the shit they do? Do they really need to be such **assholes**? No, they don't. And yet this assholery just keeps happening. Some guys fake it like **douchebags**, playing a role for themselves and others. There's the guy who's a perpetual self-declared victim, the single most important person in his own world. You know that self-righteous **dick**—or maybe you *are* that dick. And what does it mean to be a **pussy**? The term makes us cringe, but "don't be a pussy" is all too common vernacular.

Understanding and recognizing these kinds of men is the first step in living a more centered and satisfying life. Men can be **selfish**, and there's a time and a place for that. But many are also **selfless**, putting the needs of others before their own. A man might be **shameless** in one situation, and **conscientious** of others in a different setting. Knowing how and why we react to life, to new information, and to other people can help us respond better without losing our shit over nothing.

Could we say all this without all the goddamn naughty words? The Mom thinks so. I don't. We're saying it like you say it and like you hear it. Profane and profound. Sincere and authentic. The characters in this book are composites of the real stories of real people. These archetypes are all of us.

Have fun and brace yourself. This is one hell of a ride.

PART 1
THE ARCHETYPES OF MEN

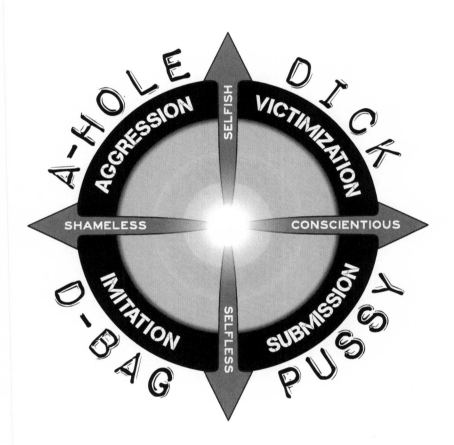

INTRODUCTION TO THE ARCHETYPES

*All of us cope in different ways. We all spin out, away from our centers, but at our extremes, we embody different archetypes: You might be a rageful, aggressive **asshole** who furiously shits on others. Or if you're a submissive **pussy**, you may roll over to avoid failure, confrontation, or further disappointment. You may be a **douchebag**, sidestepping reality as a fictional character in your own scripted story, complete with props. You might be a **dick**, the impossible victim, defiantly resisting connection and real life, because it's always rigged against you.*

None of us are exactly one of these guys; we may be a combination of these labels, with some traits more palpable than others. But sometimes—too damn much of the time—we go to extremes.

Dick State University

Do you remember all those amazing classes we took before graduating to adulthood? The courses that helped us transition so smoothly from volatile teens into emotionally healthy and fully self-actualized adults? Here are a few of my favorite crucial courses:

- *Wild and Complex Emotions and How to Navigate Them*
- *The Complex Relationship Between You and Your Parents*
- *Listening to Your Intuition and Ignoring the Bullshit*
- *QTIP 101: Quit Taking It Personally*
- *Your Spinning Mind and How to Tame It*
- *Dick Pics Are Hard to Erase: A Guide to Technology and Sex*
- *Vulnerability: The Gateway to Connection*

- *Self-Defense for Brawls*
- *Embracing Your Sexuality at Your Own Pace*
- *How to Be Alone*
- *The Fine Art of Saying No*
- *You're Beautiful and Fucking Amazing*
- *Gender and Race: A Guide to Equality and Inclusion*
- *Meet the Clit!*

Weren't those classes useful? Weren't they great? Given how important these skills are to our health and happiness, it only makes sense that our society would teach these kinds of classes. And I bet you, like me, *aced* them.

Wait, what? You never took any classes like those? No one taught you anything about dealing with insecurity or shame? Self-criticism? Addiction? Sexuality? Communication? Well, *me fucking neither*.

Calculus might be helpful for those who pursue a career in the sciences, and everyone should read *To Kill a Mockingbird*, but c'mon, man! How could we be given endless instruction on how to solve algebra problems, but zero guidance on relationship problems? Language Arts, but nothing on the art of a genuine apology? There's pressure to *appear* put together, happy, and fulfilled, but we are left to teach ourselves how to actually *be* put together, happy, and fulfilled. For the wisest among us, that's a challenge; for many of us, it's a clusterfuck of failure and frustration.

How Are You Doing Your Life?

"Why are you here?" This is a question I ask new clients at my psychotherapy practice in San Francisco. *Why* is a necessary question, but I'm always more interested in the *how*: How are you doing your life? *How* do you respond to your triggers? *How*...?

I won't say I've seen it all; I haven't. But I've seen enough to know that while the *why* is always different and unique, the *how* is the key to healing and building: How do you respond to loss in your life? How are you dealing with financial angst? How do you respond to relationship stress? If you're recovering from abuse, how do you do that? If you experience periods of self-hatred, how do you navigate them? Not why. Why invites interpretation. How takes us right into the guts.

Life will upset us; it's upsetting. It will scare us; it's scary. It will challenge us; it's challenging. But how do you respond when you're triggered? How have you adapted through childhood, adolescence, and into adulthood?

You're a unique individual with the need for safety and belonging, pushing up against family and other systems. As you moved on, you had to define yourself. But how? How did you do that? Well, however you did it, you did it. You still do it. And how you did it back then shaped who you are now. Underneath the heartbreaking *what* is the beautiful *how*. Given all this trauma, look at what you did.

How did you pull it off? Did you become a pleaser, a peacemaker? Brilliant! Did you protect your true self with a disguise? Nice move! Did you learn not to feel because feeling anything at all was just too painful? Right on! Spectacular! That's how you did it, and it made sense. Can you see just how sensical it was? Genius. You did what you had to do. You did good. Well done!

You adapted to minimize the unbearable shame, aloneness, worthlessness, abuse, and neglect. You adapted to the regular, inevitable life traumas and stresses: a disappointed parent, death, sibling dynamics. You played out these strategies in your childhood, and you're likely playing out the same adaptive strategies as an adult. You're largely the product of these strategies; your thoughts and beliefs evolved from these brilliant and necessary adaptations. Whether you're a taker, a maker, a foresaker, or a faker, these adaptations are how you've done life, and they're how you *do* life. You patched together skills to minimize what is overwhelming.

You developed strategies to shield yourself: you complain, point, fight, reject, sulk, stew, detach, isolate. Take a bow—truly. Let's honor your adaptive "how." Let's give the asshole, the pussy, the douchebag, and the dick their due. But let's take a look and see what still works and what needs to go away, because these compensations can sever you from what is good and right and true and beautiful about life.

I am not making excuses for shitty behavior. I don't want anyone to be a hostile *asshole*, and I don't want anyone to submit like a total *pussy*, either. I want men and women to be powerful and joyful. I've wanted this for all those who've come into my practice over the years, and I want it for anyone reading this book. We need generous, assertive, self-possessed men. I want us to stop acting out our fear and pain on the world and on our families. *Douchebags* front and imitate, but they lack substance. *Dicks* blame and complain, offering little else. To live life at these extremes is to live a limited life.

We're not *reclaiming* "asshole," "pussy," "douchebag," or "dick." There's no attempt here to dull the profanity or the impact of these names, but this isn't just another shock book full of naughty words. These are the words that have been passed on for generations to describe archetypes that predate our civilizations. These names sting for a reason—they hold truth. They describe us in our extreme forms.

You will ask yourself where you fit in the scheme. You may be a complete asshole, a total dick, or some amoeba-shaped blob at the intersection of all these archetypes. But facing the worst in you honestly is how you're able to become your best self. Staring the profane in the face will grant you access to the profound.

1
THE ASSHOLE

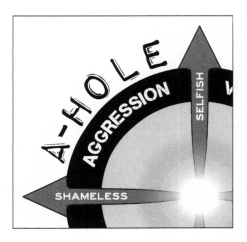

The asshole is the so-called alpha male, but that term fails to convey the impact of his danger. He is shameless. Selfish. Aggressive.

Anyone who's been hurt by one of these characters—likely a long list—may seek a diagnosis of the asshole's condition. Dr. Google Search might say that his aggressiveness, coupled with his failure to recognize and adopt social norms, puts the asshole in the realm of antisocial personality disorder.

Jonah, the Asshole

Jonah skips the mob at the hostess stand and drops himself into a booth that could easily seat six. *It's a shitshow out there,* he thinks, grabbing the elbow of a passing server. "Jack and Coke, light on the ice, and an order of wings with extra sauce."

"Sir, you have to wait to be seated. Please go to the..."

His callused hand tightens its grip on her elbow in a way that escalates and clarifies. He squints as he stares her down.

Stunned, she looks away, murmuring, "There's a charge for the, umm, extra sauce; I'm sorry."

"And there's a big tip in it for you, doll," Jonah adds, releasing his grip and focusing on his phone. The manager quickly arrives, but Jonah interrupts him before he can speak. "I'm not moving, boss, so unless you wanna try to force me out,"—Jonah smiles big here—"I'd suggest you go check on my order instead." *Oh, and fuck you,* Jonah thinks to himself, going back to his phone. By the time Jonah's drink and wings have landed, he's already reamed out his business partner for hiring "shade-tree labor" and insulted his tile contractor for not finishing a project on time. He feels eyes on him; he likes it. He meets some dirty looks, and the eyes look away. "That's right," he mutters, and he grabs the elbow of a different server to order another drink. He finishes, leaving the promised big tip; he appreciates the hustle of the servers. The manager—well, that's a different story.

"I've wasted an hour at this sagging outhouse you've pawned off as a restaurant," Jonah tells the red-faced twenty-something. He's secretly thrilled by the people in the lobby who've stopped talking to listen. Power surges through him. The night's just getting started.

He pops an Altoid as he gets into his Ford F-350, turns up Led Zeppelin, and, on his way to one of his regular liquor stores for some cheap Lodi Zinfandel, he cuts off a couple trying to cross the street with a stroller.

His interest in Megan is selfish at best. She's twenty-seven, a patent lawyer at Google. She has a nice place in the city, near many of Jonah's job sites. Without remorse or concern for anyone else, Jonah entertains himself in the company of—and at the emotional expense of—a young professional woman. It's convenient, it's hot, and it serves his ego. To Jonah, Megan isn't worth much more than the cheapest bottle of Zinfandel.

It's nearly midnight by the time Jonah gets to his suburban Piedmont home. He's surprised to see Shaylee in the living room. She greets him with a strained smile. "I made dinner for you," she says, marking her place in a Montessori school curriculum with her finger. Her silk robe fits like a pencil dress. She's a recent graduate of a yoga teacher training course and a reader of healing books. The yoga, the courses, the healthy bullshit—it all makes Jonah's skin crawl. But tonight, Jonah doesn't give a shit. He's just had some great sex, then dinner from the new Thai restaurant below Megan's hip-as-fuck San Francisco condo.

"Babe," he says, his voice trailing off, "I already ate." Shaylee starts to ask him what he had, but he's already on his way to the bathroom to shower off Megan's scent. In their sixteen years together, she's questioned him about his late-night "business meetings" only once, and she eventually apologized for doubting his fidelity. Afterward, he felt vindicated, and Shaylee got a diagnosis of depression, some prescriptions, and eventually, a personal trainer or two.

* * *

The next morning, Jonah goes over a list of Saturday chores Shaylee's been compiling and texting him about all week. *There's a reason God made children*, he thinks, with a private smile. When his oldest son comes into the kitchen, Jonah corners him. "Why are you all geared up?" Jonah says, eyeing his son's shoes and equipment.

"I'm playing soccer with some friends. Everyone's going."

"Not so fast, pal. We also agreed that you'd mow the lawn and finish getting things ready for your mom."

"But Dad, you said I—" *Snap!* Jonah's contractor fingers make an echo through multiple rooms.

"Goddammit." Jonah points to the garage until his son sets down his backpack and follows his father's pointing finger. "And don't blow the grass into the pool again," he calls after him.

Ding. Jonah gets a text. Megan is still in the same bed where they fucked last night. It's just her tits. "Up your game. Where do your legs meet?" he writes back as Shaylee comes into the kitchen and finds the coffeepot empty. Jonah cups his phone and sees another text—more of Megan. He grins and texts back, oblivious to Shaylee as she grinds her teeth and tightens her fists.

By noon, the lawn is as pristine as a golf course. There's not a blade of grass in the pool or on the pool deck. The balls, bikes, and toys are hidden from Jonah's view. The boys have raked up the shredded hacky sack that went through the lawnmower; it was something Jonah gave them. Jonah's older sons have missed their Saturday morning plans.

In the den, Jonah sits with his whiskey and beer, watching a college football game. But calling it the game is perhaps too generous: he's watching Lee Corso and Kirk Herbstreit fake-argue and predict stupid shit while fans scream doucheries from behind the set. Jonah is oblivious to the presence of his wife.

Shaylee believes, with familiar conviction, that *this* is the time she'll finally confront Jonah about passing off work and disrupting everyone else's plans. He isn't even watching the game—it's halftime or pregame, or a commercial about football. She can't tell the difference; nobody can. She steels herself, feels her ground, and this time, finally speaks up—finally, after so many years. "They're not your work crew, Jonah. They're your children. Don't you see what you're doing to them? Don't you care?"

He gives her a quick glance. "Now? Seriously, *now*?" He raises the volume.

Shaylee retreats, feeling the familiar disappointment and muttering audibly, "Fuck this. Fuck my life. And fuck him. Asshole."

Characteristics of the Asshole

Whether Jonah is disrupting a restaurant, watching characters in costumes argue about football games they don't play, bitching about a city inspector's decision, or cheating and lying, he's a familiar character.

We've seen him in real life, not just in the movies. We know this guy. We're equally familiar with Shaylee and Megan.

How would a woman characterize an asshole? Ask one, and she'll be quick to provide a litany of examples: An asshole will eye her plate of nachos and tell her it'll go straight to her hips, even though he's sporting a spare tire of his own. He'll tell her that it "takes a lot of guts" to dress like her. An asshole will hit on her best friend right in front of her. He'll make her feel stupid for wanting to use condoms. But she might also describe him as a loyal protector, a fierce advocate, or a leader.

What does it mean to be an asshole, and how does it feel on the receiving end? How is an asshole different from a pussy, a douchebag, or a dick? What kind of madness does it generate…and where the hell do these fuckers come from, anyway?

The asshole is not just impervious to social cues; he's actually *turned on* by the very situations most of us take pains to avoid. We desire peace, even if that peace sometimes means eating shit. The asshole, on the other hand, wants what he wants when he wants it, and he's hellbent on achieving it. He has no remorse or inhibition.

Laws exist to protect the rights of individuals and to maintain social order. Assholes violate those rights and disrupt stability. They can do so without *technically* breaking the law, so being an asshole often incurs no legal consequences, only social consequences—and the asshole is largely unaffected by these. Did Jonah break the law in the restaurant by seating himself at a six-top? It's a gray area. But was the manager going to risk the reputation of the restaurant—not to mention personal humiliation—by causing a scene and confronting an asshole like Jonah? Fuck no. Damaging private property is a criminal act that might result in incarceration; inflicting psychological harm is more nebulous. It's illegal to smash the beer fridge at 7-Eleven. It *is* legal to startle the clerk, let him hear you call him a punk-ass bitch, then laugh at his non-response. While you're at it, tough guy, why not insult the panhandler just outside and tell him to "get a fucking job"? There are probably no legal consequences for that thrill either.

You might hate the asshole, and you might be afraid of him. You might also wonder how it would feel to be like him—blunt, indifferent, shameless, and unapologetically self-serving. Where some of us hesitate to speak up, then berate ourselves later for not telling our truth, the Jonahs of the world push us aside on their way to the megaphone.

You can't seem to win against the asshole. If you resort to his kind of behavior and try to push back, his resilience only seems to strengthen. It's this unflappability that's so incredibly maddening. You leave an interaction with an asshole feeling ridiculed, defiled, bewildered, and crushed. The asshole, on the other hand, is invigorated. If you live with an asshole, you forever concede the last word: it's the end when an asshole *says* it's the end.

We love action movies because the hero valiantly stands up to villains, who are often assholes. Our heroes are so fearless in the face of these assholes that they'll even crack jokes in the middle of a shootout. Off-screen, however, most of us have nervous systems that are geared less to gallantry and more to survival. Indignity and regret might suck, but they won't kill us; an asshole like Jonah just might.

We are constantly monitoring and assessing threats. We're hardwired for it. One of the primary reasons we're here today is because our ancestors were capable of surviving perils far more catastrophic than Jonah. Today, most threats we encounter are from other humans, not tigers, but the same mechanisms for survival persist. We look for nonverbal cues, tracking body language, pupil dilation, vocal intonation, movement, and proximity. We keep an eye on the twitchy guy walking toward us on the sidewalk. We maintain our distance from the sketchy-looking dude at the liquor store. When a voice is raised in our vicinity, we evaluate exit strategies and weigh our options. We are hardwired to survive. It is this survival instinct, this wiring, that assholes exploit; this is how they're able to affect us on such a bone-deep level.

While most of us gravitate toward the safer survival responses (flee, freeze, or appease), assholes usually choose just one response: fight. They escalate the situation, anchoring themselves through instigation. Recognizing this, and foreseeing the discomfort and danger that might ensue, people capitulate to the aggressor. This is why Jonah gets his way—why Shaylee, for example, apologizes for doubting his fidelity. Assholes aren't merely nuisances or thorns in the side. They evoke a critical evolutionary response in us, one that's more powerful than our rational minds. Assholes disrupt our baseline experience of safety and security on another level, too: We all have repositories of feelings from our childhood years that we've worked hard to keep locked away, feelings of powerlessness and terror. Assholes target these feelings.

Jonah in His Element

By virtue of their mailing address, Jonah and Shaylee are invited to their neighbor's summer party. Shaylee and the boys are gone for the weekend, so Jonah agrees to go to the party and drop off a gift Shaylee prepared. He doesn't RSVP—*nobody pays attention to that shit*—and he arrives an hour and a half late. The bash is in full swing. He eyes the makeshift tiki bar and gets in line. After what seems to Jonah like a long wait, he arrives at the bar. "Those margaritas look good," Jonah says. "I'll have one of those." Greg, who's volunteering at the bar, hands him a drink. Jonah taps the rim of the glass. "Weak pour," he says, sliding the drink back toward Greg.

The men and women in line are surprised. Some mutter a few complaints. This only heightens Jonah's energy. Greg takes a step back. Jonah's behavior is beyond a faux pas; he's flouting the basic rules of courtesy and consideration. "Hey, buddy," Greg says.

"That's," Jonah taps the rim of the glass again, "a weak pour. And that line was slow as shit; can you go ahead and pour me a Laphroaig, too? I see it up top there. That's the good stuff."

Greg's annoyed, but he's also alarmed. He's pissed, but he's also unsettled, as are the others within earshot. The whole mood shifts. Arms are crossed. Conversations quiet down or stop altogether. A man in the corner perks up, silencing his date. All around, jaws clench.

Greg begrudgingly pours a glass of Laphroaig and passes both full drinks to Jonah without a word. Jonah smirks, as if to say, "I knew you didn't have it in you, bitch." With that, he saunters off, feeling brilliant. "You all have a fine night," he says for everyone in earshot, putting them in the same camp as the conciliatory bartender. Assholes aren't known for their subtlety. Relief washes through the group as Jonah walks away, but the atmosphere has changed irrevocably. Everyone feels dirty, somehow—disgraced and demeaned. This is no coincidence. Assholes shit on others, and the stink lingers in their wake.

The bartender chastises himself for the rest of the night. He can't get his groove back behind the bar. He should have told Jonah to go fuck himself when he asked for a second pour. Distracted, he envisions different scenarios, scenes in which he kicks Jonah's ass and throws him to the curb.

Greg tries to convince himself that he'll find Jonah later, that he'll wipe that smug look right off his face, but he knows in his heart that he never would, that if he were to see him again around town, he'd turn and walk the other way. His night has gone to shit. When a coworker arrives to take over his shift, he feels too dejected and cowardly to join his buddies for a beer. *I'm such a pussy,* he says to himself over and over again that night. The line of people who witnessed the exchange makes it all the more humiliating.

When Greg's girlfriend calls, he lets it go to voicemail.

Who Are These Assholes?

What, exactly, does the asshole care about? Jonah cares about Jonah. He's selfish. Dominance over others provides a rush, an exquisite form of exhilaration. This is the state that Jonah and every other asshole seeks. Without it, they're dissatisfied, dull, and restless. Like an addict obsessed with getting and sustaining a high, Jonah is tuned in to that feeling he got at the restaurant and at the party, that rush. He gets that rush with Megan; he gets it by browbeating his sons and berating his employees. Jonah orients himself to this rush of power and seeks it shamelessly.

George Bernard Shaw is credited with saying, "I learned long ago never to wrestle with a pig. You get dirty, and besides, the pig likes it." Conflict is sport for the asshole. He's juiced by the possibilities, and he can outlast others. We defer to assholes because the potential price of *not* deferring is too high. And this is how assholes get away with their behavior; to hell with social fallout.

From the outside looking in, Jonah is a self-made man, a hardworking contractor who has set his table perfectly. He has a devoted, beautiful wife, three healthy children, an oversized home, a job where he calls the shots, and a robust income. He also has a girlfriend on the side—and in this case, "on the side" means on one side of an imbalanced relationship. She caters and capitulates; he does not. But Jonah doesn't demonstrate any emotional attachment to anything he has. If he gave even one-half of a fuck, he'd do what it took to show that he cared for the people closest to him. But he seems not to give even that fractional fuck. Relationships that involve mutual respect, empathy, and compassion are not a priority for the asshole. There might be deep relationships, but they exist on his terms. He sets the conditions. Anyone who wants to be in a relationship with him accepts his conditions—or else.

Were your feelings hurt by his actions? Tough shit. It isn't personal, though; the asshole is oblivious to the emotions of others. Most of us enjoy bringing pleasure to another person, sharing an intimate moment with a partner, catching up with a friend, collaborating on a project with colleagues, or helping out a stranger in need. To many, these experiences are just as important, if not more important, than feeling superior, potent, and powerful. We're social animals, and we thrive on connection. The asshole is the outlier. He mocks what we cherish. If someone or something doesn't serve him, he assigns it no value.

We can identify extreme assholery when we see it from a distance. When a CEO jacks up the price of his company's exclusive life-saving drug by 5,000 percent and laughs about it on social media, it's easy to identify (and hate) that asshole. We exclaim in revulsion, and that's that. But in our homes and day-to-day lives, interacting with assholes is devastating, exhausting, and hurtful. We struggle when the asshole is someone we love or someone we thought (or hoped) loved us.

Why, you may be asking yourself at this point, would anyone spend more time than an elevator ride with a guy like this? The asshole brings absolute, shameless clarity to a situation, and some people actually find that clarity soothing. The asshole owns the space, and that makes some people feel safe. You can count on Jonah to be, well, Jonah, and if anyone (other than him) threatens his people, he's all over that fucker, ending the threat by force or intimidation. He is the ultimate protector.

You can't deny it—there's something intriguing and persuasive about assholes. In part, it goes back to that question: What would it feel like to be that uncensored and rabid? Or: What would it be like to have a true asshole on my side?

The asshole maintains his delusion of strength by seeing only in black and white. You and I know that things are never that simple. We want to shake the asshole and say, "But what if it's more complicated? Isn't it *always* more complicated?" Not to the asshole: He's right. You are patently wrong. An asshole doesn't let things get complicated. Unwavering in his beliefs and closed off to feedback, he's obstinate, immovable as a tank.

When he is primed or triggered, the asshole turns immediately to aggression. He fights because fighting is electrifying. And because he is habituated and trained for a fight, he doesn't have the awareness to resist this impulse. The asshole is hampered by a kind of tunnel vision. With only a fighter's reactions and instincts to fall back on, he can't even entertain the idea that collaboration and cooperation lead to a different kind of thrill: connection.

But back to the burning question: How do assholes get away with it? How can they be so incorrigible? In short, assholes are shameless. They don't care what the rest of us think or feel. Most of us would be mortified to speak to a server the way Jonah did, much as we'd be horrified if we shit our pants in public. Assholes seem to feel no shame when they're belittling others, cheating on their spouses, or demeaning their children.

Guilt is wrapped up in remorse and accountability. We feel guilty when our behavior doesn't match our own expectations. We feel guilty when we hurt someone close to us. It's a feedback loop that leads to course correction. It helps us understand the consequences of our behavior.

Shame is excruciating. To feel ashamed is to feel as though one's very self is corrupt. Guilt corrects, but shame, when it isn't managed or understood, cripples and isolates us. Shame is the soul killer.

Guilt says: *You are good, but you did a bad thing. Let's figure out what happened.*

Shame says: *You are bad for doing a bad thing. Go away.*

Shame taints us in both subtle and dramatic ways throughout our lives; childhood is just the beginning. And that's the tragedy of shame—it erodes our self-worth. Like me, you probably learned shame from others. We don't arrive in the world feeling like we're bad; we learn it through interactions. Shame is a social construct—we learn what is shameful from the responses we engender in others. Masturbating, eating with abandon, or even picking your nose—all of these can feel great, but somewhere along the line most of us were taught that they're appalling or inane acts that aren't even to be *talked* about. Meaning, of course, that these things are done in secret or not at all, reinforcing their shamefulness.

Now, imagine: What if a child misses out on loving arms entirely, or becomes trapped in a traumatic moment at the age of, say, six, before his conscience is fully developed? At the point of his trauma, his ability to reason with himself is stunted. Whatever skills he pulls together to survive trauma become his *how*, his default response to circumstances. Because he hasn't been shown or taught all the alternatives, he adapts as best he can at the point of the trauma. From this point forward, he reacts just as he did at this critical moment.

Consider for a moment your own experiences with shame: Did you ever forget a line in a play? Trip in front of a crowd? Forget someone's name? Think of junior high—primo shaming time.

Most of us react to shame in much the same way we'd react to touching a hot stove: we startle and jump back, trying to put as much distance as possible between ourselves and the source of pain. This isn't a conscious choice. It's pure reflex. Shame is unbearable, *literally* intolerable. We want to get away from the crippling, limiting shame and self-loathing and just fucking *live*!

This is the appeal of assholery. That shameless, give-no-fucks attitude is a freedom we crave, a reprieve from giving too much of a fuck too much of the time. Jonah demands a better pour and a second drink; most of us wouldn't choose to be that bold or disruptive. He gets what he wants, and we accept what we get. We hate him, and we envy him. Relishing the attention of a dozen eyes zeroed in on him, the asshole makes his way to the front and demands a drink, while the rest of us suckers just watch, seethe, and bitch.

Demanding that drink is the asshole's specific, calculated rejection of shame. For the asshole, shame is to be avoided at any cost, even if that cost is to do away with all internalized standards for self-measuring, to be *shameless*. And by ensuring that the victims of his assault *themselves* experience shame, the asshole avoids enduring it himself. This is why Jonah is exhilarated when the bartender submits, and why he gets a bonus rush at having witnesses who share the bartender's humiliation. "You all have a fine night," he says.

Jonah Barrels into My Office

"The only reason I'm here is because of my pansy-ass lawyer," Jonah says by way of introduction. "He thinks the judge will go easy on me if I improve myself. So here I am, trying to fucking improve myself."

An asshole compelled to go into therapy by a loved one, an employer, a judge, or a lawyer, tends to begin his therapy process inefficiently. To put it less mildly, a compelled-to-therapy asshole is belligerent. Jonah makes it abundantly clear that he doesn't want to be in my office. Initially, the feeling is mutual. After some prodding, he lays out the situation for me: at work, one of his laborers got in his face, and a confrontation ensued. Jonah pushed back—assholes always push back—and that "candy ass" tripped on a two-by-four, got a concussion, and filed assault charges.

"So you're here to improve your case," I say. "Makes sense. But what do you want to do while you're here?"

"Fuck if I know. You're the shrink, aren't you?"

I let that pass and move on. "Maybe there's a way we could figure this stuff out so you won't have to deal with situations like this in the future," I say carefully.

"There's nothing to figure out, Doc. I'm fucking fine. That guy had it coming, and if he wasn't such a pussy—with a fragile little pussy head—I wouldn't be here." He crosses his arms and leans back. "He was never worth two shits on the job, anyway. Now I have to pay this guy *not* to work while he's suing my ass; my lawyer says I can't even fire the fucker without getting sued again. But no worries. I'll put an end to this shit. This is not going to be a problem any longer."

The Look and Feel of the Asshole

And so it goes. The first three weeks of sessions, Jonah arrives late, kicks his feet up on my coffee table, and blames, bitches, and brags, sometimes brilliantly, and sometimes all in the same sentence. He curses his employees—"They should kiss the ground I walk on!"—his subcontractors, his cleaners. Architects, clients, lawyers, and neighbors all come in for a jab or two. The Middle East, the governor, the gardener, drivers, cell phone providers. If he can't personally fire someone or get them fired, he wants to make their life hell and their job impossible. He mocks my profession, ridicules the art on my walls, and asks how a real man could listen to people complain all day about erectile dysfunction and their problems with hoarding.

One time, he comes in, sits down, and cracks open a beer to begin the session. Before I can even laugh about the beer, he manages to un-leash one of his more memorable brags: "The married chick next door has been trying to fuck me since they moved in. I'm thinking about it."

Over the next few months, Jonah presents himself as omnipotent, wholly invulnerable. He is above indignity, heartache, depression, lone-liness and, importantly, shame. This shamelessness is the crux of asshole behavior.

He points a finger at me, the same striking finger he pokes into his sons' chests when they talk back. He's a classic asshole: aggressive, punishing, and unswervingly unaccountable. Selfish and shameless. He himself is the constant in all of the complications in his life, but the self-delusion that he relies upon so completely keeps him from seeing this. He both intrigues and exhausts me.

Jonah is an abusive and philandering husband, a bastard of a father, and an intimidating, even dangerous, boss. There's also a palpable desperation oozing from this guy, a frantic, hard-edged energy. His brutality indicates more than mere hotheadedness. Working with Jonah, I often picture him on a sinking ship, frantically bailing out water, trying to fill the leaking hole in the hull with the toe of his boot. He is always alone on that ship.

The intensity of a person's anger and defensiveness is directly pro-portional to the anguish and vulnerability underneath. Jonah is in a great deal of pain, and even if he fails to recognize it, I can feel it. His bravado and assholery do little to mask it; at times, they only seem to underscore it. For me, this engenders compassion for people like Jonah—and hope.

Jonah and His Asshole Ways

"Sounds to me like you're trying to change the world—and if you can't fix it, you're prepared to break it," I say, some three months into treatment, with about half the scheduled sessions paid for but not attended. "You'd be happy if your wife were happier, if your kids were more grateful, if your employees worked harder, if your lawyer charged less, if government employees would do their fucking jobs, and if I were less of a pussy. Sound about right?"

He nods vigorously, a big smile spreading across his face. Everyone likes to be "gotten," and Jonah is no exception.

"But what if there was a way for you to feel okay with the way things are? Less annoyed, less reactive, less stressed?"

"What the fuck are you talking about? I'm the one dealing with all of this shit, trying to keep my head above water, getting fucked in multiple directions. And here you are in your overpriced office, with your stupid-ass crystals, telling me I just need to be *fine* with taking it in the ass on the daily, dealing with lazy workers and government employees who don't do jack shit? Yeah, I'll be less stressed when I end up bankrupt and everything falls apart. Real smart idea. Where'd you get your degree, Doc? Online? Fuck. I mean, seriously, fuck that. Fuck them. Fuck you."

Gone is the impish smile from a moment ago. He looks exhausted.

"Jonah, man, this seems like so much to hold."

"Yeah, and it's thankless. Always more shit. It never stops, and here I am when I could be out there building or fixing all of it. Fuck this, man. I don't want to be here. Just what I need in the middle of my fucking day is to cross town and come sit here in your office."

"Jonah, I'm going to level with you," I say.

I'm feeling nervous. I'm aware of his aggression, so I move cautiously. Jonah is able to instill a certain amount of fear everywhere he goes, and my office is no exception. While fear—or a concern for my safety—is present, and it's part of what's making me nervous, I'm also concerned about losing Jonah and having him abandon the process entirely.

"It seems like things are falling apart at home and at work, and I'm afraid that things are going to get even worse if you stay the course. I see how hard you're working just to keep the ship afloat, and I respect that, I really do. It's a herculean task. But what if there was another way, one involving less stress and carnage? What if we could help you navigate your life better, make it less stressful, help you feel less alone in it all? I can help you change direction, but it will mean seeing that you're a part of what's going on. The common factor in all of these situations is *you*, man."

This stops him. For a split second, things get quiet. I feel something new: grief, so much grief—then a wave of terror, right in my stomach. The energy in the room is cold, and Jonah stands up suddenly, jabbing his finger at me. "Go fuck yourself," he says, slamming the door behind him.

Reeling, I take some deep breaths. I'm triggered. My threat system is activated. My body is in a "freeze" response. I stand up, shake it out. "We're okay," I say out loud to myself. I text a close friend. I do some push-ups. I lie on the wooden floor. I start to settle. "Well, shit," I say to my stupid-ass crystals. "That didn't go well." I begin to second-guess myself. But it was time to make a move, and I made it. Jonah may have mastered the art of finding and exploiting others' vulnerabilities, but like most assholes, he can't really bear comments that hit too close to home. It was time to try to get in there, so I tried. And if I'm honest, I was also just tired of being shat on every week. After five minutes, I can feel my nervous system start to come back online.

Deep down—and we're talking about the bottom of an abyss—Jonah knows that he's being an asshole. And you probably know when *you're* being an asshole. You may feel validated at times because the object of your assholery deserves it—a friend fails you spectacularly, your wife makes the first jab, or a coworker pushes you. But you know when you slip into asshole territory, and while it may be gratifying—even exciting— to teeter on that edge, most of us have the strength and foresight to step away. We're aware of that line, even if it gets fuzzy when we're pissed.

Being a true asshole requires total disconnection from other people. You must stay within the confines of your self-deluding story, your air-tight narrative. Otherwise, you'd empathize with the person you hurt. Or you might feel the same pain, and it would motivate you to correct your behavior. Jonah isn't ready for that yet. But I figure he'll come back when things get worse and his defenses start to crumble—and that's exactly what happens.

Jonah Feels the Consequences

Months after Jonah told me to go fuck myself and stormed out of my office, I get a text message from him at two in the morning asking for a session. I wake with a jolt and, seeing who it is, feel another. The body remembers. Mine remembers being told to go fuck myself, the contempt, the fear that he might attack me, the slamming door. I breathe. I feel the warmth of being under the covers. I need my reply to be level. Deep down, I know—I knew months ago, and I know in this moment—that his "go fuck yourself" to me wasn't personal. But what I *know* and how my nervous system responds to the perception of threat are two different things.

That's better. My exhales are getting longer. Jonah is a man I care about, and he's worth it. I can't *not* do it. Beyond my professional obligation, I'm drawn in. Settled, I propose a time for us to meet a few days later.

The man I see in the waiting room is changed. As he follows me into my office, his steps are halting; the bluesy rhythm they used to have—*one* and a *two* and a *three* and a *four*—is gone. He's chewing gum that doesn't stand a chance against yesterday's whiskey and cigarettes. Shit, maybe *today's* whiskey, I think nervously.

Jonah's eyes are red, and his face is puffy. He's unshaven. There's a stain on his Ben Davis shirt.

"Fuck, David. What the fuck else can go wrong this week?"

Namaste, Jonah.

"Fucking hell, man. She...she did it. She left me. Fuck." Jonah isn't waiting for introductions. He's not interested in catching up. "She fucking left," he says flatly. The whiteness of his knuckles makes the scars stand out on his hands. He's trying to hold it together. "Told me she knew about Megan. Pictures. Texts. She said I'd sent a 'fuck me' text to another woman while we were in Tahoe together. She took the boys to her parents and made plans to move out. Some bullshit about email threats, and now I've got even *more* legal bills—and fuck, man, I didn't know what the fuck else to do. Just saw your number in my phone."

He shifts in his chair. He's looking around my office. *Stay here,* I think to myself. *Stay.* A minute passes.

Jonah breaks the silence. "My boys haven't talked to me. That's the only thing I need help with." He bends over when he mentions his boys. His strong hands are clenched so tight that I can see the scars on his hands change colors. He releases his grip. "Because fuck her. And fuck her lawyer. Some bulldog bitch from San Francisco who sent me these goddamn letters telling me how many feet away I have to stay from my own wife—"

"Jonah," I interrupt. "I'm glad you're here. I get that you want help with your boys. We can dive into that. But I'm also curious about how you're doing with Shaylee leaving."

Jonah is quiet, then says, "I fucking hate her." He tries to say more, but nothing follows. Again, he opens his mouth to speak—nothing.

I watch him closely. He's lying, but I feel his dilemma. Jonah feels it too, and this is new to him. Even in this moment, with me, in this room, Jonah doesn't want to feel the gravity of this situation. He doesn't want to change. He's a builder. He's a fixer. He isn't here to feel this out—he just wants to *fix* it. Saying aloud that he hates Shaylee is meant to fix an immediate problem; it means she's off the table for reconciliation. But he can't bring himself to pursue his own lie. He doesn't hate her. He loves her. Jonah's defenses are breaking down.

"Maybe a part of you hates Shaylee, and another part of you misses her," I say. "Is it possible that there's both inside of you?"

"Don't fuck with me," Jonah snarls.

My heart pounds. *Boom.* "I'm not fucking with you," I say. *Boom.* My heart is thundering in my chest. *Boom.* "Things are fucked up in your life right now," I tell him. *Boom.* "On multiple fronts. So, let's understand how things got so fucked up, and—if you want to—figure out how to unfuck them." I pause. "I'm not the one fucking with you. I'm the one trying to help you."

Jonah is quiet again. Crickets. "I fucking hate this," he says at last. "I miss my life. I miss my wife. My kids. I fucked everything up." The room seems to exhale.

This is the first time Jonah puts aside his asshole strategies, revealing a glimpse of the fragility that's always waiting underneath guys like him—and hell, all men, for that matter.

2

THE PUSSY

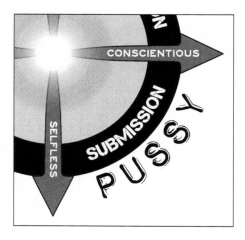

"What are you, a pussy?" How many times have you heard that—or perhaps said it to yourself? "Don't be a pussy." The sentiment can be conveyed with a simple look, a tone, a dismissive wave or a shaking of the head.

*This word, aggravating and derogatory, is full of impact and implications. The judgment looms over us all precisely because we know that sometimes we **are** pussies, complete and total pussies, the very thing we tell ourselves we're not allowed to be.*

George, the Pussy

Once awake, George looks around and appreciates his familiar surroundings. Equally familiar is the grim nervousness that rises in his chest like panic. He takes a fast shower so Kayla won't run out of hot water. He checks his Fitbit; he's managed to shower and get dressed in less than sixteen minutes. The shower and bathroom are tidied up and ready for Kayla.

George is beating the eggs when he hears Kayla get out of the shower. By the time she descends the stairs, her hair is tucked back, her lipstick perfect, her scarf just so. Ten months of living together, and George still marvels at her ability to go to bed looking polished and wake up looking…what's the word for it? Together. Confident. He puts some eggs and extra-lean bacon on their plates and sits down next to her. George wants to kiss her on the cheek, but he also doesn't want to interrupt her.

Kayla is picking at her eggs. When she looks up, he realizes he's been staring at her. "Didn't you wear that tie yesterday?" she asks, not waiting for the answer. "Okay, George. Today's the day, right? You've been there three years. If you don't talk to your boss about that open commercial mortgage lender position, I'm going to march right in there and talk to him myself."

George blushes. "Yeah, I'll talk to him today. Can't have my better half coming in and making a scene, can I?"

Kayla winks at him. "I talked to the contractor. He's coming at one; you'll have to meet him here and show him the bathroom."

Dammit. George thinks. *I'll have to take a long lunch for this. The area manager won't like it. And I never know how to talk to the contractor guys. Oh, well. I guess I'll figure it out.* The day has just begun, and George is already silently strategizing, figuring out how he's going to navigate the day's choices.

"Pick up the delivery from the farmers' market too. It's one box," Kayla says, giving him a kiss on the cheek on her way out the door. "And make sure you load the dishwasher." Kayla moves briskly. She oversees a team handling title searches and title insurance in Alameda and Contra Costa counties. She prides herself on decisive planning, and she never brings her work home.

Distracted by the requirements of the day, George doesn't realize he forgot the dishes until he's already in the car. His anxiety shoots through the roof. *Kayla hates this sort of thing.* At a red light, he sends a quick, apologetic text to Kayla; fearing her response, he puts his phone away. He cranks up the AC, turns down Nickelback, and slows to let in a truck that's passing a long line of cars for the on-ramp. When the man behind him honks and shoots him the finger, George cringes, slouching in his seat. Humiliation clusters behind his eyes like a migraine. He looks at the San Francisco Bay and thinks of ways to make it all up to Kayla, to the world.

* * *

Wells Fargo promotes from within. Six months into George's new role, he still feels more comfortable doing basic teller duties; even when there's no pressing need, he schedules himself to work the teller position. "How may I help you?" he asks. The simple routine of teller tasks makes him happy. Serving customers makes him happy, and he's able to competently perform any and all actions that might be required of him. Sure, the bank sees its fair share of upset clients—people on the brink of financial ruin or simply pressed for time—but George understands. Money is a very personal matter. He takes great pains to apologize profusely when customers are overreacting or emotional.

"You're so deferential," says Marge, the new teller. Outwardly, he responds with a smile to avoid making Marge uncomfortable. But he feels ashamed, and he wonders if Marge just called him weak.

Assuming a defenseless position is second nature to George. He considers himself one of the good guys. He values kindness, loyalty, and patience. He selflessly puts the needs of others before his own, and he's proud of it. But the pride he feels in serving others first is often smothered by inward judgments and criticism.

Jack, one of his tellers, strolls by and doesn't look up to give George his usual morning nod. George feels a pang of fear and racks his brain, trying to recall their last interaction. *What the hell could I have done?*

George avoids conflict or supervisory interaction with others. Around Jack, he tends to be quiet. Well, even quieter.

"Hey, Jack," he says, noticing his own voice breaking—and with that, he's questioning himself again. "Can I, um, get you a coffee? I'm just about to step out for a Starbucks run."

"Thanks, boss man. That'd be great," Jack says, and he reaches for his wallet.

"No, no, it's on me," George insists, heading for the door before Jack can protest. "The pleasure is all mine." *The pleasure is all mine?* George can't identify exactly *what* his pleasure is in picking up a coffee for Jack, but he feels obliged to try to patch something up with him, even though that 'something' is imaginary, existing only in George's mental loops. George breathes a huge sigh of relief, but he's soon questioning himself again: *The pleasure is all mine?*

* * *

Kayla is home when he arrives later that evening. She's on the couch, reading. He brings her a bottle of Perrier and waits for her to say something about dinner. "Thanks," she says softly, engrossed in her novel.

Thanks? George's stomach clenches, rumbling so loud he's afraid Kayla will hear it—he skipped lunch to meet the contractor. He opens and closes the refrigerator door, cautiously opens a cabinet, searches the freezer without moving anything out of place.

"George," Kayla finally says, marking her place in her book. "If you're hungry, just say something."

"Well, yeah, if *you* are," he says, watching her carefully. "I could probably go for something to eat, but only if you're hungry, too. Are you?" *I should surprise her with a night out in the city. She's always wanted to try the roasted chicken at Zuni Café. That place looks so fancy! What would I wear? What would it cost?* He fidgets with the loose change in his pocket; he always wishes he had something to do with his hands. *Dammit. I didn't talk to my boss today, either. I hope she doesn't ask.*

"George?"

He blinks, but his mind still won't clear.

Kayla is exasperated. "George, I don't really care. Why don't *you* pick a place?"

George feels his temperature rise and turns away, fearful. Kayla makes him so anxious sometimes. She always wants him to pipe up. She wants his input on where to eat, what movie to see, whether he wants stemless wine glasses or flutes for the wedding reception, which side of the bed he wants to sleep on, and where he'd like to go for Christmas. *Doesn't she know I'm perfectly happy letting her decide? She always has better ideas, anyway. Dealing with the contractor today was stressful enough. Now this? Besides, what if I choose something she hates?*

"Do you want to get some Mexican food at that place on Shattuck? I know you like that place," he says, looking up at the ceiling. "I know you like it."

"But what do *you* want to eat?" Kayla asks, sitting up straight and turning the full force of her gaze on him. George hesitates. *Why does this matter so much? What does she really want?* Frustration flashes across Kayla's face. "Just say what you want, George. Seriously! Just say 'I want pizza and beer' or 'Pad thai sounds great' or even 'Fuck you, Kayla.' Or 'Fuck *me*, Kayla.' Just add something to the mix."

"What do you want me to say?" George starts asking, then cringes. Even the sound of his own voice fills him with shame. He can feel his sweat, and he crosses his arms. *Fucking wimp*, he can hear his father saying, and this just makes him shakier.

"Just make a suggestion!" Kayla says, throwing up her arms. "It's not that hard, George. Think about what you'd like to eat, then say the words. *Out loud.* Or at least narrow it down, and I'll weigh in! But for God's sake, say *something*."

At this point, a rush of terror. *You failed her.* George's stomach drops. Tunnel vision. The world starts to tilt, and he sits down.

Kayla pauses. George sees her face turn to something close to pity.

"Oh, honey. It's okay," she says. She reaches for him and gives him a hug. "We can go to that Mexican place. It's totally fine. I'll go get my coat; you know how cold it is in there. Do you want yours? Should I get yours, too?"

"No, no," he says, waving her off with a plaintive smile. He's so relieved he could cry. A rogue thought resurfaces—Mexican food gives him heartburn and gas—but he brushes it off as barely a sacrifice. For now, he's full of the hope of feeling Kayla's care and her approval of him. This is what he wants most, just to know that he's okay in her eyes. He would do anything for that.

* * *

Thirty minutes later, they're seated at a corner table. A mariachi band clamors through the restaurant. The bar is jam-packed. The waiter comes by with chips and salsa. "Kayla, why don't you order something for both of us, and we'll share?" George asks, his head in his hands, not even bothering to glance at the menu. Kayla sighs loud enough for George to hear and asks for a margarita.

She catches George watching her. She does love him. *He's so devoted,* she thinks. *I know he'd never leave or do anything to hurt me. I can count on George to be, well, George. And he's super cute.* Kayla remembers the contractor visit. "Oh, hey, where are we with the mold situation? How did it go today?"

Oh, God. "Well, I met him, showed him the bathroom, where we think there's black mold. He, um, shined this light in there, and said that there was. He said it needed—what was the word?—remediation. I think. I didn't know exactly what that meant, and I didn't know what to ask him. He seemed really busy, and I didn't want to ask too much. I just figured that, well, you could call him and talk to him about it; you're so good at handling stuff like this."

Kayla, shaking her head, quickly orders another margarita. In the silence, George picks the cuticle of his ring finger, and when the blood pools on his nail, he puts it in his mouth. Kayla is about to say something, but she decides it's just not worth it. She *is* good at handling things like this, and it's always less trouble this way, but sometimes she wishes...

George relaxes, watching her take a sip from the salty rim of her second margarita, believing the storm to have passed. *Thank God. Maybe she forgot about the mortgage position.* George grins, reaching for her drink as she puts it down, careful to position his lips on the part of the rim where the salt's already gone.

What Is a Pussy?

George is a pussy. A big, fat pussy.

There, I said it—and for the record, I don't feel good about it. You see, I'm a pussy too. I fear repercussions for using the word, and I'd really like someone else to address this for me. I've tried to make alternatives work; "pussy," after all, is a charged and offensive word in this context, but it's the right word—the *only* word—and I'd be even more of the very thing I'm describing if I didn't use it.

We all know "pussy" is slang for vagina; it would be disingenuous to ignore that connection, although "pussy" has other origins and points of reference. It's also a name for a cat. But honestly, is that what anyone is thinking when it's used to describe a dude—that he's a cat or a vagina? Of course not. There are three distinct uses of the word "pussy": a cat, a vagina, and an extremely submissive person (usually a man). We're using the word in the third sense, to refer to the submissive, selfless, and conscientious archetype. It's a word commonly used to describe men who are always afraid, always deferential, and who fail to meet expectations for male behavior. It's the only fitting word for this archetype.

The pussy is essentially selfless, and highly conscientious of the needs and wants of others, to the point that he negates himself. He burdens others with the responsibility of directing the parts of life they share with him.

How would you describe George, or someone like him? He might be described as basically a good dude—a trustworthy friend, an attentive co-worker, a helpful neighbor, a reliable son. One thing should be perfectly clear at this point: a pussy is not an asshole. In fact, the pussy's behavior is *diametrically opposed* to the asshole's.

The asshole reflexively attacks; metaphorically speaking, he's a bull charging a red cape. The pussy, in contrast, deftly evades, like a fancy bullfighter, sometimes even with the bullfighter's smiling panache. De-escalation is a useful and necessary skill, but the pussy perceives every person he meets as a raging bull.

By being unthreatening and making peace at all costs, the pussy avoids conflict and wins a degree of love and loyalty from others, but not their respect. The asshole and the pussy both achieve peace, each in his own way. The asshole enforces *pax assholia* by imposing his will and silencing opposition. The pussy promotes *pax pussifica* by removing his will from the equation and accommodating the opposition. Taking control and giving away control are both useful approaches in different situations, but neither approach works all of the time. But that's what we find George doing—always trying to give away control as a way to feel more in control. Yes, you read that right. He's only at ease when others have all of the control, when others carry the burden and exposure that comes with responsibility.

The pussy and the asshole are two sides of a single coin. Here, for example, is a passage from the asshole chapter that can easily be rewritten to describe the pussy:

> The ~~asshole~~ <u>pussy</u> brings absolute, ~~shameless~~ <u>conscientious</u> clarity to a situation, and some people actually find that clarity soothing. The ~~asshole~~ <u>pussy</u> ~~owns~~ <u>cedes</u> the space, and that makes some people feel safe. You can count on ~~Jonah~~ <u>George</u> to be, well, ~~Jonah~~ <u>George</u>, and if anyone ~~(other than him)~~ threatens his people, he's all over that fucker, ending the threat by ~~force or intimidation~~ <u>craven</u>

appeasement. He is the ultimate ~~protector~~ <u>peacemaker</u>. You can't deny it—there's something intriguing and ~~persuasive~~ <u>disarming</u> about ~~assholes~~ <u>pussies</u>.

You get the point. Peace by aggression or peace by appeasement—they each want the discomfort to end.

You might hate the pussy, and you might pity him. You might also wonder how it would feel to be like him, so careful, caring, conscientious, and deferential. Where some of us can't help butting in and offending others, then kicking ourselves later for our lack of discretion, the Georges of the world seem to skillfully navigate around these incidents.

But appearances can be deceiving; the Georges of the world are constantly kicking themselves anyway. They live their lives from a position of presumed fault. The pussy assumes he is wrong—or *probably* wrong, or *about to be* wrong—and absorbs all of the resulting guilt, blame, shame, and fear.

It's perfectly natural, of course, to be apologetic and deferential when you know you've fucked up, like when you forget her birthday, or when you get drunk and make an ass out of yourself. In the pussy's mind, however, he has *always* somehow fucked up. He wouldn't be able to respond to his need to take a piss if it would inconvenience anyone around him. This is one hell of a burden.

A loop is constantly running in the pussy's mind: *Are you happy? If you're happy with me, I'm okay. If you're unhappy with me, I'm afraid. I'll do anything I can to make you feel better. How do I need to be to make you okay with me?* He cannot soothe or reassure himself, and he cannot trust his own judgment; he derives his sense of stability and reality from others. The pussy feels safer when he's being selfless, avoiding the risks of personal rejection and deferring responsibility for choices he's sure he'd just fuck up. The pussy is willing—even glad—to place everyone else's interests above his own. But the submissive choices he makes to get through the day are themselves subject to his second-guessing and doubts, so the cycle continues.

What happens when you believe that occasionally wanting things your way is inherently selfish? What happens when you grant every preference of those around you a greater priority than your own needs? If you only submit to others' priorities, making everyone's needs more important than your own, you suppress your own *aliveness*. Eventually, the massive energy it takes to kneel, supporting everyone else on a pedestal of importance, is a burden that cannot be borne. Chronic submission leads to greater and greater deadness.

George the pussy is not merely steeped in his mediocre routine and complacency, he's *drowning* in it. Achieving more at work would require a certain conviction that he can't seem to stir up. Unable to face his fears, he's stuck in tedium, lacking power and purpose. His primary aim is to keep others from being upset with him, and this is profoundly limiting. He wants to advance at work, but he can't abide the possibility of being rejected, or maybe even the risk of succeeding and losing jealous friends. Even his future-tripping is a gauntlet of submission and conscientiousness. He convinces himself that if he tries in the light of day and fails, he'll disappoint others and feel like a bucket of shit. If he doesn't try, he can't fail. He chooses not to try. Wrong choice, pussy.

George Tiptoes to My Office Door and Knocks Gently

"Hi! It's so nice to meet you. Thank you so much for meeting with me; I really, *really* appreciate it," George says. "Um…" He glances nervously around. "Where should I sit?"

I gesture toward the sofa, and he sits quietly, looking at me with saucer-like eyes. I smile, and he visibly relaxes, leaning back into the cushions but keeping his hands tucked under his thighs. It's clear that George is a compulsive pleaser. His eyes never leave mine, and he takes his cues entirely from me, mimicking my body language without realizing it.

"I'm glad to meet you too. I'm curious what it's like being here right now. What do you notice happening inside of you?" I want his attention on himself, not on me.

George's hands clench in his lap. "Well, um…What do you mean? What do you want to know?"

I smile again. "Well, we're meeting each other for the first time. Maybe you're nervous? A little tight in your chest or stomach, or your neck? You may have thoughts running through your head, or maybe you're concerned about whether you're doing this right. You may feel warm or cold. There's always a great deal going on inside of us, and part of what I do is help teach my clients how to pay attention to that inner landscape."

George fidgets for a moment and looks confused. Finally, he speaks up: "Well, my chest is sort of…sort of tight. My jaw is kind of clenchy, and I guess my hands are hot. I'm nervous. Is this what you wanted me to do?"

I feel an impulse to take care of this man, to reassure him. I motion for him to continue.

"This is a great space, by the way. Love the ficus. Am I missing something? Is this what you want me to do?"

I see sweat starting to glisten on his forehead. "Good awareness," I say. "So, your chest is tight, your jaw is clenched, and your hands are warm."

This process is called reflective listening; it builds connection and safety, establishing confidence that what's being expressed and what's being heard are the same thing. Sounds simple, but as the saying goes, "The single biggest problem in communication is the illusion that it has taken place."

"I feel this way a lot, actually," George says. "It's kind of why I'm here, I think. I guess I can't ever seem to make her happy—sorry, make Kayla happy. My fiancée. She's always so frustrated with me. I love her. She's frustrated, though. Since she moved in, we got me another promotion and we fixed up the house, but I'm afraid she wants to leave me, and that makes me more nervous, and then I have an even harder time being who she wants me to be—and now I'm just rambling. I'm so sorry. Sometimes I just, like...I don't know. I'll shut up now."

"I notice that doubting voice just came in again, questioning whether you're doing it right." I wave off his second round of apologies and try again. "There's no right or wrong here, George," I say, a slight feeling of tension in my jaw. His face changes from confusion to terror. He's *that* attuned to my state of tension. I deepen my breath, soften, and feel my interest and care for George. Right away, he softens too. "We're going to pay attention to you, be curious about you. As you begin to live closer to yourself, you'll feel more settled with Kayla, and the relationship will likely improve."

"How, though?" George asks. "I mean, I try so hard, and it never seems like enough, and I can't even concentrate at work. You know, I just keep worrying about conversations we've had and things she's said—sorry, am I talking too much? And the way she looked at me this morning or last night, and..." He takes a deep breath and looks at me pleadingly. "I feel like I'm walking on eggshells. All of the time."

Try so hard...never seems like enough...can't even concentrate...walking on eggshells...

"That sounds intense, George, that level of constant worry. Tell me more about 'trying so hard,' and how it 'never seems like enough.'"

"Well, I'm always trying to figure out what she wants, you know. But often she wants to know what *I* want, and I usually don't know, or don't care. I just want her to...you know, to decide."

"Right," I say. "Then you could just go along with what she wants, knowing she's happy because she chose."

"Yes! That's what I want!" he almost shrieks, then looks down shyly. "Sorry, didn't mean to get so excited. I just wish she understood where I was coming from."

I'm lit up by his excitement. *There you are.*

"I loved feeling you there, George, your 'yes.' You were so clear; you really want her to get this. What else?" I ask enthusiastically. "What else do you wish others got about you? I won't tell them, I promise," I say playfully.

"Well," he says, "there are some work issues…"

It turns out that George has opinions about lots of things, and he really gets some momentum going, almost ranting at times.

"So, George, you're clearly a thoughtful and intelligent guy. You see what's going on around you. What happens when you think about letting folks know what's going on in there?"

He stares at me blankly, as if I'm asking him if he's ever considered ballroom dancing with a polar bear. The man who was confidently sharing his insights a moment before returns to his hunched-over self, eyes down. He says little for the rest of the session. I learn a great deal from this; going forward, for a time, I avoid encouraging George in this way. It's not time yet. My couch is a safe space for him to share whatever he wants, however he wants. That's plenty. He's building his confidence, and it's a pleasure to feel this man bring himself forward in our sessions a little bit more, week after week.

Months Later with George

"I see how much you care about her, George," I say as he's telling me about Kayla, "and how much you want to make her happy. But she wants to know what *you* want, right?"

He nods.

We're three months in, and now it's time to encourage him.

"She wants to hear from you, George. You matter to her. She wants to do what *you* want sometimes, something that would make *you* happy— or she wants to decide together. Does that make sense to you?"

"Yes, of course I understand that. She wants me to, but how? I don't know how to do it. She wants me to. Sometimes I try, and I get shot down. I know I'll lose her if I don't figure this out, but I just can't. I don't even know why I can't; I just *can't*. What do I do?" His eyes are on me now, wild and pleading.

George is relying on me. He's strategizing. He's trying to give me his power—but I'm not taking it. He doesn't know it yet, but he's here to take ownership of his own power, not to take his cues from me or anyone else.

When I don't answer his stare immediately, George is visibly uncomfortable. His eyes get wider, and he rocks back and forth.

"George," I ask, "what's happening right now? What do you notice in your body?"

"Throat tight—sweating—chest feels heavy," he says in a rush, his voice panicked.

"So, right now, your throat is tight, your chest is heavy, and you're sweating," I repeat back to him. "You're doing great." And with this, he settles a bit.

"Okay, sure, I guess. It's just that Kayla always tells me I'm too fearful..." His voice trails off, and tears come to his eyes.

"Let's you and me try to be with that fearful guy for a moment. He's here right now," I say. "No agenda. He gets to be here." George's breathing accelerates. "Can I sit next to you?"

He nods.

I gently place my right hand in the center of his upper back. He tenses. I stay there for a few moments. Slowly, I increase the pressure. I listen with my hand and with my own body. After a certain amount of pressure, I feel it: the moment of deep contact. Our nervous systems settle noticeably. *Here he is. Here we are.* I stay here, at this point of connection. *We're okay because we're together. You're not alone.*

"Hi, George," I say, five or twenty-five minutes later. "I'm going to slowly remove my hand from your back now, but I want you to continue to feel the connection. Got it?" He nods. "Keep feeling it, even as I go back to my chair." He smiles. He gets it.

"George, slowly open your eyes. See if you can stay with this feeling of connection when we're making eye contact."

"See if you can still feel our connection if I close my eyes."

"Look around the room; come back. What do you notice?"

We experiment. We practice.

Sitting with George

Notice the way George speaks: *kind of, I think, I guess, I don't know, um, like, sorry.* Communication, for him, is something that must be framed and filtered. These are strategies to water down his voice and his beliefs in the hope of protecting himself from the pushback and judgment of others. These "fumblers" are a powerful protective strategy. They help to convey an unsure, apologetic, and nonthreatening position. They say to the world: *I'm not sure what my opinion is or where I stand, so no need to pay me any heed. Let's do it your way.* Selfless.

Is it unorthodox to sit by George or touch his back? You might think so, but think again. When we were very young, we learned to feel safe and comforted through touch, and touch remains one of our primary channels of regulation. We're no different from most mammals in this regard. My own balanced (in this moment) nervous system encourages George's to settle; my hand on his back supports the part of him that's afraid and reassures him that he's safe. George's adult, conscious self knows he's okay when Kayla is upset with him or when another driver flips him off or when his father expresses disappointment to him. But this very anxious younger part of him, the one breathing shallowly, the one feeling intensely triggered, is experiencing a life-or-death situation and responding accordingly. He shields himself with the behavior he knows best: deference. He's responding as the lonely little boy inside of him, whose very attempts to achieve love, acceptance, and safety thwart him from finding love, acceptance, and safety as an adult.

The Complicated Relationships between the Pussy & Everything

We pity the pussy's living death, bless his heart. We fail to notice, however, that the pussy is one of the most familiar figures in the community. He hides in plain sight within the parameters of a "normal" life, complete with job, home, family, grimace, paunch, slouch, aching knees, and empty platitudes. He doesn't make much of a first or lasting impression. Frequently described by others with flat, ambiguous non-descriptors like "a nice fellow" and "reliable," he's the completely forgettable man you see without noticing. In his attempt to stay safe and secure, he becomes the backdrop.

Intimate relationships are out of balance when one side refuses to show up. Whether it's a sports match or Match.com, an exciting match of any kind requires both sides to show up.

Kayla wants to connect with her partner; intimacy is vital to the survival of their relationship. George's selfless sacrifices and his goal of making her happy are the beginnings of intimacy and connection—but only in one direction. Kayla can feel the potential. But mutually fulfilling intimacy and connection involve both giving *and* taking; they require George to show up for Kayla with his own needs and desires, something that feels risky to George. It's too threatening, too much of a gamble. In fact, the very idea of prioritizing his own needs scares the hell out of him. And the more upset Kayla gets at his lack of mettle, assertiveness, and agency, the more selfless he gets—the more desperate he is for Kayla to save him from this overwhelm—which triggers Kayla even more. She feels abandoned by George's unwillingness to show up. All of that frustrates the goal of intimacy and connection, of course, and breeds more desperation and more reactive passiveness in George.

* * *

Men, we're goddamn hard on ourselves. We beat ourselves up and call ourselves names for shortcomings both real and imagined. Society doesn't like an asshole, but it doesn't respect a pussy. No one wants to be seen as a pussy. And the harshest judgments and accusations on that front are often self-inflicted: Already putting in a sixty-hour workweek and missing your wife and kids? *What are you, a pussy?* Boss needs you to work on the weekend? *Man the fuck up.* Feeling sick? *Suck it up.* Exhausted? *Don't be a fucking liability. Push through it; don't be a motherfucking pussy.* We wreck our health and relationships to avoid being seen as pussies.

From clinical experience, I can assure you that we don't become the men we want to be by telling ourselves not to be pussies—but we try. And try, and try, and try again.

These insults are bullshit, and they're hurtful. Nobody wins here, especially the guy telling himself to grow some balls. Not having testicles has never been the issue—and having an extra set would be awkward. This kind of abusive relationship with yourself can be brutally harmful. Stop this shit. The name-calling, including what's happening in your own head, isn't working. Deal with facts, with reality.

In addition to the self-inflicted insults designed to motivate us, there are parts of us that resist with bullshit excuses. The single most common of these is that things are "good enough." Translated into reality, this just means that change is really fucking hard. When we want to try something different, the anxious voices inside our heads prevent us from doing anything risky, new, or bold.

The self-told excuses are clichés. You know them all already:

- *Don't embarrass yourself!*
- *You already have a good life!*
- *What will people think?*
- *Just be grateful for what you have.*
- *You're going to feel stupid.*
- *With your track record, why risk it?*
- *It's none of your business.*
- *Someone else can do it better.*

Why do we beat the shit out of ourselves with these crippling rationalizations? Simply put, we're subjected to them so much that we've become accustomed to them. We tolerate and believe them, and they shape our inner lives, often in extreme, maladaptive ways. The asshole, for example, absorbs these expressions of derision and spits them back out at the world, leaning harder into his shameless aggression; he opts out of the dilemma entirely. The pussy accepts the criticism and becomes paralyzed over the impossible choice between being disappointed and being disappointing. He internalizes the idea that he can never get it right unless he sets more of himself aside.

In some ways, all of us act like pussies, half-asleep at the proverbial wheel, lulled into fatalistic inaction. I've been a pussy, for example, in the process of writing this book: I had a good enough life in my private practice without writing stories about assholes, pussies, douchebags, and dicks, or so I told myself for years. *Couldn't you just write a sweet little self-help book instead? You're going to be judged. Humiliated.* For months at a time, I cycled through this internal argument and couldn't get any work done. Guess what I call myself when I'm churning, unproductive, and frustrated? You guessed it: a pussy.

But so what? So what if you don't make an unprecedented leap? So what if George gets a little heartburn and has Kayla on his ass for not just telling her whether he'd prefer turkey or pastrami? So what if George doesn't make president of the bank? No harm done, right? Not necessarily. The status quo can be seductive, but "good enough" just ain't working out for everyone. I know. I've seen it in my practice. I've heard it from—and about—men. Let's be clear: the meek will not inherit the earth. Nobody is turning this planet over to the pussies. Now, more than ever, we need men and women who are intensely alive, who have the guts to take risks for something better—for themselves and for each other. To quote Andy Dufresne from *The Shawshank Redemption*, "It comes down to a simple choice, really. Get busy living, or get busy dying."

We *need* to be pushed and challenged in life, and all of us would benefit by mixing it up a little. George stands a chance at happiness if he'd just show some verve, which he can only do if he can engage with his fears and experiment with different behavior. Otherwise, he'll remain where we met him, in a trap of angst and stagnation. There, a decade goes by in the blink of an eye—and I say this because I want to terrify all you pussies into meaningful change.

The Big V: Vulnerability

Vulnerability. That grownup word is so often misused. We throw it around as a synonym for weakness, susceptibility, likelihood of being hurt or killed. The vulnerable wildebeest is the one that gets mauled by the lioness. The invading army attacks the most vulnerable spot in the defender's line. An underperforming salesman is vulnerable during layoffs.

Dr. Brené Brown, professor at the University of Houston and best-selling author of *The Power of Vulnerability*, says something quite different. She suggests that vulnerability is the birthplace of innovation, creativity, and change. Vulnerability sounds like truth and feels like courage, and it's the only way to experience real connection. Vulnerability is strength.

She's right.

Internally, we have our private thoughts, feelings, and sensations. We pick and choose what we let other people see. We only share with others that part of our experience that we want them to know about. This may or may not be congruent with how we actually feel. How often do you say you're okay when you actually feel like shit?

Being vulnerable means acknowledging what's going on inside and sharing your authentic experience. It's showing yourself to another, being real, dropping pretense and agenda. It's not cowardice; it's an act that calls for great courage. It's the revelation of your true face, the one underneath the protective mask that each of us wears. Vulnerability opens the portal of connection. And connection, after all, is what the pussy so desperately desires. As do the asshole, the douchebag, and the dick, for that matter—whether they know it or not.

All of these grand pronouncements aside, vulnerability is about being honest. Tactful and compassionate? Yes, but also frank:

- *Whoa. Hold on. That really stung. I'm feeling set back.*
- *This, frankly, makes me sad as hell. I don't know what to do. I don't even know what to say.*
- *I'm worried; I didn't get the deal done, and we're going to run out of money this month.*
- *I feel invisible.*
- *I feel so lost in my life right now, and I don't know what to do.*
- *I don't believe you.*
- *We need to talk about STDs. I'm nervous. This is awkward to discuss.*

Simple, right? You check in and offer a report. But also difficult. When you take a chance by expressing your emotions, shit actually starts to get real. The elephant in the room is named, the boat is rocked, the apple cart is upset. Vulnerability is a high-stakes, high-risk game. With candor, assertiveness, and vulnerability, there's the possibility of loss, but there's so much to gain. Vulnerability is valiant.

You aren't being vulnerable when you acquiesce, nor when you stifle your inner experience, nor when you apologize for something that doesn't warrant an apology. There's a substantial difference between being vulnerable and being submissive. Real vulnerability in George would sound like this: *Kayla, when you demand an immediate answer from me, my throat gets tight, and I feel scared.*

Vulnerability addresses what's on your side of the street—what you know is true for yourself. It means disclosing that you are human and imperfect, which is key to genuine connection.

We all want support and comfort, but men often feel conflicted in expressing those wants. And that perception—that men aren't supposed to want comfort—*that* is some bullshit. Real fucking bullshit. Men not only want these things, we *need* them, far more than we let ourselves admit or express.

Men strive for invulnerability, even though it's through honest, raw reflection and expression that problems are truly solved. It's the addict gathering the courage to attend his first twelve-step meeting and ask another man to be his sponsor. It's picking up the phone to make a sincere apology. It's admitting that you're acting like an asshole when you're acting like an asshole. It's gracefully explaining why you're leaving a job—or a relationship. Expressing vulnerability is often the first step toward peace, progress, and redemption.

The modern male ethos of independence and strength clashes tragically with our natural need to be understood and emotionally supported, and most men make the choice to sacrifice their vulnerability—whether by acting like assholes and driving away those they love, or by repressing themselves to the point of paralysis. We turn against the best parts of ourselves and mistakenly despise that which makes us most human. We sacrifice the parts of us that create connections. We end up feeling alone. We end up being alone.

"To run from vulnerability is to run from the essence of our nature," says the poet David Whyte. "The attempt to be invulnerable is the vain attempt to become something we are not." The asshole and the pussy are both trying to feel invulnerable. The asshole finds a false sense of security in domination and aggression. The pussy finds it in submission and cloaked feelings. Both are losing out. Both damage themselves and those around them. Being untouchable means living life deprived of touch, and that is a high price to pay.

3
THE ELEMENTS OF MEN

The asshole considers himself the most important person in the room. The pussy considers himself the lowest priority in the room.

The asshole doesn't give a fuck about anything but himself. The pussy gives a fuck about everyone but himself.

Who's more important, you or someone else?

Do you give a fuck, or not?

Words are Just Words

Words, with their nuanced meanings, implications, and secondary definitions, can be tricky. The word "nice" used to be an insult, meaning "ignorant" or "foolish." As we've already observed, sometimes the right word is not the nice word. And sometimes the right word just doesn't exist. Nice, right?

We call the asshole *selfish* and the pussy *selfless*. But what exactly do those words mean? *Selfish* and *selfless* are not just about how many cookies you share (or don't share) or whether you shovel snow off your neighbors' driveways. This has nothing to do with greed or altruism. For our purposes, selflessness and selfishness are measures of how much of a man's true self he brings to the situation. Do you make yourself important, or do you make yourself invisible and irrelevant? Are you the single biggest priority in everything you do, like Jonah? Or do you make yourself the lowest priority, like George?

We also call the asshole *shameless*, and the pussy *conscientious*. Jonah, in the immediacy of any moment, doesn't give one fuck or one goddamn about consequences, shame, or other people. George is considerate of everyone else, often to a fault. George shows care; Jonah shows none. To be free of care, to be completely removed from social contracts, to feel no shame—this is what it means to be *shameless*.

To be *conscientious*, on the other hand, is to be meticulous and careful. That much you can learn from a dictionary. What your dictionary won't tell you, however, is that a conscientious person can make himself sick with worry and shame over the smallest of misunderstandings, like a pussy. Thus, we have arrived, once again, at the simultaneous awesomeness and limitations of the two words on our care axis, and we don't give a fuck about the dictionary's feelings on the topic.

The Self Axis: Selfish and Selfless

This is not about you! Or: *Why is everything always about you?* Do these lines sound familiar? Have you been hearing them your whole life—or do you say these things yourself, feeling like you're crazy because you can't figure out how the hell someone can make *everything* about them?

Selfish and *selfless* may sound like value judgments, but the way we look at things, they're simply points on an axis, each with their own positive and negative consequences—no judgment implied. The dick and the asshole, who are on the selfish end of the axis, protect their self-interests; for them, the self is present in everything they say or do. The pussy puts everyone else's interests first; his self is barely there—weightless, invisible, not very important. This is the essence of the **self axis**: Is your self present or absent in your engagement with the world?

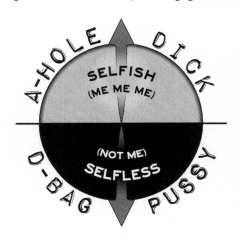

In life, there are times to make your own experience the priority and be very selfish, and times to put your self aside and act selflessly. We're used to praising selflessness and condemning selfishness. It seems obvious, for example, that Jonah's extreme selfishness is destroying his family, his business, his relationships, and himself. What may be less obvious, however, is that George's extreme selflessness is having a similar destructive effect on his life. Abandoning yourself in a conflict isn't exactly generous. Just ask Kayla, George's fiancée, as she deals with the contractor, manages George's promotions, and decides for the fifty-fourth straight night what they'll have for dinner. After a while, that shit isn't just boring, it's *heavy*—back-breaking and soul-crushing. Kayla cannot carry George's abandoned self forever, and she doesn't want to. And submission is not fucking hot. Beyond being a burden, selflessness can be, in a covert way, manipulative and demanding.

On the axis ranging from entirely selfish to entirely selfless, the pussy and the douchebag share the selfless side. The pussy doesn't even think about protecting or prioritizing what's his, and the douchebag completely ignores his real, authentic self, including his real, authentic needs.

Hold on. Wait a goddamn second now, I hear you saying. *Aren't douchebags those insufferable frat-boy clowns who are always flaunting their success? Are you seriously calling a dude who keeps a catalog of sexual conquests in his phone 'selfless'?* Yes and yes, but I understand your confusion. This is another case where the old words are imperfect, so our use of words departs from dictionary usage. Remember, when we talk about selfishness or selflessness, it's not about altruism or greed, it's about whether the *self* is present or absent. And in this regard, the douchebag's whole motivation is to convince the world—including and perhaps especially himself—that he is some other person entirely. He is the great imitator. When you see the douchebag behaving with shameless avarice, he's serving *that other dude,* not his authentic self. You think his behavior represents how he really feels, deep down inside? Well, you're falling for the act.

The Care Axis: Conscientious and Shameless

I'm doing this, and I don't care what you or anyone else thinks! How often do you say that? I know you feel it. We all feel it. Are you ever on the verge of doing something and just *know* that, goddammit, nothing is going to distract you or hold you back? At the other extreme, do you ever want to do something, but just *can't* because you're too worried about what others may think, say, or feel?

On what we call the **care axis**, which ranges from total shamelessness to total conscientiousness, the asshole and the douchebag are on the shameless (or no-fucks-given) side. They go about their day insensible to—or indifferent to—disgrace. Oh, you don't like being shit on? Well, the asshole doesn't even see you there. He damn sure doesn't take into account your feelings or the consequences of what he is doing. The asshole is not concerned with the wounds and scars he leaves on others, and the douchebag doesn't see or acknowledge the damage he does to you or to his true self. They don't give one fuck about shame.

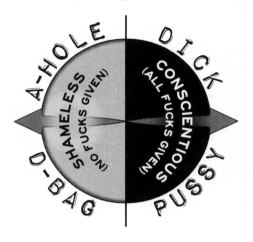

Jonah doesn't seem to have a care for others' experiences, feelings, time, or lives. But he *does* care about the rush of getting what he wants. He still cares, but not about anyone or anything else; the asshole gives a fuck about himself, but not much more.

Shamelessness is a potent and necessary force. We *need* shameless people to make the deepest dives into entrepreneurship, manufacturing, science, and the arts. We need people who exercise no caution, who feel no remorse if they miss the mark or just downright fail. They pair ambition with selflessness and do humanity a great service—and we can be passengers on their ride.

Conscientiousness is defined as being careful. We are not implying that these men are fragile. I am not describing their handling of kittens and fine crystal. Do not think fragile; think only that they care. They give a fuck. They care a lot. Conscientiousness is the application of care and effort. It is care in action, which is not always positive or always negative. Conscientiousness, like care and shamelessness, is neutral.

The dick and the pussy are both acutely aware of the effect they have on others, but this conscientiousness manifests differently in each. If, for example, the pussy is shushed for talking too loud in the theater, he'll selflessly submit; he'll apologize and feel bad for disturbing the shusher. The dick, on the other hand, feels victimized by the bastard who had the nerve to shush him when he wasn't even talking that goddamn loud.

The Four Archetypes of Men

The self axis and the care axis combine to create four distinct archetypes:

Asshole:	*selfish and shameless*
Douchebag:	*selfless and shameless*
Pussy:	*selfless and conscientious*
Dick:	*selfish and conscientious*

When it comes to dealing with life—threats, information, triggers, or stress—none of these combinations is inherently bad. No specific combination is better than another. None lack merit, and they all have benefits. You need access to the basic elements of all four of these combinations. All four! To the extent that you are heavily or exclusively reliant on *one* combination, you are limited. When you take one of the four orientations too damn far, you become one of these insufferable archetypes.

4
THE DOUCHEBAG

You can "douche out" over just about anything. You might be a:

Sigma Alpha Epsilon douchebag
Google employee douchebag
New York Yankees douchebag
Legacy family name douchebag
Triathlon douchebag
Tesla douchebag
Yale douchebag
Burning Man douchebag
Wokeness douchebag
Conservative/liberal douchebag
Vegan douchebag

A douchebag relies on something outside of himself—a group, a status, a belief system, an activity—to stand in for himself as the measure of his worth, and to serve as protective armor against the risks in his life. His obnoxiousness, his bravado, his aloofness? All an act to deflect attention away from the fact that he has abandoned himself.

Jed, the Douchebag in the Wild

It's Friday night, and Jed's got shit to do.

Drake blares from his custom McIntosh home audio system. He pauses in front of his reflection, flexing and tucking and sucking in, and says—actually says out loud—"Damn, I look swole." CrossFit, creatine, two personal trainers, and a daily meal plan delivered from a hip startup—it's paying off and then some. He's looking sharp as fuck.

"It's you, baby. It's your night tonight. It's Jed time," he says to his reflection. "You are the motherfuckin' *man*." He bites his lip coyly, duck-face smirks, then throws himself down on the imported tile to pop off twenty: enough to look jacked, but not enough to break a sweat.

* * *

Now he's walking sockless in SoMa. He's meeting "his boys" before they hit the club. His Range Rover is parked on the street in front of the bar, in a delivery zone. He's parked it illegally, figuring that any worthwhile establishment would be done getting deliveries for the day—and of course, he only "does" worthwhile establishments.

He fist-bumps his boys outside the Vested Option, a trendy new bar best known for overpriced artisan drinks served on fire and twenty-dollar pizza appetizers. It's a place where posers in Zegna suits and Tom Ford shoes can hang with hipsters in Zuckerberg uniforms and Toms shoes. The pizza appetizers are "fired" in a truck that parks inside the bar for happy hour and in the food-truck courts by Costco during the day. Jed and his homies all "know the guy" who owns the bar and the pizza truck:

allegedly retired after allegedly making it big in a startup that allegedly made it huge, now the guy just slings pizza and cocktails.

Jed and his homies dress alike, think alike, act alike, flex alike, and probably fuck alike (on top, so they can watch themselves in their mirrors). Their near-identical distressed jeans were all bought from the same guy. They have a "jeans guy" at a storefront right next to their "beard guy," who's next to their "shoes guy," who's next to their kava bar. Their "t-shirt guy" makes shirts for Simon Cowell, or so they say.

Jed's waddle-swagger looks like it was perfected in front of a mirror (it was). Pimp Scotty struts to his left, while behind them Danny exhales a refinery-sized vape cloud in Brad's face. The stories of conquest fly in this Friday night circle jerk, where high fives are freely given, and no one bats an eye at blatant exaggerations.

"I turned down 30K on that commission this week; I took the equity piece instead. Fuck yeah!"

"I got five calls this week from headhunters working on shit for Kleiner Perkins."

"She came four times before she even saw my cock."

"I bought three percent of a new cannabis company that will definitely go public," tries Brad, making an effort to keep pace with the bigger alphas in this pack.

"Yo, Brad, I maxed out this morning at two-seventy-five!"

Brad takes the jab in stride; he's always in fourth place in bro contests.

The top-shelf shots, Red Bulls, and some CBD from their other bro's dispensary are working their magic. They all claim to have had five or six of everything, including the live resin that "won huge at the Emerald Cup," but really, each had a few drinks and a couple hits off a standard vape pen.

The energy of the evening is building toward their final destination, the new club opening on Folsom. A startup client has booked the entire venue. Anticipation is everything, and these dudes anticipate getting VIP stamps and bitches. The Vested Option is just the first stop.

A pair of women walk past them, and the conversation grinds to a halt, the group's full attention now on the lovelies. "We're negotiating another round right now," Jed is saying. "We definitely want to grow…" Jed pauses his bullshit and reaches a hand out to brush against one of the girl's elbows.

The brunette rolls her eyes, and both women keep walking.

"Where you going?" Jed calls after them. "It's my man Brad's birthday. Don't you want him to have a birthday he'll always remember?" It's not Brad's birthday; Jed is merely shifting to wingman for the inevitable rejection (the beta won't even know). "The mixologist here is my bro!" The bartender is *not* Jed's friend. In fact, he always adds a gratuity to Jed's bill without telling him. "Let me hook you up with a mythical concoction beyond your wildest dreams."

"Fuckin' wanks," the blonde says, never breaking stride.

"Oh, cockblocked. Fuck 'em," Scotty says, tilting his head back to drop in Visine.

The scene repeats with similar results until Scotty suggests, "Let's head to the club, boys."

"Aww yeah. What *what?*" And the group is instantly reenergized, like they've been struck by a lightning bolt.

"And fuck it," Jed says, "Let's take the Rover." With the ladies and their rejections forgotten, and new possibilities awaiting, they jump in the Range Rover for the short drive to the new club. Almost in unison, they reach for the window controls, even opening the sunroof to let in the cold San Francisco fog. If the lights on Folsom are in sync, their drive will only be about three minutes longer than the short walk they could've taken. The lights are not in sync.

Waiting at a light, Jed gets a text from Mandy. *Shit, that ain't good. Forgot to turn this fucker on vibrate.* It's the "Where are you?" text. She fucking hates Scotty and the boys. And Jed hates that she calls them "Sleazy and the Orbits." *Fuck.* He starts to text a lie back to her, saying that he's going to the office, then catching a red-eye out—that would give him a full weekend pass—but he changes his mind and deletes her text without responding.

This Jed Bro Rolls Deep

Step a little closer to Jed—if you can stand the cologne and the smugness. Feels familiar, doesn't he? How would you describe him? A tool? Well, yeah, but a tool tends to be a bit of a slacker, and Jed is no slacker. A simple poser? Maybe his entourage is faking material success or skills, but Jed himself has the receipts—for his ride, for his pad, for his bankroll, for his lifestyle. Is Jed another manifestation of the quintessential asshole? While Jed may be bold, he isn't deliberately going for the jugular in an attempt to dominate. The asshole asks himself, "What do I want?" then says, "Now get the fuck out of my way." The douchebag asks, "Who do I want to be?" and does his best to become that guy. He is more ridiculous than scary. Is he a species of pussy? Nah, he's too lost in his own act. Jed is not regularly checking on his bros or deferring to their ambitions. These dudes are props in his shtick. They are showing up for him, not the other way around.

Okay, so we can see who he's not, but who the fuck *is* this guy?

Simple. Jed is a douchebag. The douchebag is always hard to identify by what he does, because what he does is act like somebody else, and he does so with great conviction. In trying so hard to be someone else, he loses access to his authentic self. He is invisible in his own illusion. Like a pussy, he is selfless. How could this image-conscious, Prada-wearing clown be selfless? A douchebag abandons his own basic needs and authentic *self* for something else. In some ways, this has worked out quite well for Jed; replacing his own needs with the company's interests pays off in options, commissions, advancement, and prestige. But Jed takes it too far. He discards the good core parts of himself, to the point that he believes his own bullshit. He's convinced that this is all working. In his head, those chicks in the bar would really be better off with the distorted version of the Jed-I. That douchebag bullshit is going to wear his ass out.

Jed pumps himself up—and not just at the gym—often referring to himself in third person in a completely non-ironic way ("Jed's the man" and "Jed likes" being the most frequent usages). He reviews his body as if it were a separate entity, mentally approving what he sees if it fits squarely into what he believes to be the male ideal: sculpted abs, ripped arms, steampunk tattoos, high-maintenance haircut, dope threads. His appearance is a requirement for membership in this club. He shares stories of conquests and bravado with his crew, an assortment of dudes who follow his cues, put up with his shit, drink on his tab, stay at his cabin, and wing bitches.

He's got all the working parts, from the trendiest of lofts right down to a James Cameron Deepsea Rolex. In his mind, he's accumulating what a winning man should possess. He likes his fancy shit, which he always manages to bring up in conversation. To get the right kind of attention, he *wills* himself to be the dude that gets attention—from a certain kind of lady, from a certain kind of dude, and maybe, just maybe, from the venture capitalists. It's not about who he "really" is; the douchebag doesn't care about that shit one bit.

Having neither the interest nor the capacity to self-reflect and reevaluate saves douchebags from the pesky but necessary tendency to question themselves, to feel self-conscious, to change course based on outside feedback, or to *feel* like douchebags when they *act* like douchebags. And to some extent, we all act like douchebags.

Impervious, prideful, unaware Jed. His spoken code: *It's my world; you're just living in it.*

Jed Struts In, Wearing Prada

I see the suit before the man, which is the whole fucking point. Jed is immaculate, as if he's on his way to his best friend's wedding or about to start posing for a Saks Fifth Avenue advertising shoot. Even his nails are buffed. Still standing, he looks me up and down, pausing at my shoes, then takes in my office, slowly, letting his eyes rest on the furniture, the rug, the plants. I'm feeling self-conscious. I notice the knot in my guts. What is it, inadequacy? My eyes rest on the end table, the cheapest piece of furniture in my office, and I feel embarrassed. It's from Target, and I've been meaning to upgrade it for months now. Without a word spoken, I have some understanding of this man, and a bit more of myself, too.

"Not sure why I'm here," he says with a shrug, still staring at his phone.

I offer him a seat. He sits at the end of the sofa closest to the door.

"A friend—well, my ex, Mandy—said maybe I should talk to someone, and you had good reviews, so..."

"Tell me about yourself," I say.

Given the opportunity to talk about himself, he puts his phone down. "Well, I came back to the Bay Area right out of college. Scholarship for tennis, but fuck that. It's been a fucking dream, though. Been here seven years now. I live not far from here, in a loft in SoMa. It's cool. I've busted my ass. I sell so much shit now, I'm untouchable. The selling's almost automatic now. Now all I have to do is 'fuck like bull.' I can say shit like that here, right?"

"You're fine."

"Right now, I'm the global head of sales. I'd be worth more if I hadn't fucking listened to my dad. When we go public later this year, I'll be set. I'm going to ditch the Range Rover lease for my dream car, pay off the loft, and build a cabin in Tahoe so I don't have to deal with people bitching about Scotty's fucking parties."

I notice he's mentioned the loft at least twice. I wonder if he's listening to himself, or if he's just running through the list of shit for me to know. I think he's lost his place on his balance sheet of the things he considers assets. And who is Scotty?

He grabs his phone and thumbs through images. "You gotta see this," he says, and I oblige, looking at his homes, his rides, his ladies. He glides through pictures of his "vacays."

"All of this sounds great," I say, "but there seems to be something off, right? Something that shouldn't be, given how 'dialed in' everything is?"

"Yeah, I mean, I don't know." He adjusts his posture. "What I can't figure out is why I'm not the happiest man on the planet. I fucking *made* it. I'm *that* tech-success story. My stock and options are worth millions, and they're bound to go up a fucking ton when we IPO this bitch. Plus, you saw the photos! But I don't know. I'm not sleeping. Maybe that's the problem. Maybe I just need some Ambien or something. I'm always tired. I work out and train like a motherfucker, but I'm always cold. I think it's the summer fog and shit. Fuck, man. Goddamn, I get cold. Maybe it's some thyroid shit. Mandy thinks maybe it's that, too."

"It's always a good idea to get your blood work done and rule out things like the thyroid, but I'm curious about you, Jed—how you're *really* doing on this great ride."

"Yeah, I mean, I don't know. Mandy noticed I wasn't in the game like I used to be. I broke up with her and shit, but we still talk. Need my edge back. But fuck, man. I just don't feel like I used to, which doesn't make any sense, right?"

"Maybe something else is going on, Jed. Externally, things may be going well, but that doesn't always equate to us feeling well inside."

He looks confused for a moment, then smiles, pitying me. "I *got* that something else. Solid connects everywhere. I got every kind of something else any man could ever want."

He's powerful. He's a salesman; he wants me to be a buyer.

"You've got a ton going for you, Jed. Truly, you've killed it," I say, and with this, his eyes widen. "You're successful, you're a good-looking guy, the world is your playground. Yet somehow, I sense that you're not feeling satisfied. You said you were cold. It's warm in here. I'm curious: Are you cold right now?"

He ignores my question, but he softens a bit. "I mean, yeah, I *have* done well," he says. "And, yeah, I *would* like to feel good. I used to, at the beginning, when it was all new and shit. But now, man, it just feels, like, whatever. Here I am complaining about my life when I'm living the dream. Pretty fucking weak, huh? What do they call it, 'first-world problems'?" He pauses. "You know what, man? I'm all good. I'll lay off the booze and coke for a bit. Scotty and I are taking the plane to Cozumel this time next week. Going to do some diving. I'm sure I'll feel better then. You wouldn't believe the ladies down there, man. And when you've got a penthouse suite, you have to turn it away."

There's a lot in this rant, and I'm trying to process it quickly: *lay off the booze...coke...Scotty...the plane...ladies.* "Maybe," I concede, knowing with absolute certainty that this upcoming trip is not the solution. "But what if we were to try something that might help you feel better *before* you and Scotty go diving? Experiment by giving some space to the parts of you that are struggling, for a start."

He's looking at his phone again. "Huh? Xanax? Because I don't know, I don't want to get all zombie and shit. People expect me to be a certain way. I can't just check out."

"No, I mean exploring..."

He looks away, then checks his phone again. I stop speaking when the phone lights up. With a little smile on his face, Jed taps out something. I'm already losing him, if that's possible; there wasn't much there to begin with. Putting the phone back inside his jacket, he tells me he'll think about it. "Gotta jam." We're only twenty minutes into the session.

When the door shuts, I stand, shake off the interaction, look at myself in the mirror, smile, and say, "Hello, David."

Stop It, You Fucking Douchebag

The evening news, social media, *Dateline*, and *SportsCenter* are full of stories about douchebaggery leading to extremes, including death. Lies, acts, and a fantastical self-image or presumed authority come to define the douchebag. Eventually, the douchebag who can't accept reality becomes the douchebag who can't tell his wife or partners that the money ran out or that he's in too deep. To avoid being exposed, douchebags can and will resort to desperate and extreme acts, including life-changing crimes. They may do anything to avoid being exposed. Abso-fucking-lutely anything.

In my practice, I've seen the restless desperation in men who are "successful," who have partners, children, and lifestyles they love. What they *don't* have is themselves. They've played the game according to the rules, done precisely what was expected of them, and succeeded. But these men have insatiable gods—usually corporate ones. I've seen countless men, good men, sacrifice themselves on these altars. They hollow themselves out. Having everything, they feel nothing.

I've seen them struggle to continue the charade. I've seen them struggle harder to *stop* the charade and find out what's inside. The douchebag is a complex character. He's a practiced imitator, and psychotherapy, which calls for total authenticity, puts this imitative faculty to the test. What you see is another person, another character in another life. He has trained himself to give everything away, sacrificing it all to be something else. And too often, the douchebag keeps this going until he just cannot fucking do it any longer.

You may know a douchebag; you may be one. You may cry watching one of these characters spiral down, while in his own mind, in his self-image, he is spiraling *up*. You can laugh at the absurdity of the act, but in your guts, in your heart, you're wishing the douchebag you know and love could just set the act aside and be real. You want to scream at the douchebag you know, "Be *yourself*, goddammit! Be *yourself!*" Well, that's the overwhelming hope I have for Jed and for the real people whose stories contributed to this outsized composite portrait. The douchebag tries desperately to convince himself that all is well, but when he finally lets his guard down, he's just a guy like the rest of us, doing the best he can and sometimes fucking it up.

Daniel Gilbert, Harvard professor of psychology and author of *Stumbling on Happiness*, has done a substantial amount of research on what makes us happy. Turns out, the things we're convinced will bring us happiness fall short, in both duration and quality. "Among life's cruelest truths," he writes, "is this one: wonderful things are especially wonderful the first time they happen, but their wonderfulness wanes with repetition." Jed is learning this firsthand.

All this posing takes a toll. Jed can no longer have a good day unless it's amplified in some way: press about his company that mentions sales, a woman affirming his charm and good looks, cocaine, a new and shiny purchase, or some sign from the universe asserting his specialness. On ordinary days, which are becoming more and more frequent, a desperation begins to creep in, particularly when he's alone. Jed feels dissatisfied, even if he can't identify the source of his unrest. He's unsettled. Untouched. Unfulfilling days often end in a late-night call to the escort service, another example of the kind of connections that keep Scotty on Jed's ride.

When people started treating Jed as though he were indeed special—which, let's be clear, money can and does buy—he began to believe his own propaganda, and he wants that feeling of specialness *all of the time*. This is the douchebag trap: you start to believe that your fantasy is real. Change your thoughts, change your life? Well, look what we have now. It's a very seductive trap.

Jed lacks the solid foundation to get him through what all of us have to endure by virtue of being human: stomachaches, frustration at work, the death of loved ones, life sometimes being "meh" instead of "on fucking fire." He is, in Buddhist terms, a "hungry ghost," impossible to please. Problem is, he wouldn't dare let on that this whole shtick is getting old. He has an image to uphold, thank you very much.

It should go without saying that not everyone falls into the douchebag trap. Plenty of people, including people with douchebag tendencies, are able to remain humble in the face of success, prestige, power, and acclaim. With the right tools, instead of losing themselves in the hype—and that's exactly what it is—they remain who they are, staying grounded and using their status and success to help others.

Concern of the Jed-I

When Jed returns for another session, he's dressed as impeccably as last time, but his eyes are red and puffy, and his posture is deflated.

He tries to put some juice into his spiel; he starts off by sharing photos of penthouse views in Cozumel, then goes on to catalog other recent exploits, but he quickly loses steam.

"To be honest," he says, "I'm exhausted."

I watch Jed. He leaves his jacket on. He's content not to rush. He looks around. I notice him looking at his shoes as he crosses his legs. He adjusts his watch and polishes the watch face against his leg. Still silent.

I match his silence.

He takes the time to turn off his phone, which he didn't do last time. He polishes his watch again. In his silence, he's looking at himself and his stuff, unaware, in some way, that I'm even here. Finally, he looks at me.

I nod. I make a gesture to him. *I'm still here.*

"Scotty and I had fun, I guess, but I don't know, big fucking deal. Everything feels the same. Same strange pussy, different panties. Fuck, we could barely go diving after I paid for that fucking plane Scotty's people hooked us up with. That shit was *nice*. Had to do some international finagling just to get the fuck home. Same crazy shit. I hooked up with this super-hot chick down there, and I'm lying next to her the next morning, all hung over and shit, nose clogged, and I don't even remember her name. That's rock-star shit, right? But it just feels, like, so...you know what I'm trying to say?"

I think I do know, but I want Jed to get there on his own. I simply move him along: "Keep talking it through, man. You're doing great."

"It's like, I know I have this kick-ass life. It's what everyone dreams of, right? But it feels, like, empty. And it's fucking expensive. Something must be wrong with me, right? Maybe I'm depressed or some shit like that? It's not like hanging out with my college friends, but fuck, those guys couldn't hang."

"Jed, I don't think that's it. I think something inside you is trying to get your attention. On the outside, you may be living the dream, but inside you're struggling. I'm interested in the parts of you that are struggling, that miss your college friends, and I want you to be curious about those parts of yourself, too, man. I think that's why you're here."

"Okay. Fuck. Okay. But what the fuck does that even look like? I just want to feel good. I don't give a fuck about struggling; it makes no sense, anyway." He pauses. "I remember feeling like this at tennis sometimes, like when I won a big tournament or ranked nationally. Man, my coach was so proud, but shit, I remember lying there at night afterward, feeling lost, cold."

"Got it. Let's start there. Tell me more about feeling lost, Jed—or feeling cold. Let's shine a light right in there and see what we find."

"Man. Fuck. Fucking fuck. I've got no reason to be having a hard time. I'm having so much fun. I'm kicking ass and taking names, not like this place—"

His provocative dig at me isn't even subtle. I cut him off, "According to who, Jed, and at what price? You're accumulating a hefty tab for your lifestyle, in more ways than one. There's a theme here of 'doing really well' while feeling like complete shit. We've got to understand this." I'm hoping to shake him out of his redundant narrative. While my patience for Jed the person is solid, my tolerance and patience for the douchebag narrative, especially as a psychotherapist in the Bay Area, is clearly not as firm.

He's silent for a noticeable amount of time. But when he speaks up again, his tone is unchanged. He blocks introspection: "Nah, you're jealous, like everyone else. But that's cool, I get it, those with limits are always jocking the limitless. It's all good, David. I got this. Maybe

I'll settle down with this one fine-ass lady I've been seeing," he says, vigorously rubbing his eyes and looking juiced again, his typical self. "A little stability...I could have her move into the loft. Yeah, maybe it's time for the Jed-I to settle down, stay in more, get some rest, but still bring the party to his pad sometimes."

He sits back and sighs loudly. "Fuck me," he says. He can't buy his own bullshit, but he can't stop dishing it out, either. "Fuck me," he says again. Our session continues, but the conversation stalls; we don't get much more than Jed's acknowledgment that there's something he doesn't know or get, that things feel empty, and that he "knows" he shouldn't feel this way in light of, well—I'll call it his douchebaggery.

With that, we begin our regular meetings. Sometimes he shows up, and sometimes he just sits on my couch.

Conditioning of a Douchebag

You come into the world as a blank slate. You learn by watching others and doing what they do, talking the way they talk, dressing the way they dress, assuming postures they assume. We're little imitators, all, and it continues: teenage boys look to powerful, tough, successful, cool men and imitate them. In our culture, the message is "be like *this*," not "be yourself."

In the end, the douchebag is no different than that attention-seeking side of us so determined to earn Mommy and Daddy's approval and praise. The seven-year-old boy wants his parents to watch him dive into the deep end because a witness makes the experience more real. It makes *him* more real. He grows up into the man who wants approval from his peers and from society. He wants to be told that he's doing it right, that he's winning, that he's...the best.

The difference between you and me and the complete douchebag (or maybe not) is that the douchebag is completely reliant on the external world for his sense of self. We appreciate the nods, but we find security some other way—something other than real or pretend coolness, association, or wealth. For the rest of us, these douchebag remedies are fleeting. We don't use the world's gaze to shore up the entirety of our self-esteem.

There's an underlying anxiety that we immediately sense in the douchebag: no matter how completely he merges with his affiliation, image, or persona, he remains a slave to outside input. To us, he quickly becomes absurd and desperate. Sad, even. It irks us; we want to shake the dude and tell him that he doesn't need to try so hard. This urge to rattle the douchebaggery out of the douchebag is strongest in those who know and love the complexities and beauty of the underlying person.

But we all pretend, don't we? You have to put your best face forward in a job interview, or with your in-laws, or on a first date. You can't be authentic all the time. *But can't you?* If you pretend to be someone else, you may score the job or get the girl or impress a new acquaintance. You may rise in the proverbial ranks in the short term, and for that short term, the rise will feel great. But if you persist in this act, presenting to the world only a particular version of yourself—one shaped by outside expectations and opinions—while the rest of you remains squirreled away, you'll be living a fractured, angst-ridden existence, fearful of being found out and of the cracks deepening in the façade. And then there's the exhaustion and complete depletion of the soul that happens in the process.

It's tragic what gets left behind in all that posturing: the beautiful soul, sacrificed on the altar of cool. As Lester Bangs says in *Almost Famous*, "The only true currency in this bankrupt world is what you share with someone else when you're uncool." The opposite of cool is vulnerable, and vulnerability is as real as "cool" is unreal.

This is not to say that you shouldn't *play* in the world of cool. Enjoy it for the ride that it is—I know I do. But remember that it's just a ride. It's like going to Vegas; you enjoy all of its obnoxious ostentatiousness and debauchery, but then you get back to the real world, where buildings and people are made of more than glitz, neon, and silicone. Don't mistake the fantasy for reality. Play with cool for fun, but don't invest. Opt instead for authenticity and vulnerability. You are most beautiful and deserving of genuine praise when you are fully yourself—warts, thinning hair, empty pockets, and all. This is when connection is possible: with yourself, with others, and with something greater than us. And connection, y'all, is the true doorway to freedom and joy—no Maserati required.

Losing or merging your identity to become something else doesn't *necessarily* make you a douchebag. You can become a monk or a marine and adapt the ideals and values of that group. There are countless groups and affiliations that serve others and require some level of assimilation. Marines live lives based on the higher principles imbued in them by the Marine Corps: honor, humility, diligence. They're not inflated by these ideals; rather, they're humbled and inspired by them and attempt to live up to them. They aspire to something higher than ego gratification.

A douchebag uses status to engorge his ego. A douchebag soldier, for example, hasn't *really* given himself over to being a soldier; he's merely using his status and skills to feel more badass than others. The douchebag uses affiliation to feel superior, to garner attention and exaltation, and to make his heroic façade feel credible.

While the asshole might punish and ridicule you, and the pussy might kiss your ass or just give you room, the douchebag will exclude and ignore you or indulge your "ignorance" with pity—he can't have people looking behind his façade. If you happen to find yourself in a dreadful conversation with some douchebag, you'll feel the disconnect immediately. He'll talk over your head, give you patronizing smiles, speak in jargon that pointedly excludes you. Should you snag his interest for a minute (attention span isn't one of the douchebag's strengths), he'll say, "Oh, yeah" and nod, but he won't be able to repeat what you just said. Don't bother redirecting the convo, either, bro. There's one script here, one purpose: to enroll you into his version of himself. If he's successful, and you think or say, "Wow, this guy's really great," you fortify his story. This is what he wants most. He is the consummate salesman, and the product he's peddling is his image or his doctrine, and the two are always intertwined.

After interacting with a douchebag, you'll often feel, well, *douched*. As though you've just participated in something unwholesome—something gross and kind of rubbery and just plain weird that's been done to you against your will. When you squirm out of it, headshaking often ensues, and then some deliberate grounding in your surroundings to make sure you're still part of a living, breathing, complicated world where buses go by streaming exhaust and people look a bit scuffed up by the end of the day.

You'll also tend to feel mighty suspicious. You can't trust a douchebag, and trust is the crucial ingredient in effective communication, the foundational principle that supports relationships. Mostly, though, you'll feel like a prop in his act. The douchebag generates a glaring question: Is this dude for real?

Um, no. He's not.

You'll probably laugh uncomfortably at his efforts, but only at first. There's more. The douchebag—and this is vital to note—wants you to compare your life to his and feel awe. Fuck whoever said "comparison is the thief of joy." In the douchebag's relentless search for confirmation of his baller status, he needs his persona to feel valid and legitimate. He's comparing his act or status to yours. He may look and sound like an asshole as he puts you through this wringer, but he's not seeking the assholish thrill of defeating you; he's getting a douchey charge over persuasively abandoning himself.

You drive a Honda? You live in the East Bay and not in The City? For shame. You haven't tried French Laundry? Don't lift, don't swim, bike, or run? Well, the douchebag is checking it all off his list. Are you not convinced of his coolness?

5

THE DICK

The dick has a narrative, a creed: The world has fucked him over, and it's not his fault. The world is fucking him over, and it's not his fault. The world will continue to fuck him over, and it will not be his fault.

Eric, the Dick

"Fuck."

Fuck this pile of unfinished work. Fuck these essays gathering virtual dust on my piece-of-shit company laptop. Fuck the shitty Imogen Heap-listening neighbors, and fuck the ones on the other side with their fucking Office theme song. Fuck every cheapskate landlord for never soundproofing these fucking apartments. Fuck you, garbage trucks and horns and sirens and Muni and all that yammering coming from fucking Church Street.

"Fuck."

Fuck four-dollar coffee with eight-dollar organic avocado on artisanal toast. Fuck Fox, MSNBC, Black Friday, Amazon Prime, Jonathan Franzen, and fuck you, Jack Fucking Dorsey.

"Fuck you, Bill Maher," Eric says to the screen.

"Eric?" Annie, his girlfriend and the real target of every one of the fucks in this particular but terribly familiar diatribe, responds to the three audible fucks.

"What?" he says, with a quiet voice and shaking fingers. He blinks, but the world refuses to go away, and his frustration still thrums.

"What are you thinking?"

Eric sits back in his ergonomic chair, flicks a bit of lint from his shoulder, and scans his apartment. *What a fucking shithole. Three fucking grand a month to live in squalor.* That's what he's thinking, but he keeps it to himself.

"Eric?" Annie says, leaning closer as if pulled in by some invisible force.

This is the routine. She leans in; he pedals back. He needs quiet. Distance. Space. He sighs, briefly shuts his eyes against being alive. He opens them, and she's still there, and just the sight of her in this moment makes him feel harassed. *Why don't people ever let up?*

"What's up?" she asks.

Fuck, does she rehearse this shit in the mirror? "Nothing," he says. He tries to soften his face and look Annie in the eye, but he can't bear it right now. He knows she tries hard.

"Are you sure?" Annie asks now, ripping him out of his reverie, which he much prefers to all this reality around him. Her hands are clasped between her knees as she peers at him, her face crisscrossed with good intentions and concern. "Are you overthinking this party?" She doesn't wait for an answer. "I know this sort of thing is hard for you. I know, sweetie, but I really, really want you to come with me. It's just a holiday party, and all of my friends at work really want to meet you. I just think it's time, you know? You're so mysterious to them! They think you're in the CIA or something." She smiles, suddenly worried that calling him mysterious will set him off.

Spending a Friday night at your company's holiday party sounds about on par with getting fisted by King fucking Kong. The thought is so insistent that Eric fears he might actually say it, but he doesn't. He recognizes that he's put off this kind of thing with Annie for so long that he should probably just suck it up and get it over with already. "Um, sure, yeah," he says. "I mean, that's not really my scene, the whole work party thing, but okay, sure, I'm in."

"Okay, grumpy pants," Annie says, and pats his knee. He retreats further. "You might even have a good time. I'll make dinner reservations at seven, and we'll go to the party from there." She gives him a quick kiss before he can protest, grabs her purse, and walks out the door pumping both fists in the air. Victory.

Fuck holiday work parties. People just standing around talking about nothing. "Hilarious holiday sweater, man." "Have you been to that new place in the Mission? Their truffle fries are dee-lish." "Oh my God, thank you, you're the best!" What do people actually get out of these conversations? Marcona almonds. Undeserved LOLs. Everything is not fucking lovely; it's just the same old crap wrapped up in a different package. Fuck. While this powerful voice inside him rages, the true feelings emerge: He tends to feel excluded at this type of gathering. Awkward. Uncool. *What the hell is wrong with me? Why can't I just Rodney King this and get along?* He shuts that down fast. *I'm fine. Fuck stupid, vapid holiday parties and everything they do to me.*

Eric is frozen in his chair, which he can never get to feel quite right. He feels screwed—by Annie, by his boss, by "expectations," by the world, by the fucking Thai place that still hasn't rung his doorbell. As he sits alone, he feels faint, impatient. He opens up Facebook. He resents Facebook...

Bzzzzzz. Bzzz Bzzz.

About fucking time.

Two minutes later, after thanking the delivery guy in such a tone that he'd have to be an idiot not to hear the sarcasm, Eric is eating mediocre, lukewarm curry. He scrolls through his feed; it's an itch he can't help but scratch, even if social media leaves him feeling like he has mental herpes. "So fucking phony," he says out loud to a photo of a college buddy volunteering at Glide Memorial. "Right on, dude. You just keep changing the world!"

An hour later, he's in the middle of posting a pointed deconstruction of someone's grossly misguided views on who was the biggest fuckwit at Theranos, and he can feel his ass falling asleep. Annie's status update flickers at the top of his screen: "Eric and I are confirmed for the holiday swar-ay this Friday, peeple! EXCITED!"

He feels his eyes burn. *Goddammit. Seriously? Why does she have to broadcast it? Is nothing sacred anymore?* He wishes he could delete his name from her post, but all he can do is untag himself. He'll explain later if she brings it up. *Besides, it's my fucking right! I've told her that I don't want anything personal about me posted on Facebook. The photos from the "anniversary dinner" last month were bad enough. Now this? She shouldn't have even asked me to go to this "swar-ay." I fucking hate these things. And learn how to fucking spell, "peeple." Doesn't she know these kinds of things are offensive? Typos! Facebook! Does she even care about me, or is it always about her, her, her?* He stares at the computer screen, livid. Positively boiling.

He can hardly sleep that night.

* * *

Feeling wronged, he pulls away even more in the days that follow. He tucks himself into his own misery and keeps himself more zipped up from the world than usual. He's slow to respond to Annie's texts, and when he finally does, his answers are short and distant. He makes sure never to ask a question. Calls go to voicemail. Facebook posts are retroactively unliked. Each time he commits one of these relationship crimes, he feels a pang of regret and shame for acting so childish, but the justice he feels overshadows it and then some. He is a man of principle, and he has a point here, goddammit.

Friday night rolls around, and Eric dicks around on Twitter until half past six, then throws on a suit and rushes out the door. He's feeling miffed about having to leave his apartment. *I didn't even get to my writing project, and now I have to leave, dammit.* The restaurant is now his least favorite. *I'll have the tiny cut of grass-fed beef crusted with sea salt aged in a bamboo barrel. Fucking pretentious San Francisco diners. Fuck me.* And just to remind himself: *Stupid startup party, and stupid fucking commercialized holidays.*

He arrives fifteen minutes late to find that Annie has already ordered a drink. She sits at the bar, and he has to admit she looks sexy as hell. He pauses in the doorway and is taken by her radiance. Her long, glossy hair covers her bare back. *Those legs. How did I get so lucky?* He feels something unfamiliar spreading across his face—the hint of a genuine grin—but then he remembers what she's making him do, and he feels his eyes squint, his lips setting into a thin line. He stiffens, taps her on the shoulder, and says a flat "Hey." This is not an affectation; *fucking hell* does he not want to be here. She is comfortable. He is about to lose his shit, and he wants a reaction.

"Hurry," she says, rising to give him a quick kiss on the cheek, "or we'll lose our reservation."

Fine by me, he thinks, recalling the gyro truck on the corner. But she's all business, and this grates on him, too. The hostess gestures for them to follow her into the hipster restaurant, where ten-year-old tech millionaires are jabbering away over three-hundred-dollar plates of California fusion douchebag deliciousness. He and Annie sit, and he's immediately annoyed—even more so than usual.

Her hair is freshly blown out. Her nails are a rich holiday red. It's a new look. She's beaming with excitement, gushing with enthusiasm. This is an Event, and that alone makes him recoil; he hates bald attempts at doing something memorable. She tries to coax him out, peppering him with questions about his week, about work, telling him he looks handsome even though his shirt could use some attention.

He keeps his eye on the door as if plotting his escape. He's remote, offering perfunctory answers, getting testy from all this energy around him. He's fuming inside, and he makes no move to hide it, folding and unfolding his napkin. He's clearly on edge.

"What's going on, Eric?" Annie finally asks.

He rolls his eyes, sensing the drama train right behind her. "Nothing. I'm fine," he huffs, wishing he were at home. "Why do you call me Eric when you're sitting across the table from me?" he snaps. "I *know* you're talking to me. It's annoying."

Tears spring to Annie's eyes. She looks away, then back at him, thumbing away the running mascara. "What's going on with you?" she asks, quieter now, more composed. "What's wrong?"

"Nothing is *wrong* with me," he says, air-quoting "wrong" and slumping back in his chair. A waiter runs by, and Eric narrows his eyes, riled that the server seems to have so much purpose. *Doesn't she realize that this is all a fucking façade? Here we are at a nice restaurant before going to your big party. What's wrong with you, Annie? You're getting everything you wanted. You should be happy.* He cycles through his bitching and moaning internally, saying nothing.

"This is about the party, isn't it?" Annie says.

He says nothing. *Let her figure it out. This isn't rocket science.*

"Please, Eric," she says. "You've been putting me off forever. Please just do this for me. Don't ruin the evening. I love you; I just want my friends to meet you."

"For starters, they're not your friends—they're people you work with. Pretty big difference there, *Annie*. Two, I'm not ruining the evening. I just fucking got here, and I'm just being me. And how long do we have to wait to order? We've been sitting here for ten minutes with our menus closed. What's up with this place? I swear you only like it because your friends come here." He sees her shake off his needling comment.

"I never ask you to do anything," she says. "It's just this one time. It's just a party. My friends don't bite."

Eric hears Annie's words, though he is only listening to the voices in his head. *She must have learned this technique in HR training, along with how to spout meaningless platitudes to new hires and how to hold court at boring holiday parties.* "They don't bite, but they sure do suck."

"Just. Give. It. A. Chance. Please, try to have a good time. I'm begging you. For me, for us. Just do this."

"Fine," he breathes, feeling that his willingness to see things through deserves a colossal pat on the back. For now, though, he sullenly orders his food, bitches about it, eats in strained near-silence. They summon an Uber, and Eric grudgingly makes his entrance with Annie at her douchey boss Jed's "pad," a loft in SoMa that's far finer than anything Eric will ever be able to afford—one more reminder of the unfairness of the world.

Eric helps himself to one of the martinis being passed around by a woman who looks like she's advertising her OnlyFans account. *What is wrong with the world?* He tries to make small talk, flinching inside all the while: "Yep, it sure is foggy; thanks for enlightening me." "Totally, this year just *Zoomed* by; hilarious." "Yeah, I've heard The Maldives is a good place to vacation." He has a scotch, and that helps—a little.

A political conversation gets heated, and Annie pulls him away right when Eric is actually getting interested in something at this sorry excuse for a party. He hears stories about the workplace as Annie sets off to mingle: "Bonuses were *suh-weet* this year." "We def need to upgrade the pinball and Skee-Ball machines in the lounge." "Parking is a *total bitch*." *These poor souls; they've known real heartache.* He tries to jump in on a conversation about the restaurant where he and Annie just ate, but when he starts cataloging his list of gripes with the place, he's met with blank stares.

Drink in hand, he assumes a position alone by the window, the night outside glittering with lights, and wonders why bloggers don't make more money than this Jed wanker. Inside, he's dying, and at a certain point he simply can't stand it any longer. He feels like a cornered animal. He checks his phone; it hasn't even been an hour. *Fuck*. He hears Annie's tinkle of a laugh and looks up to see her by the bar, laughing with some tall guy who's been groomed from birth for J. Crew and tee times and Breckenridge winter breaks.

But hold up—Annie actually seems to be enjoying herself. Like, truly enjoying herself. She seems so relaxed around this dude, Eric thinks, feeling his stomach drop into the center of the earth. She's never that quick to smile around me, he thinks, and a crushing pain shoots through his guts. Self-doubt and recrimination bubble up through his body but quickly dissipate. There's no way he's going to let those bubbles reach his conscious mind.

"I came to your party," he types out in a text to Annie as he hustles down the stairwell to the street below. "Have to bail. Got to write. You seem happy talking to Bradley Cooper anyway, so see you later, I guess."

Ah, relief. Righteous clarity. Freedom. Victory.

With that, he switches his phone off. He feels a kick in his step; he's looking forward to swinging by his corner market for a six-pack and settling in to write. But the moment Eric plops down into his chair and pops open an Anchor Steam, the image of Annie with Bradley Cooper overwhelms his thoughts. Eric proceeds to pick it apart in meticulous detail in his mind: shallow, phony, flirty.

Fuck his essays for a bit. Recon is needed. He checks Instagram, scrolling through Annie's photos, hoping for and fearing another photo of her and Coop at some "work event." Forty-five minutes pass. An hour. Nothing.

A knock at the door disturbs him from his fervent search. He hides his beer below the Thai takeout containers in the trash, pulls the hard copy of his manuscript out of hiding, and minimizes the browser on the screen. Annie bursts in, full of fire he's never seen before.

"You had to bail?" she starts, her face red. "*Bail?* To write? I can't believe you left without even saying goodbye to me! After only what, thirty minutes? How could you do that to me?"

"Look," he says, flattening his tone to emphasize how high-pitched and insane hers is. He slouches casually against the wall. "I didn't—"

"Fuck you."

"Listen, Annie, I didn't—"

"Fuck you."

"Will you hear—"

Annie interrupts him, "I will look, listen, and hear when I *feel* like looking, listening, or hearing. Let me guess: you didn't do anything wrong tonight?"

"Listen. Easy. Calm down. I didn't *do* anything to *you*. Let's be really clear about that. I didn't want to be there. I said I'd go, and I did. I hung out in the land of the contrived and phony for a while, and now I'm working, which is how I want to spend the rest of my Friday night—and I don't need to ask your permission for that."

"We were supposed to spend the evening together." Annie is desperate, buzzed, exasperated. She is also on fire. Her anger and sadness are finally surfacing in this showdown. Her anger says, *I dare this man-child to tell me one more time that I sound like his mother. Oh my God, I dare this dick to say it. I dare him.* But her overwhelming sadness wins out. "Eric," she says. "You make me feel so…unwanted."

He senses her sadness. He has the upper hand now. "Don't turn this on me, Annie. Don't try to make me feel guilty. I went. Why would you want me to be someplace I don't want to be, anyway? And by the way, you looked perfectly content giggling with that dude."

"Who? What? *Joel?* Give me a break! He's just a friend. He works in marketing. And besides, he's married!"

"Oh, so if he *wasn't* married, you'd be interested? Well, too bad for you, I guess. You could cavort all over town together, taking in all of the important parties. Seems like you two have similar priorities. What's on sale this weekend at Anthropologie?"

"Fuck you," she says slowly, calmly and deliberately.

The words themselves don't phase him, or even the tone; it sounds meek compared to the previous fuck-yous. But something about it... holy fuck-you of fuck-yous. The intent startles him.

"I was joking, Annie. But come on, you were all over that guy."

"Don't try to make this about Joel," she says. "You are *not* the victim."

She hasn't taken off her jacket yet, and this confuses, frightens, and elates him all at once. It means she might bail soon. It also means she might *really* bail. Soon.

"You left without even giving me the courtesy of a goodbye, making me look like a complete fool in front of my friends. You knew what that would mean. You didn't even care."

"I *do* care. Don't take this personally," Eric says with a sigh. "It's just not *me*. I don't like these kinds of things. But clearly Joel loves these 'swar-ays,' and while I was talking to the three most uninteresting humans on the planet, you guys were having a grand old time. So, I left."

"Oh my God! You act like I'm some controlling, philandering bitch when I just wanted you to be a part of my life." Tears drip from her face; she makes no attempt to wipe them from her cheeks.

Eric sees only desperation, and he's pissed. *What a complete waste of time and words. Now she's my fucking puzzle to solve. Now I have to carry her desperation around, when in fact—in fucking fact—I was the one put out by her fucking party.* "Don't cry, Annie. Just, just...don't expect me to be some pussy who follows along everywhere. Or some douchebag who gets off on rubbing elbows at some tech millionaire's SoMa loft. I mean, Jed? Come on, *that* guy? You should know this about me by now. And if you don't, you might as well get used to it." He takes a breath. "Now, I've seriously got to get some writing done before I lose an entire night because of some party."

With this, Annie walks out. The door doesn't close behind her.

Later, but not much later, Eric is home, still feeling angry, wronged, inconvenienced, misunderstood, and unappreciated. Another day, another conflict. He goes through three beers, a bag of chips, Facebook, and a forum of freelance writers. He dives right into the online kerfuckle of the day. But his vitriol for other peoples' lives, both on Facebook and in the forums, has lost momentum. He ends his night apathetically buzzed, dick in one hand while awkwardly trying to maneuver the mouse with his left hand. He clicks through free porn videos. He finishes the night with a climax but without satisfaction.

The Glory of the Malcontent

It's safe to say that Eric is in no way sacrificing himself to please Annie—quite the opposite. An aggrieved creative genius? Well, he'd like to think so. But for the sake of brevity, let's just say it: Eric is a dick.

We all know "dick" is slang for penis; it would be disingenuous to ignore that connection. With the exception of some dudes legally named Richard and a spotted British pudding, a "dick" is a penis or an aggrieved person. We use the word to refer to the victimized, selfish, and conscientious male archetype. Is it just coincidence that the penis and the selfish dude who thinks he's been wronged are both super-duper sensitive? Probably not. The regard that the dick (person) has for himself and for his dick (penis) is likely the greatest connection between the two definitions. "Dick" is the only fitting word for this archetype.

The dick combines an extreme, self-serving worldview with fastidious awareness of others, generating the infuriating superpower of victimhood. He can tell you how everyone and everything is fucking him over, and he'll probably make it your fault. An asshole shamelessly forces you to submit, but a dick meticulously needles you to quit. Where a pussy takes the blame and placates, the dick assigns the blame and irritates. If you try to show a dick where he stands with our model of male archetypes, he might call it an insulting, confusing, reductive attack on his complicated identity—when he finally starts responding to your texts five days later.

From the way Eric tells it to himself, you would think the whole universe was conspiring against him—the coffee, the noise, the Thai restaurant, the world. Something as simple as going to a party with his girlfriend is treated as a universal conspiracy that deserves his resentment and disdain. He's a victim, goddammit, and poor fucking him. He arrives late to dinner and proceeds to make the evening miserable, feeling fully vindicated in his reasoning and actions. He never wanted to go; she manipulated him—end of story.

The dick mantra is consistent: Whenever you do something, I will determine the fairness of what you've done—to me. If I decide it's not fair, I'm entitled to pull out, pull away, and behave selfishly, and it's *your* fault. For the record, I'm just being real. You're very fucking welcome.

Eric's dickish worldview is on full display when he accuses Annie of something inappropriate between her and her coworker. To Eric, this is something deliberately done to him—she and Joel are colluding against him—and it's part of why he leaves the party. If you've ever dealt with a dick, you know that this is another dick move: deflect and project.

The asshole is a dangerous threat who sets off our survival responses. The dick is more of an impossible pain in the ass who can't be pleased. He's perpetually tuned into KSUK radio. Beautiful day in the park? Yeah, but there's trash on the ground, it's cloudy, and there's flies. Lovely dinner out on the town? Sure, but the waiter could have been faster with the bill, and that screaming kid—why do they allow children into restaurants? What the hell is wrong with the parents who bring them along? Scowl, point, accuse, deflate, sulk, complain, blame. He rarely laughs unironically.

The asshole likes power. The pussy seeks a sense of safety and, to serve this need, puts others in charge. The douchebag seeks adoration. All of these are understandable benefits, however fleeting. So, what's the dick's shtick? The dick derives a level of validation from opposition—casting himself as the heroic truth-teller, the only honest man. He justifies making himself his own greatest priority, while experiencing the world as an invading entity that is trying to corrupt or rob him.

Sounds like fun, doesn't it? Well, if you're wondering how you can become more of a dick and delude yourself in this very same self-victimizing way—if, in other words, you want to be *more* dickish—here's what I suggest:

- *Create a compelling narrative about something unfair being done to you by someone: your girlfriend/wife/partner, your children, an institution, a colleague, the government. Really, there's no limit to who or what you can identify as wrong, unjust, or threatening. Eric often looks to Twitter and the pundits to get started.*
- *Play your narrative on repeat in your head. Revel in the wrongness and injustice of it. You are completely right; they are totally wrong. Solidify your case. Hone your points. Tell yourself you are brave and honest. Your ego is sacred.*
- *Utilize black-and-white thinking, or create a million shades of gray, or any combination of the two—however inconsistent or hypocritical your position may be—to serve your interests in the moment.*
- *Gaslight and manipulate at will. Get creative, but don't hesitate to let social or mass media do the heavy lifting for you.*
- *Believe your narrative completely. This is crucial: you must convince yourself that these points you've honed are, in fact, objective truths. Resist different interpretations of events, even if they are backed by actual facts or science. You are obviously correct.*
- *Never surrender; defiance is necessary and valiant. Others who think differently are wrong, ignorant, dumb, or evil. If somebody stumps you, take a well-deserved break from that bullshit to collect your thoughts until you've figured out how your adversary is still wrong. If you never figure it out, you never need to discuss it with them again.*

- *Police yourself. If you ever do back down and concede a point, berate yourself for being a pussy or a sellout, and firmly resolve never to let yourself be bullied or tempted away from your truth again.*
- *Never, ever, be curious about what you're feeling underneath your narrative. Do not go there. Your position has nothing to do with the way you feel. Tell yourself, "Fuck feelings."*

I shouldn't need to say it, but I will: I want you to be *less* dickish. These tactics, shared tongue in cheek, will help you be more dickish, but they won't help you make friends, keep friends, or find any true satisfaction in your life.

Eric sees himself as the ultimate truth-teller on a planet of complete posers, assholes, and pussies. The demands he makes on the world are prerequisites for his participation in it. He wants authenticity, rawness, and engagement. He thinks the rest of us are full of shit for behaving like good sports while he cowers behind a veil of supreme disappointment and self-pity. He knows we're putting on an act, and our real purpose is to make him look bad, because, well, everything is about him.

The dick only considers himself, but he ceaselessly accuses others of being inconsiderate toward *him*. He is mindful of others only in this way: *How are you fucking me today?* He's the guest of honor at his own pleasure party and at his own pity party.

Eric Slouches Begrudgingly on My Sofa

By the time we walk the twenty feet from my waiting room to my office, I'm feeling a tiresome drag. *Will I be able to help this guy?* I get curious. By paying attention to my own experience in my office, I learn a great deal about how my clients engage with the world and how they do or don't make contact with others. I notice Eric do a double take at the speaker near the door, the source of white noise. He shakes his head deliberately, as if, somehow, this fake noise is symbolic of some bullshit yet to come.

He has a degree from Sarah Lawrence. He considered law school, even going so far as to take the LSAT. Almost thirty and single, he lives alone in a small apartment close to my office. He's a writer working unhappily at a publishing startup. He has changed jobs frequently. He thinks his writing prowess is unappreciated in today's online media, which targets wankers with short attention spans and compromised cerebral cortexes. These basics are reported in a flat, distant tone.

"Your intake said, 'Maybe some shit to deal with.' That seems like a great place to start—maybe some shit to deal with. Sound good?"

"Well, I'm pretty sure it said, 'Some fucking shit to deal with,' but hey, you read my form, so that's good."

"Yeah, 'some fucking shit.' That's right." There is another noticeable pause. Eric is still guarded. I feel awkward. He plays his game well.

"Why are you here?" I ask finally.

He scratches his face. "You know, I don't even know, really. Annie— she was my girlfriend, kind of—well, she was always on my ass to talk to someone. Said I complained too much and acted like I was depressed. I hate it when anyone tells me what to do, so naturally I refused. But in hindsight, some of what she said may...I mean, I'm a glass-half-empty kind of guy. But shit, I think I just see things as they really are, man. And things aren't so great, you know."

"Got it. So, you're just being honest, seeing things as they are," I say, reflecting his narrative back to him.

He nods, settling just a tiny bit. "Annie and I broke up. Great girl. I liked her. But it went to shit like it always does. She was good...good company. Yeah, she was good." His stammering when he talks about Annie stands out. His tone is flat again.

"So, how does this all—"

"I'm tired, and I'm tired of always being tired and whatever. I'm frustrated. I'm sick of everything, all the shit around me. Fucking San

Francisco. This town hates everyone who isn't either a billionaire or shitting on my steps." He stops when he's out of breath, just as abruptly as he interrupted me. He's staring at the base of the door. He waits. He pauses, listening to the white noise, barely audible through the small gap below the door. "I put it on my intake form, so I know you're going to ask. I guess I think about suicide. Sometimes. Sometimes I just don't care if I live or die, and when I'm driving, I think about how easy it would be to jerk the wheel and fly off the side of Highway 1—you know, after that tunnel at Devil's Slide? Usually by the time I get to Taco Bell on the beach in Pacifica, the feeling is gone. But then I go through that fucking tunnel, and those lights flash at me, they reflect off of everything. And I don't know, man, *wha-booosh!* Off. Over those rocks and into the waves. Relief."

"Yeah, so some part of you wants out, wants it to end. Do you ever get serious, with a specific plan, a particular day, a way you'd actually do it? Would it be off the 1?"

Eric doesn't respond instantly. "Sure," he says finally. "Fucking sure. Sure. Yeah. What's the fucking point? And you can add *this* experience to the list of pointlessness, too, by the way, since I'm sure you're astutely keeping track of my issues. But I would never do it; don't worry about your liability. I wouldn't give the world the fucking satisfaction."

Wow. He's just said so much. By the end of our first session, he's convinced that not much good is going to come from meeting with me, my fee is too high, and the walk from his place was a bit of a shlep. There's something energy-sucking about him. Nevertheless, I'm optimistic that he'll be able to see himself and the world through a different lens.

The Dick Pic

The dick is selfish. There is nothing in this world that is not about him, for him, to him, at him, or from him. Nothing happens that does not revolve around him or his interpretation of events. He is omnipresent in his own reality. Selfishness, for the dick, is not about a lack of generosity; rather, it's about his presence in everything that ever was or ever will be. The shit that is about him is limitless in scale and frequency. When Napoleon marched his army into Paris in 1800, even that was personal and about the dick who is now living in the twenty first century.

His conscientiousness, in its extremely dickish spun-out form, is only about doing the right thing *for the dick*—a distorted version of a moral conscience—and it's just plain fucking ugly to the rest of the world. It's useful to be aware of our own and others' feelings and their social and psychological impacts; it's disturbing when the dick weaponizes that awareness.

The dick deftly uses our responses, concern, or interests to draw us in, then uses the same concerns to push us away. Just when it seems like he's on the verge of using his awareness of us and our feelings to build a connection, he spins the story back to his own feelings. Our hopes are raised and dashed, over and over. If you feel like a human yo-yo, it might just be that a dick is skillfully playing you.

* * *

Eric is sad. He's scared. He's angry. He's hurt. He's profoundly disappointed. He needs to grieve—my God, does he need to grieve. But for all of his outward expressions of disappointment and grievance, he's not actually allowing himself to authentically feel any of his own personal grief. What he does feel is the distracting satisfaction of victimization.

Eric is married to his own rigid life narrative. This is true for most of us too; we believe what we believe in order to understand our feelings. If it's too damn hard to figure something out, we just create an explanation that works well enough. "He's just an asshole," for example. And with a simple explanation, we end the process. That convenient story we tell ourselves is a simple solution to complicated feelings and to the complexity and insecurity of life. When we experience disappointment, hurt, and loss, and it's painful as hell, living and coping with it all means finding a way to move on. The dick soothes himself by concocting a story of blame that's plausible enough to reassure him that he's not the source of his problem, so he can move on to the *next* thing that's wrong.

These internal narratives start with a *feeling*. Nothing more. You experience some hard feelings, and your narrative, which attempts to make sense of those feelings, usually implicates someone or something as a triggering cause: *This is your fucking fault.* This narrative shifts your attention to the perceived cause of the irritation: *Now look what you made me do* (or worse, *feel*). Examine the hard feelings and take full responsibility for them? No fucking way. No chance. No. For the dick, that's never an option. He'll choose blame over feeling pain any damn day of the week. The narrative, instead of being a tool to help you understand your feelings, becomes a tool to help you *avoid* understanding.

Can you see it now? What looks like somebody working through their shit is often somebody just working up *new* shit to cover up their *real* shit, just so they can get on with their day. But getting on with a day is not the same as getting on with a life. Show me a life made of these narratives, and I'll show you a life made of Groundhog's Days— feedback loops of dissatisfying climaxes, without real relief, self-understanding, or healing.

A dick's narrative cuts him off from his hard, deeply-rooted feelings, keeping them from moving through him. Those hard feelings— which he judges to be humiliating, "unmanly," or otherwise unworthy—remain buried and suppressed beneath the momentary feelings his victim narrative generates. His most reliable narratives rigidify; his beliefs rigidify; his body rigidifies; his *life* rigidifies, leaving him in a rut. A dick like Eric holds onto his stories for dear life, even as they strangle him.

For the record, feelings *are* manly; feelings are cool. Dickishness is not cool. It hurts people, and hurting people sucks. Stop that shit.

Eric's Dick Therapy

"Doesn't feel like much could ever be different, huh?" I ask quietly at Eric's second session.

"Nope," he says, and his eyes briefly light up—it's some small comfort to have someone else acknowledge the disgruntled pain he's always in. "Same shit, different day. You know?"

"I do," I say. "Let me ask you this: When was the last time you truly felt alive?"

"Good question." He sinks back into his seat and thinks. "Probably when I squared off with this guy in the office over a piece the other day. That really got my juices flowing. It was like...I was like...I was able to get out of the fog for a few minutes, you know?" His face tightens for a moment, and he glances away. "Annie and I had some fun, I guess. I mean, before. At first. We used to laugh. In the end, she wasn't fun. Anything *but* fun."

"When you talked about Annie just now, I noticed something. A sadness. Right here." I place a hand over the center of my chest.

This pisses Eric off. He holds out his hands as if to fend me off. "Dude, you don't know me or what I've been through, so you can knock off that whole 'compassionate therapist' thing."

This is unexpected—or somewhat unexpected, at least—but I decide to stay real. "Whoa," I say. "I didn't expect that; now the sadness is replaced by a jolt. You didn't like that one bit, eh?"

"I hate it when people presume things about me, and here I am in therapy, which is a fucking cliché in itself. You might as well have me lie on my back and offer me a tissue and tell me it's not my fault, *Good Will Hunting*-style."

I nod, knowing what it's like. "You don't want any bullshit from me."

"None."

We sit together for a moment in silence.

"No bullshit," I say. "What if things could actually feel different in the world, Eric?"

"*Right.*" He pauses, then sits up a tiny bit. "Different how?"

"For starters, what if you didn't feel so put upon all of the time? What if life had more energy?"

"Well, yeah, I'd take that. But I don't see how you're going to do that."

"You're here. Why not give me a chance? See if this isn't all just a cliché. If nothing works, no harm done. Anytime you want to know anything about what I'm doing or why, just ask. I'll be open and honest with you, and if I slip up in some way—which I do from time to time—I imagine you'll let me know, and I promise I'll be real with you if that happens. For the record, and for whatever it's worth, I did feel a pang in my heart when you talked about Annie. I did feel sad. That was not bullshit." I pause for a moment and add, "Not everything is bullshit."

This is me setting the contract. Eric is a straight shooter, and he's distrustful. He's a dick. I get that. I want him to see that things can be honest here, real, which is the very thing he's starving for.

"I don't know, man," he says, not yet ready to commit. "I mean, come on. Look at all the bullshit in the world. Everyone is just so inauthentic. Look at our political leaders! Look at every single fucking person on TV! It's all just so sickening to me. It's all such a lie, and it seems like I'm one of the few to even notice. I used to write about it. A lot. I had this…" Eric pauses. "I had this blog."

Chills run through me.

This may seem like an odd point in our conversation to get the chills. So what if he had a blog? Everyone's had a fucking blog. But right at this moment, Eric is beginning the process. I sense a shift. He's talking about something meaningful. And that gives me chills.

"I had this blog that we tried to roll into a video production—

YouTube-type shit, with a podcast." The pause changes his expression. "I had this idea that I could say real things about real people and be real or something. I dunno. I just had this idea that people *wanted* something. Fuck it all, though. I couldn't get enough subscribers to get revenue, I ran out of money, and I had to take a job at this news gig. We create content for corporate video websites like it's real news or some shit like that. We don't report the news; we tailor the news for people to link to. It's all over websites, and you'd have no idea that we were writing it. The elite's version of reality that helps them control the masses—"

Another rant.

I cut him off. "I won't argue with you on that," I say. "But the way you respond to it—I want us to be interested in that. I'm interested in you. I want *you* to be interested in you. I get chills listening to you talk about your blog and what it meant to you. I want you to be interested in *you* and not get sidetracked by the giant agenda."

I've interrupted him mid-jam, and I'm curious what he'll do next. The urge to dive back into his rant and move away from the vulnerability of his blog is clearly tempting him. What I want is for him to move in from the perimeter, away from the safety and miserable familiarity of his self-righteous dickishness, and toward his center. To do that, he'd have to *feel*. He touched upon it for just a second; now I'm encouraging him to try it again.

"Am I wrong, though? Nope, I'm fucking right, and I'm not going to change who I am to fit into this bullshit system and be like everyone else, just eating whatever shit is on my plate."

Oh, well. Goddammit, Eric is exhausting. His conviction in his interpretation of reality is absolute. He's a fundamentalist. But a few times each session, we share a moment, a human moment of connection, of recognition, of something outside his airtight narrative. He returns week after week. I'm worn out after our sessions, but also hopeful.

Moby Dick

Bitterness and resignation are Eric's chief experiences. He only knows how to feel alive by resisting wrongs—and even then, only from behind his walls. He watches porn, peruses Instagram in a state of infuriation, comments on forums under a fake name, and tweets. He achieves some temporary reprieve, but "temporary" is the key word here. To him, his resistance feels essential, obvious, and necessary. He derides as "castrating" norms like marriage, holiday parties, meeting the parents, and widely adored restaurants. But this resistance is the limit of his self-expression and creativity. Without his cherished wrongs—his Moby Dick—his life is pointless. Call him Ahab.

Like all of us, Eric has an unconscious bias to absorb information and perspectives that support his arguments. Seeing the world through his own lens, with token corrections, he imagines that he is seeing the world objectively. Through that lens, it's a world that's absolutely deserving of every one of his complaints. He blames his exes, his work, his landlord, his server, his accountant, and the goddamn air conditioner for his unhappiness, but he brings no alternative to the table. This is key. To bring an alternative would be to risk himself, and that's not something he's ready to do—yet.

Underneath his pain-in-the-assness, the tragic truth is this: He doesn't realize the impact he has on people and that he does indeed matter. He feels alone in his version of reality and in his fight against that reality. He lives his life guarded against further hurt. His attempts at bringing himself forward haven't worked out in the past—or so he thinks. *So, fuck it.* Instead, he creates tension and drama, and he fucking thrives on it.

* * *

No one really wants to be seen as an asshole, a pussy, or a douchebag. But calling other people out? Being a pain in the ass? There's something badass about that, at least the way the dick narrates it.

And we see that narrative reflected, imitated, and celebrated in our media landscape: being an outraged newscaster, writer, or politician—a champion of call-out culture—is lucrative. Many of these champions, however, while claiming to be bold and courageous, are just being *dicks*, dicking around and offering up commentary that means *dick*—as in nothing. They criticize without solutions, in order to incite looping, distracting emotions in gullible audiences—the very audiences these champions, as dicks, also disparage and detest. The irony would be delicious if it weren't all so goddamn evil! I can't even—

Wait a second. Has this little rant of mine become a bit dickish? Good catch; I'll cop to that. The point is to own that shit and be a little *less* dickish.

The dick tries to convince us that he knows something we don't. We all find ways, even without the dick's help, to question whether we're good enough, smart enough, exceptional enough—or even, tragically, whether we're deserving of love. The dick plays into these deep insecurities; the less willing the dick is to offer a compliment or approval or commiseration, the harder we try. The douchebag, whom the dick abhors for his fakeness, craves an audience to legitimize his fantasy of himself. The dick appreciates an audience, too; in fact, he often *needs* one for his shtick. But the dick's audience is there for him to manipulate and criticize, to legitimize his martyr's narrative, in which he is the only honest man—and the one true victim.

Eric is hesitant to participate in therapy because the possibility of feeling better daunts him. If Moby Dick were captured, all the wrongs righted, and satisfaction achieved, Captain Eric would stand to lose his purpose, his power, and his individuality. Who would he be then? What would he do with himself? Without his cherished wrongs, Eric the dick, the bitcher-in-chief, doesn't exist. This is why Annie could never make Eric happy. Sorry, Annie, he simply can't afford to make himself *available* for happiness. To Eric the dick, it feels like a life-or-death choice.

Dicks carefully sting, wounding you and leaving you wondering if you deserved it. The dick, this needling fucker, teases you, tempts you, taunts you, and dares you. He calls you names, insults you, and dismisses your feelings or ambitions. Sometimes he's subtle, but he's always deliberate. Then he pretends to care, or says he cares, just enough. Or he suggests that he never tempted you at all. Then the fucker needles you again, tempts you further, and turns up the pressure—but only enough so that he can pull back without leaving a mark. Finally, jabbed at and exhausted, you crack—you reach your limit. You may snap and leave, like Annie did. You may scream at the dick. Hell, if he picks an asshole to blame and manipulate, the dick may get punched right on the goddamn chin. And what does this reaction from the taunted person mean for the dick? Success! The dick is a victim, and he was right all along. You cannot fucking win.

In Eric's view, the world is not just uncaring, it's actively hostile to him, having deprived him of something essential—and perhaps something about that sentiment rings true for all of us. He engages the world with a chip on his shoulder, criticizing and poking, finding ways to deprive the world right back in retaliation for what he feels it has done to him. The universe has already mugged him, and now it demands that he go to a goddamn holiday party? *That's bullshit*, he says. *You're gonna regret it.* Eric's manuscript remains untouched. A world that has rejected him in so many ways is now baiting him into sharing his creativity? So it can inevitably mock his efforts? *Fuck that game*, he says. *I'm not playing.* Dicks live by the rule of self-imposed impotence. But does he piss and moan? You fucking bet. He's a victim with a vendetta. A narrative. A purpose.

Life is hard—and not just for dicks. The dick can have a pity party for himself in Dick City, where he is the biggest priority and the biggest victim. And we might be willing to meet him there—until we aren't. At some point, people choose to not accept his terms and conditions. Annie reached that point with Eric. Others are bored with him. He's alone. He's scared.

PART 2
IDENTIFY THE SPUN-OUT BULLSHIT

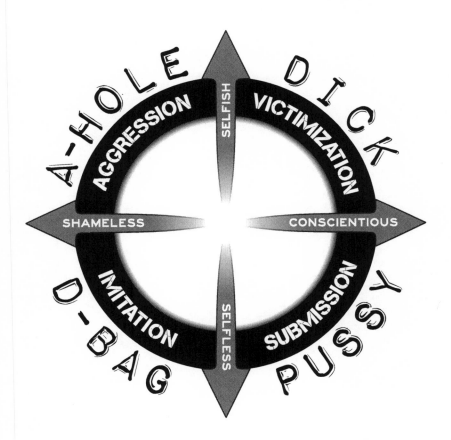

6

THE PERIMETER

We track four basic motivations and behaviors on a scale that radiates outward from a point of balance and neutrality in the center to extremes at the perimeter.

When you "spin out" to the perimeter, your worldview is contorted, and your behavior is less rooted in reason. You're unmoored, restless, reactive, and chaotic. In the center, there is an alert calm.

You Are Way the Fuck Out There

When you have an extreme reaction to information or events, you "spin out" to the perimeter. This is what's going on when you make a total dick move or act like a complete asshole. You act reflexively; you're out of control, out of your head. This reactionary behavior leads to a lot of regrets. As a rule, when you spin out, you make your life worse—and you make someone else's life suck, too.

When you're centered, you understand that sometimes making yourself the priority is okay, and sometimes it's important to make others the priority. You can decide when it's appropriate to give a fuck, or not. At some point, however, as you move from the balanced center to the extreme perimeter, being assertive becomes blind aggression, or surrendering to circumstances beyond your control becomes submission to any opposition. You have spun out.

Strictly speaking, an asshole—Jonah, for example—is not an asshole only because he's selfish and shameless in orientation. He's an asshole because he's too often spun out at the perimeter, where his responses are dialed up to eleven. His habitual and chronic behavior at the perimeter is aggression; this has become his go-to solution for challenges in life. He's lost track of his center completely, and he can't even see it. We all have to be assertive, selfish, and free of care sometimes. We *don't* have to be aggressive, selfish, and shameless assholes *all the time*.

The serial asshole, pussy, douchebag, and dick live out at the perimeter, meaning they have little or no access to the center and little inclination to interact in other ways. You can see this in the therapy sessions: Eric fails to see things except through his own self-victimizing filter. He's right, dammit! Just ask him. George submits to everyone, including me, the therapist he's paying. Jonah aggressively invites me to go fuck myself when I get a little too close to the truth of his situation. Jed writes me off as being low-status and jealous of his crafted persona.

They all interpret reality through the extremes of their limited perimeter orientations. This is the problem. Life pushes them to grow; they ignore the hints and double down on what they think is working. When life insists—as life does—Jonah slams doors, Jed does blow in Fiji with Scotty, George begs Kayla to order pancakes for him, and Eric ignores Annie so he can troll on the internet. Perimeter behaviors.

When you're spun out, the extreme move doesn't just seem like the *right* option, it seems like the *only* option. You may not even think it over—you just do what you do. We all do what we've always done. We get triggered, and we react in predictable ways.

You don't have to be losing your shit all day, every day. You don't have to be so reactive. Even raging assholes and petrified pussies can learn to recognize their own spun-out behavior and do something different. Just knowing how we react and behave is beneficial in staying centered, even when life gets intense, whether you're the dick or the one being triggered by the dick.

We're out on the perimeter too damn often, and typically we don't even know it. How do we accomplish this miracle of obliviousness? If we're spun out there often enough, this becomes the new normal. Plus, we're masterful at distracting and numbing ourselves, or finding some other creative way not to fucking deal. When you live on the perimeter, you become inflexible, incurious, and self-righteous in your thoughts—and your behavior follows. You build a life and identity out there. You plant a flag, saying, *This is just who I am!*

Right, asshole.

Sure, douchebag.

Whatever you say, dick.

C'mon, pussy.

We all roll our eyes at your justifications. This isn't your identity; it's your shitty habitual behavior, and *you can change it*. Step back from the perimeter. Find your center.

Aggression

Aggression is the perimeter behavior of the asshole. It is the shameless extreme of the care axis, and the selfish extreme of the self axis. The asshole makes himself the priority, living his life without meaningful recognition of what his actions do to others. Jonah personifies the kind of man who finds relief in—and even gets a kick out of—aggression. In the moment, the asshole may not give a fuck about what will happen, but ultimately, he cannot avoid the consequences of his actions.

Aggression threatens, harasses, and abuses. It can be conveyed with a fist or with just a tone, a look, or a gesture. Aggression is always *felt* by its object. That's the whole point—it hurts. It puts us on notice: *This is no longer a discussion. Meet my fucking danger.*

Most of us are not complete assholes, but most of us *do* engage in one restrained form of aggression or another. We do so because we're "in a bad mood" or we're "stressed and tired." We use simple and irrefutable justifications: *She started it! He had it coming!* And so it goes.

In most situations, aggression is not a strength. The centered man uses aggression with calculated discretion—a behavior we call "assertiveness"—and only to support himself or others. No matter what's going on, we can learn to stay clear, open, and curious. To get there, we need to practice staying centered in the face of intensity and uncertainty.

Jonah Learned It from Somewhere

After several sessions spent processing shameless behavior, Jonah comes to see me with a lot of energy. It's sunny outside. He's clean-shaven. He closes his eyes, claps his hands, and motions that we are getting started *right fucking now.* No delay. As he sits down, he begins, "I've been thinking...my dad smacked me around a lot. He was always putting me down, fucking with me, especially in front of my friends. But I got what I deserved—I was a rotten little fucker. I was always getting in trouble at school; I couldn't sit still, always fidgeting, like now. See? My dad always used to yell at me to sit still, but for some reason, I couldn't. *Couldn't.* Tried. Couldn't pull it off. I can still see that finger coming at me sometimes. He was a cool dude, but goddamn, that finger in the chest was a thump."

"I can't tell if you recall the finger thump fondly or not." These are the first words I've said in this session.

"Yeah, it wasn't that bad...and he always said, 'Jonah, listen.'" With a huge grin on his face, Jonah mimics his father thumping his chest. "'Jonah!' Yeah, if I'd just listened, things would've been good, but I couldn't ever just fucking do what he said, I suppose."

"Did you *want* to do the things he wanted you to do?" I ask.

"Hell, no! I was a kid. God, no. It was always be still, mow the lawn, clean the garage, go to bed, shut the fuck up, grow the fuck up, be a goddamn man. That sort of thing. Fuck no. No, no, no. I didn't want to do what he wanted."

I take a deep breath, then ask, "What did *you* actually want to do?"

He looks at me as if this is the first time anyone's asked him what he genuinely wants. A minute goes by. "I don't know. Fuck around, play the drums, be a kid, draw, climb trees. Drive his truck—my dad's truck. Shit, I don't know. Funny, right? He was cool. He shouldn't have taught me to drive for my eighth birthday. Oh, man, man, there was this one tree I *loved*, a big-ass live oak in the shitty park down the street. It was huge, with huge branches coming out in all directions. Have you ever seen a live oak with a branch that hits the ground and takes off again?"

I'm laughing. Until now, he's never asked a single question about me, even a more-or-less rhetorical one. It's clinically significant, and it also feels damn good.

"I would climb all over it," he continues. "I'd pretend I was some different type of human that lived in trees. Man, that was fun. And I really loved climbing all the way to the top of that sucker and just sitting there above it all, taking it in. You know the kind of tree?"

"I'm from southern Louisiana. I love those live oaks; I grew up climbing them too. Stay there for a minute. I'm curious about the 'it.' What was the 'it' you were taking in from the top of that tree?"

"Aww, fuck, man. I don't know. Just peaceful, away from all the bullshit, the fucking yelling, the homework I probably wasn't going to finish. Up there, I could be left alone and feel free. Fuck, I don't know. That was forever ago."

Free. Free. Free. My body buzzes with the word.

His face is transformed. He's relaxed; his smile is natural, whimsical, different from the sadistic smile I've seen so often. His eyes half-close, look away, then drift back for another moment.

"I feel like we're up there together right now," I say. "It feels amazing." For the last five minutes of the session, nothing and everything happens. I'll never forget this feeling. We share the space. We pass the time together in the freedom of that tree. My God, it's beautiful.

On his way out, he turns to me. "Hey, man. Remember way back—*way* back—well, I'm glad you didn't go fuck yourself. Thanks for that." The door closes gently. The door opens again, and I see his meaty head. "Or maybe it was the crystals," he says, and we both bust out laughing. "See you Thursday, Dave." (I go by David, not Dave, but Jonah is not one to color inside the lines.)

"See you then, Jonah."

* * *

He's moved out of his home, the home he built for Shaylee and the boys. He misses that home. He's living in the carriage house of a customer's place in Pacific Heights. It's a temporary arrangement. He's a regular at the Balboa, even though none of the cougars there look even a fraction as good as Shaylee. He walks, often drunk, through the Presidio to the base of the Golden Gate Bridge. The fog rolls in. The foghorns are loud at the bay's only ocean entrance. Hanging on a gate at the base of the bridge is a plaque with two hands outlined on it. Evenings after work, Jonah walks to the hands; the douchey triathletes pass him by with scorn. While they pedal and run, he smokes and drinks. He gets to the gates, touches the hands, and turns back for the long climb and sobering walk back to the top of Pacific Heights, to the carriage house.

A fucking gazillion-dollar view of the East Bay. A long way from home. This is hell. This is hell. Those hands are on the gates of hell.

Jonah occasionally shares his moods and thoughts in text messages. Without Shaylee, the boys, or Megan, he does his job, walks past the "whine" bars, and buys whiskey by the half-pint. When the mood hits, he texts or emails. He writes mostly to me. It's a raw, untutored stroll through his anger, hate, love, and drunkenness.

Jonah's Return to the Tree

Three days after our last visit, Jonah arrives back at my office.

"Did you get to do any of the things you wanted to?"

"This week, or when I was a kid in that tree?" *Whoa. He's back in the conversation we left days ago. Back in the tree.* "This week, I just avoided people and walked to the bridge a lot. It's been my routine for months now. I'm hooked. I don't have my home office, so I just send myself emails and text messages to remind me to do shit. This week, though, I got drunk enough and tried to text the president of the United States—asked him to pardon the Red Sox or some stupid shit. Did I get what I wanted when I was a kid, though? Not really, 'cause I was always in trouble, grounded, always in some sort of shit. Got to play football; I liked that, but I got kicked off the team for fighting. Sucked. I was pretty good, but I fucked it up again. I'm sure I deserved it."

"So, some part of you blames yourself for everything, right?"

He nods.

"Does that critical voice in your head sound familiar?" I ask.

"It sounds just like my Pops. I never noticed that before. There all the time, riding my ass just like he used to do. Man, I got the hell away from there, but that fucker's still with me."

Jonah looks different in this moment. Gone are the sharp eyes and tense jaw. He looks sad.

He starts again, slowly. "Dave—goddammit, man. Goddammit. I keep walking to that spot at the bridge, and this story...this story keeps popping into my head. Same story. I was about nine, and my dad—"

"Jonah," I interrupt, stopping him. "I want you to tell the story as if it's happening right now, first person."

"I'll try. Sure. That's weird, man. Fucking weird. But whatever, man, sure. I'm nine. My dad is slapping me upside the head for something. Hell, I don't even know why. Now I'm walking down the street fucking fuming. I see this kid from the neighborhood. Parker. He's about seven or eight. He's riding his bike and humming some song. One of those TV theme songs—*The A-Team*, I think." Jonah is rocking back and forth. His voice rises and falls slightly with the movement of his chest. "And he looks so happy, so happy. Singing his song. Something comes over me. I'm not even thinking about it. I'm crossing the street and—*bam!*—I knock him hard off his bike into the dirt. He's crying. I'm laughing. Shit, I'm laughing. Why am I laughing?"

Jonah is silent for a moment. The rocking continues. "I did it, then I just walked away. But I felt different, good, strong. Pretty soon I was roughing up other kids. They were scared of me. They'd run off when I walked by. Other kids started looking up to me; I got a rep as someone not to fuck with. I started making friends that were older and bigger than me. I liked that. I felt like a badass, like *somebody*. I was maybe ten years old, or eleven. I was kind of a punk."

"Let's get to know this kid, the one who roughs up the others. Tell me about him."

"Doing that stuff made me feel strong, like my dad—my dad was a bad motherfucker, and I wanted to be just like him."

"Tough like your dad? And what did being like your dad keep you from feeling?"

"Oh my dear fucking God. Seriously? It kept me from *being* weak, from *being* afraid all of the time. Fucking feel *this*." He makes a jerking-off motion. At least he's laughing—and he's still in the conversation.

"Jonah, you found a way to deal with all that pain and abuse, to feel powerful when you felt powerless. You did what you had to do."

"I loved my dad," Jonah said. "He was a cool-looking dude. I idolized him. But it was all so fucking confusing. I hated him, too."

Jonah Is Not Just an Asshole

With tremendous pressure from the outside world, support from me and my crystals, and copious profanity, Jonah inches his way back from the perimeter and toward his center. To do this (and this goes for all of us), he has to feel the really hard shit and realize it won't kill him. Literally—he has to realize it won't kill him. As kids, it's too much to feel, so we develop strategies. As adults, we can and must return and engage with the times in our lives when we went off the rails. Jonah is putting his story together, trying to understand how he ended up out on the perimeter in the first place, how he ended up being an asshole. He's just getting started, but he's in. He senses what's possible and knows that this is the ride he wants to be on.

When Jonah restarts the sessions, he says he needs help talking to his boys. That's it. He thinks he's come back to *fix* something, not to face everything. Folks usually come in with a "presenting problem," as it's known in my profession. The presenting problem leads us to underlying pieces of the whole person. For Jonah, maintaining a connection with his kids means changing his relationship with, well, everything—especially himself. At the beginning of his process, he can't do it just for himself, but he *can* do it for his sons. Even though he's treated them poorly, those boys are still his greatest motivation. The connection with his sons gets him far enough to feel the possibility of something different for himself.

Jonah has been living with the embodied history of habitual threat. It's colored his entire experience of life. He's never left his father's table. His nervous system has to adapt to sitting still, to feeling. He has to learn how to feel his pain instead of living in reaction to it.

He learns that he's not just the bad kid who deserved the abuse his father heaped upon him. He's the kid who did the best he could in difficult circumstances. He's the kid (and the adult) who learned how to lessen his own overwhelming pain by being an asshole to others. As a boy, he associated the people he loved with disappointment, so he created protective strategies to use against those who hurt him, and he has carried forward this confused and immature framework for living into his present. He's a guy who needs connection, and until now, he couldn't risk it.

Now, does this excuse all of his abuse and philandering? Hell no. No, it does *not*. He's got to take responsibility for his actions. He's got to feel and acknowledge the pain he causes in others. And he can do that now because he's acknowledging and engaging with his own painful past.

While Jonah is responsible for his own life, he's not to blame for every development *in* that life. It's on me to help him see his behavior as an understandable response to the larger system he was part of, including family, school, and community. Jonah had an asshole father, and he didn't fit well into the traditional school system, and both of these factors shaped him. This doesn't mean he deserves to suffer. Jonah grew up in a rough world, a bare-knuckles world. He was conditioned to think that weakness of any kind was unacceptable, and he responded by not feeling it. Jonah is learning to understand what this means to him.

The big live oak tree is a powerful metaphor in our work together. It symbolizes freedom, playfulness, a sense of safety, and connection to something bigger. This is the goal of our work: to help Jonah find these things again and bring them into his regular life. We have a long way to climb.

Victimization

In my professional training and education, Lu Gray was one of my most impactful teachers. She said, "We all have to come to terms with our own victimization." She didn't just mean those of us who have been severely victimized; she meant all of us, because we are all victimized. We are all hurt by life. We all live in response to the history and challenges of our circumstances, and there's a cumulative effect over time. We all push up against structures and people that confine us. We all have to figure out how to move through a life that can and will continue to hurt us. I'm not being morbid when I say this. I love life, and I still feel hurt by small things and by not-so-small things. I may feel hurt tomorrow too.

"Everything can be taken from a man but one thing: the last of the human freedoms—to choose one's attitude in any given set of circumstances, to choose one's own way." Viktor Frankl, who was a Jewish survivor of the Holocaust, grants all victims their victimhood, then points out—from his ultimate experience in victimization—that there are parts of you that can't be victimized or taken away from you if you don't allow it. Being victimized is not the same as playing the victim. Even when you've suffered abuse or atrocities, you still have choices; you don't have to accept the role of victim. This idea has been developed and taught by people like Frankl—bona fide victims—for millennia, including the former slave Epictetus, in one of the foundational Stoic philosophical texts, the *Enchiridion*.

To victimize someone means to single them out for cruel or unjust treatment. The spectrum of unkind or downright awful forms of abuse and mistreatment is wide. Some just represent an inconvenience, but some are life-changing. Some folks are physically and emotionally harmed beyond recovery. In my practice, I've heard horrific stories of abuse. I have seen victimization up close. I do not, and will not, diminish actual victimization and trauma. Trauma is real. Pain is real.

Victims of accidents, abuse, violence, illness, betrayal, or anything that deeply wounds us physically or emotionally, need our support and compassion. But I never see my clients exclusively as victims. They were victimized—yes, absolutely—and they are not to blame for the horrible things that happened to them, but my hope is that they come to realize that they are also capable of dealing with their circumstances and their futures.

If you assume the *exclusive* identity of a victim, you shirk your responsibility for your own experience and limit your path for healing. You stay stuck, and you build an orientation around the things that happened to you, both real and imagined.

I'm not dismissing the horrible things that happen to people. I'm saying: Don't let them own you. Don't let the fuckers win. If you continue to make your experience about what happened to you, about what *they* did to you, they continue to victimize you. Don't define who you are by what happened to you. You are powerful, and there's so much more to experience on the ride of life when you're willing to take on your life as your own responsibility.

The dick? Just like the rest of us, he may have been victimized, but instead of taking responsibility and dealing with his pain, he takes on the identity of a victim. He's a victim whether he's really been wronged or not. Fuck the facts, pal. What *actually* happened is not a priority for the dick. He's the most important guy, the most important victim—the VIV, Very Important Victim, both entitled and victimized.

Self-victimization, for our purposes, means positioning yourself as a victim, whether it's true or not, and then paying it forward by victimizing others. No matter what happens, no matter the circumstances, there's always a victim, and the dick has decided that it's him. The dick's self-victimization is different from the aggression of the asshole. The asshole hurts someone else and may be unaware of, or unconcerned about, the effects. To the asshole, it's not personal. You just happened to be the one in the room. To the dick, on the other hand, it's very personal. *He* has been hurt or wronged by you, goddammit—and fuck you, it's *your* fault.

Me, me, me, says the dick. First and foremost, how does this affect *me*? Is someone going to ask *me* what I want? What was unfairly done to *me*? Why is *my* table not ready? Is someone else getting something instead of *me*? I know you're not in the mood, but I am—what about *me*? You're not considering *me*. The dick thinks only of himself, but in a textbook example of projection, he judges others as selfish for not considering him: I'm just being real, being myself, he thinks. *You're* the one being selfish. Self-victimization is holding others responsible for how you feel and demanding that they make it right—or punishing them when they don't. It's a rigged game, though; the so-called culprits can never make it right *enough*. That is the perimeter behavior of the dick.

Crisis of Credibility

The dick cares a lot about people's disapproval of his behavior and attitudes, and he feels shame. Shifting blame for his harmful behavior onto other people—becoming their victim—is an adaptation that allows him to ignore and excuse the shame he feels, and project guilt and shame on anybody who tries to shame him. If it sounds circular, that's because it is. It's impossible to keep up with this merry-go-round of bullshit. When this deflection, blaming, and shaming becomes chronic, the dick is no longer a believable witness; he's just a fucking nuisance. His imagined grievances make him the town's wolf-crier whose actual condition is ignored.

As we pointed out earlier in the book, the dick is convinced that the world has fucked him over in the past, and that it's not his fault. He can't wait to advertise his righteousness. The dick is sure the world is presently fucking him over, and it's not his fault. He insists on making his victimization known even when he's not really a victim. He's sure that the world will continue to fuck him over. *Wolf, wolf, wolf!* And who the fuck cares?

Because his victim story is often not actually true, the dick loses credibility. An adult on the receiving end of the dick's blame will see the facts, determine that the dick is off his goddamn rocker, and no longer trust him. This distrust may not be significant among infrequent acquaintances, but it is devastating in relationships and families. It's exhausting to live with someone you don't trust, or to live with someone who doesn't trust you.

If the dick is a pain in the ass for an entire family vacation, then blames the family for his poor experience, he won't have much luck spinning his victim story. He can try. He *will* try. But when the family spent most of their vacation listening to the dick bitch and moan, his fictional version of events is not going to fly. After consistent repetition of these tales, the kids conclude that if they can't even trust their dad to tell the facts about a vacation, they really can't trust him *at all.*

The dick's children, forced to cope with their father's whining, will slowly but surely lose respect for him. A teen in particular will see that the dick is just making shit up: *Seriously, Dad, are you upset over nothing again? Did the younger generation conspire to spill your milk?* If the teen concludes that the dick is untrustworthy when it comes to dishes and dinner, the same kid will eventually conclude that the dick isn't credible when it comes to money, sex, booze, and grades either. If the dick can't tell the truth about his own experience, he can't tell the truth about a damn thing. Guess what, dick? Now your kids think you're lying about everything. Now the kids are parenting *you.*

Eric Is Spun Out in Victimization

Eric's progress is slow, but it's steady.
He shows up for another session. His curiosity is just enough to keep him trying, to keep him moving along. We have the same conversations, but I keep trying to bring him back to his own experience: "I appreciate your passion, your hunger for things to be different in the world. It's admirable. What if you could keep your passion for change but not feel so negatively affected by the world around you?"

"But it's all so messed up," Eric insists. "I don't *want* to be unaffected. I don't want to be put on meds, like my hack doctor suggested. And now you're trying to peddle your shit again. Please, no new age affirmations, no what ifs."

"I think I just triggered your bullshit detector. Let me try again. I appreciate you wanting to be yourself, man, I really do. We want similar things in this world, believe me. But the way you're going about your life and your fight with it, right now, is causing you a great deal of suffering. You don't like your job; you want a relationship—which never seems to work out—and you're having thoughts of suicide."

"Well, that about sums it up. Great work, Doc. Now I see why you make the big bucks."

Now I'm triggered; I can feel my jaw getting tense. Eric and I have a lot in common. I've spent most of my life struggling with my own deep distrust of the world, and I've turned a corner. It's difficult to be faced with a ghost from my own past. But life has a habit of presenting me with qualities in others that I'm still resolving within myself—which is pretty damn cool, actually. I close my eyes and take a deep breath, go inside for a moment, and settle myself down. I connect with my care for this man. "Here's what I see; you tell me if I'm right. There's a part of you that feels deeply disappointed in other people and deeply hurt and alone as a result. You probably feel that way toward me right now. Is that right?"

"Yeah, you seem well intentioned and all, but shit, I don't know—you just don't seem to get it."

"I may not get it yet, but I know that I want to." This is true. I'm interested in this guy, and I care about him. And, man, is he tough. When Eric resists introspection, I listen.

"I don't think this is working."

"Tell me," I respond.

"Well, I've been coming every week for three months, and yeah, you want to get where I'm coming from, and I don't feel you judging me, but shit, I still feel the same. Nothing's changed."

"I hear that. Can we delve into the question of change or the idea of change? I'd like to know more about what you expect to change and how."

"Sure, whatever."

"Well, every time I try to get closer to you, you push me away. I'll share my experience, I'll offer an insight, I'll invite you to try something on, and your reaction is to push me away and keep me at a distance. Essentially, you're telling me to fuck off. Do you know what I'm talking about?"

"Yeah. It feels like you're trying to control me."

"Right. I get that it feels that way, and that's what I'm interested in. Your experience of feeling controlled by the ways I'm trying to connect with you."

"Why are you trying to connect with me?" he asks.

I pause for a moment. "Well," I say with a playful smile, "I want to help you get something valuable out of therapy—it's actually what you're paying me to do." I lean toward him. "But more importantly? It's because I like you, and because I think connection is one of the major keys to feeling joy and fulfillment, and I think you're terrified of letting other people close, and for damn good reason."

"What do you mean?" he asks. It's one of the first times he is curious rather than dismissive.

"I'll use an analogy. When I was sixteen, I drank gin for the first time. The last thing I remember before blacking out was thinking to myself, *This stuff tastes just like water.*"

Eric smiles.

"I was violently ill that night and all the next day. Since that day, the smell of gin makes me nauseous. My body reacts as though it were poison. A threat. While I know rationally that gin is not poison, my system responds as though it were. Do you see where I'm going with this?"

"I think so. I got super sick off of hummus one time, and I couldn't eat it for years."

"Does it make sense to you that you would be protecting yourself from even the *possibility* of more disappointment, the possibility of more frustration, the possibility of more manipulation?"

"Yeah. I mean, shit, I feel enough of that stuff all the time already."
He pauses for a moment. "You're saying that I don't let anyone close
because I got hurt before. My system has the same kind of reaction, an
automatic aversion to the possibility of more?"

"Exactly. And it's not just you; it's me, too. When we experience
mis-attunement as children or trauma or deep emotional pain at any
point in our lives—all of which is inevitable to some extent—we organize to prevent that kind of thing from reoccurring: *Never again, fucker.*
Nothing gets over this wall."

"Man, when you say it like that, I feel like a big fucking pussy. I'm not
even making my own decisions. Like I'm on automatic lockdown. But
yeah, I can't say it's not true. Fuck. I don't want to feel like someone is
fucking with me. So, yeah, I head it off. So, what do you *do* about that?"

"We've already started. We give those painful experiences a voice
in a safe and connected space. We start to understand the parts of you
that never processed the painful experience all the way through. Me, I
got bullied by older kids when I was a boy, so I got really quiet, didn't
want to give them any reason to go after me—but then I stayed that way,
and I had a hard time expressing myself as a result. A survival strategy
became a life strategy, and it was not a good one. I isolated myself to
protect myself. But then I was all alone."

"Yeah. I can relate to that. Fuck. I get it, man."

This is progress. I'm no longer someone to be kept out. Getting there
can be slow—it's taken Eric and me four months—but he has damn
good reasons for those walls, and I always, always, honor the defenses.

* * *

Eric is very quiet when he comes in for another regular session. "There's
something I've been avoiding talking about, but it keeps popping into
my head. I wish it didn't, but man, it still bugs me all the time, even
though it happened so long ago. I really loved this girl in college—Jodee.
We lived together with a bunch of other people off campus. I thought

she was the one. I was so happy when I was with her. I was even looking at rings—I mean, I wanted her to be my wife, David." He pauses here.

"Take all the time you need," I say.

When he speaks, his voice is distant. "She was, you know, fiery. I liked that. I was crazy about her, and all of my struggles seemed to fall away when I was with her. I was a different guy, someone I liked so much more. I was editor of the college paper. I was fucking chill—funny even. I really liked my roommates; it felt like family, finally." He's getting choked up. "Finally, I felt like I had this group of people, a girlfriend. I was good, really good. I was happy. For the first time in my life, I was happy."

Something big is coming.

"I can hear the words in my mind. I want to tell you—I have to tell you—but I can't." He starts to shake. His eyes go wide. He's scared by what's happening in his body.

"Eric, your body knows what it's doing. You ever seen ducks tussle? They swim away and shake it out. That's what your body is doing. You can trust it. It's processing trauma, and we just have to let it do what it knows how to do." I say this to provide him with some understanding so he doesn't freak himself out. The wave passes, then settles. When the shakes return, he starts to cry; he fights it, but it's coming through. I stay with him, bringing my calm and trusting presence to the chaos. This wave passes, and things get strangely quiet. He looks at his hands, around the room, out the window, then back at me.

"She had been sleeping with one of my roommates for months." He hears himself say it. Another wave; the tears and shakes come back. This time, no resistance.

"No need to force anything, Eric; let it happen."

"No," he says forcefully, "I want to finish it. I want to say it all. Fuck them. Fuck her. I want to tell the whole story." He gets up from the sofa and paces. He shakes his arms and hands out. "She would sneak upstairs to his room. When I was in class, at the paper. Lots of my so-called friends knew about it, even the other roommates, my chosen fucking family, and no one told me about it, and that was even worse."

Humiliation.

"I tried to talk to her. I still wanted her. Can you believe that? I asked her to move out with me, said we could go to a different school together, start over. Pathetic, right? She was really drunk. She, she, she..." He's still pacing back and forth. "She started telling me all these terrible things, how I was a shitty boyfriend, that she was glad I found out. I packed my shit up and left that night. Never talked to any of those fuckers again. I've never talked to anyone about it, anyone. Until now."

"You've been all alone with this," I say. I'm not asking. I'm making a point.

"I drove. I don't even remember where I drove, I just drove. I slept in the back of my car, and drove again. It was the worst time in my life. It took everything I had not to turn the wheel into oncoming traffic. I trusted her completely. I never even imagined..." His voice trails off. "I thought what we had was real. Turns out I was a sucker. A dupe. I was living in a fucking fantasy world looking for wedding rings; meanwhile, Jodee's getting it on in the room right above mine after telling me she wasn't in the mood, then crawling into bed with me. *That's* who I was. That was me, a total fucking chump, a joke—and everyone was in on it but me."

"Holy shit," is all I can say.

"Exactly. Fuck me. That happened to me, David. It really happened. You can't make this shit up. I lived that. I was that guy, that chump."

"That happened to you," I mirror. "You lived through that. You found a way to keep going."

When trauma from the past is left unhealed, that means it's still happening *right now*. There is only ever right now. And now. And now. Unhealed trauma robs us of our lives. Please take this in. We all live in perpetual reaction to our unhealed trauma, and most of us don't know it. Eric is still in the hell of this betrayal. He sees newscasters, politicians, bosses, friends, family, coworkers, and especially girlfriends as threats; they're trying to set him up and crush him. Make him a chump again. He's fighting against this *all the time*. Alone. That's a hell of a fight to be in every day.

Submission

Submission is the perimeter behavior of the pussy, who lives at the conscientious extreme of the care axis and the selfless extreme of the self axis, and who believes that things will go better if he can just withhold his interests—his desires, preferences, opinions, thoughts, and feelings—in deference to the interests of others. While aggression negates the other person, submission is an act of *self*-negation. *I'll be better off if I can be invisible.* Or, *others will like me better if I just go along.* Is there a time and a place for this? Absolutely. Think of a dog tucking tail and rolling over, exposing its vulnerable belly. It's a disarming act. It calms the aggressor. In some situations, systems, hierarchies, and relationships, standing down is the right move.

When you orient toward submission, it is often to escape judgment and blame. It's an attempt to avoid exposure and minimize risk. In rare circumstances, submission is a useful tool, but as a life strategy, it's a refusal to play. When you submit, you offer nothing to push up against; you abandon yourself—and you abandon those who need you to be you.

We all do this sometimes, especially when we feel overwhelmed. We disappear in plain sight. After a suggestion of yours is met with firm or emotionally charged resistance, you might say something to smooth things over: *I don't care. Whatever you want to do.* Or maybe you submit resentfully: *Whatever. I don't give a shit.* There are healthy expressions of selflessness and consideration for others; this is not one.

Absenting yourself to clear space for others has consequences. Submission isn't always harmless; it can be extremely dangerous. If, for example, a chief financial officer is overly deferential and submissive to outside or superior forces, he can do a lot of harm. Submission allows atrocities, from the intimate to the global. Making yourself invisible, offering no resistance, is making yourself complicit with whatever the hell is happening, for better and worse.

We Are All Pussies, Pussy

You know what you want. I know what I want. Fantasizing about what you want is one thing—it's completely risk-free. But being assertive and going for it is something else entirely. You have to choose your moment, and it never seems to be the "right" time—or so the pussy tells himself. All the while, he's trying desperately to quiet his inner critic, who's always ready to give him the business.

The pussy opens his mouth to speak, but his nervous system has a different idea: his heartbeat accelerates, his chest tightens, he feels dizzy, and sweat beads on his face and arms. *Speak, dammit. Be a fucking man,* he tells himself. But his nervous system says, *Hell no, fool. What if the conversation goes sideways? What if I get rejected? Fucking terror, that's what. Nope. Not risking that!* His needs, including his need for connection and security, are overpowered by fear of rejection.

The pussy lacks confidence that he can survive intensity and un-certainty, so he remains in a state that he genuinely hates—dissatisfied, irritated, and anxious—but at least he finds safety in his flat, predictable life. And on the level of DNA and evolution, where little matters aside from rudimentary survival, that's just fine. The guy who wandered off and ate the strange-looking berries on a dare from his buddy got bred out in the same way that farmers bred out curious sheep. Just submit and go along with the program. Why rock the boat? That's how deep our basic needs run; George may *want* respect at work, but from a survival standpoint, that's significantly less important than his baseline *need* for consistent income (safety) and the sense of camaraderie he finds at the bank (belonging).

We're all wired to be pussies, cowering in our comfort zones. There are so many things we want to do: eat healthier, exercise regularly, stream less video, read a real book with actual paper pages, have fulfilling relationships, or play the guitar. But we don't. Why? Because it can be triggering to make changes. This sounds like an impossible bind: If making changes is a trigger, how can I change my triggers?

If we leave our pussy wiring and instincts unexamined, we stay asleep. We dream and immediately un-dream, stuck as shit. This is the natural state when we don't know how to deal with triggers, and since none of us are taught how, there are areas of all our lives where we're pussies. Total pussies. We can live in submission to our fear and resistance, or we can practice being assertive and bold. Or we can just say, *Fuck it. My life's good enough. I'll order something on Amazon Prime.*

George Is Spun Out in Submission

George sighs, announcing, "I can never say what I want, what I think, anything. Nothing. Everything. I don't know. I just can't say what I want. You've helped me see that I *know* what I want, darn it; I just can't say it."

"What did it feel like the last time Kayla pressed you to make a decision? In detail. Close your eyes, see her, see the room. What do you notice in your body?"

George knows the drill at this point. We are months into our therapy sessions. "I feel hot, I feel sick to my stomach, and my throat feels tight." His hand moves to his throat.

"Great awareness, George. This is your body responding to the threat."

"But there *is* no threat. This is what I don't understand. She's just asking me where I want to eat. I don't know why this happens, why I get all choked up."

"While there's no actual, objective threat, some part of you is triggered when she asks you where you want to eat, and your body reacts."

"I just wish I didn't react that way," he says. "I just keep thinking that if I could just be normal—you know, not get so panicky—we would get along so much better."

"What if we could help the part of you that's triggered feel safer in those interactions with Kayla?"

"I *hate* that part of me."

"Okay. This is good information. One part of you hates another part. Is that what you're describing?" George nods. *Internal division.* "Does that make sense to you, that there are two parts of you at work here? One part freezing up, and another part hating the part that freezes up?"

"Yeah. I feel so weak when that happens."

"Does hating the scared part make you any braver?"

George thinks for a moment. "No," he mutters. "I just end up feeling worse. I remember this feeling though. It's not like this is new. It actually reminds me of something. This is kinda funny. This reminds me of when I was a kid and we had one of those ugly plaid couches. You only see them now in the movies, but we really had one. It was scratchy. I'm sure ours was used when we got it. They're classic. I wish I still had one.

"Anyways. I was just a kid on this scratchy plaid couch. I was an easy-going kid. My parents told me that too; they told everyone that. I believed them. But this one day, I can't remember what I wanted, but I was worried about bugging my mom. So I sat on that couch and worried. Should I? Shouldn't I? Should I do this? Or shouldn't I do this?

"Sitting there on that couch, I started playing tic-tac-toe against myself with pushpins in the couch, trying to decide if I should bug my mom. If blue won, I would bug her. If red won, I wouldn't. It was so rough, that couch, you couldn't see the holes the pins made. I played tic-tac-toe against myself until I fell asleep without deciding, and my mom was sad when she saw pins stuck in her couch."

"So, this conflict of asking for something goes way back. Do you recognize the pattern?" I ask.

"Yeah. In fact, I remember poking holes in that couch that day, but I don't remember why I didn't want to bother my mom or why I was arguing with myself. I just remember playing tic-tac-toe because I wanted something, and I was worried about asking her. Still, after all that worrying, I ended up disappointing her because of the pins in her old couch."

Over the next few months, memories and images surface from throughout George's life. He retells his stories and his experiences.

Lost on the perimeter, selfless and conscientious George is still dependent on and deferential to others, submissive. By recognizing his internal conflict, he's learning how to connect with himself and to self-soothe; he begins crawling toward his center, where his true power lies. With practice, George is finally extending his care and consideration for others to himself, the person who needs him the most.

Imitation

The douchebag is at the shameless extreme of the care axis, and the selfless extreme of the self axis. Selflessness and shamelessness can be admirable qualities, but at the perimeter, this combination makes the douchebag a copycat, a faker in life, one who has sacrificed his complex, true self for an alternative look or feel, without a thought to those who might mourn the loss. He plays the game of life by throwing himself on the discard pile, and that's a tough strategy to sustain. Very tough.

There is pressure to imitate others. We are status-conscious mammals, and we're wired for safety and belonging. We're inclined to fit in. We seek assimilation with a work culture, friends, family, religion. We're asked constantly to be imitators. Corporations use this wiring to sell us things; they draw on our need for acceptance to create loyal customers and brand emissaries. The Facebook and Google algorithms (douchebagorithms?) know us better than we know ourselves. Employers want us to be selfless in our dedication to our jobs, shameless in our enthusiasm. We wear and praise the logo. *Isn't it awesome?*

Imitation can connect us, and it can be amazing. I love being one of a hundred thousand LSU Tigers fans wearing the purple and gold at Tiger Stadium in my hometown of Baton Rouge. But I also know I'm David going on a ride. That's important to remember: play here, but don't get lost here. If you don't lay claim to your core self, someone else will.

Jed Is Spun Out in Imitation

Jed finally shows up again. "I think I've basically got my shit totally together. Sorry I missed a few appointments. Mostly, I just came in to talk for a bit. Maybe we shouldn't schedule anything more. You been busy? I know I need to pay you for the missed appointments. Not a lot going on?"

"Have a seat, man. Jed, goddammit, man, I love you. You look like hell. Let's dive in." Jed feels more comfortable with this kind of approach, so I bro it out with him sometimes.

Jed stares out the window and runs his fingers through his hair. He nervously styles it back into place. "What the fuck is wrong with me? Yeah, no. Fuck. I may not have it all together today. Fuck. Why do I feel like this? I've got it all, so why, uh...? Hey, man, um—"

"You've had awesome adventures, you made bank, and you should be proud of that. What if the experience you're having of feeling empty is telling you that you're winding down on this ride you're on or moving in another direction? What if these triggers are trying to tell you something?"

"What the fuck are you talking about?" he asks, looking down at me once again. "Don't go all self-helpy on me, David."

I ignore this. "Jed, who really knows you? Like, *really* knows you, and not because you're 'the man' and can take them to Fiji, but because you're *you*?" We've been scheduling meetings for months now; it's time to hold his feet to the fire.

He looks dazed for a moment before rushing ahead: "Lots of people know me, man, all over town. My sales team, my bros, my CEO. I bet

I know more than twenty times the people you know." He's doing his bravado shit, but I have an in with him at this point. We've built some trust. He fucks with me, but I can tell he values our work together.

"That's not what I'm asking; I know you're well-known all over town. I'm asking about something else. Who can you talk to when you're having a hard time? Who can you be real with?"

"I don't know, man. That's not how me and my people roll. We don't talk about stuff like that, and man, honestly, I don't *want* to. I don't want to be talking about this shit with you. I just want to feel good like I used to."

"I hear you, man, I really do. It's hard when you're not feeling the good stuff when it seems like you should be, right?"

"Yeah, man, it's killing me. I shouldn't be trippin', but I'm just—fuck, I don't even know—and here I am in this fucking office with bad art on the walls, and I don't—"

I cut him off. "Who really knows you, man—the *real* you?" I ask again, firmly this time, leaning in.

His foot starts tapping; he notices and makes it stop. He looks out the windows. He opens his mouth to spout more bullshit, but he can't keep up the façade. The tension in the room rises.

I feel a blend of rage, hurt, frustration, and grief—deep grief. I deepen my breath. I hold the silence. I feel it all. I trust the process.

"Shit, man, *no one*, okay? You happy now? Is that what you wanted to fucking hear?" This explodes out of him, causing me to lean back in my chair. I've never experienced him so raw and uncontained. He spews this at me, and I'm rattled. My chest gets tight, my stomach clenches—threat response—but I know it's not really about me. I work with my responses while staying present with Jed.

"The only ones who did, I sent packing. And now it seems like I have everything, but I feel like I got *nothing*. Fuck. Fuck. Fuck. My whole stupid-ass life feels like an act, like it's not real. I don't feel like myself anymore, whoever the fuck that even *is*." His lower lip quivers. "I have it all. I walk around like I'm on top of the world. Fuck, man. I'm dying. It's like—fuck, it's like I'm a shell."

Jed is at "the impasse," a time in his life when he can't keep doing the same thing anymore, but he doesn't know what else to do; the next thing hasn't arrived yet, or it's too scary to see. "The impasse" is paralyzing, terrifying. Volatility fills the room. He's right where he needs to be. I'm filled with nervous excitement. "Jed, make a sound, one that expresses how you feel right now."

His chin drops. From his throat comes a low, guttural sound, and I match it with a sound of my own. I'm just following. His body starts to tremble. We get louder and louder; three floors of offices hear us. I don't care. Deeper and deeper we go. We look at each other now, snarling, then smiling. I'm nodding to him: *This. Yes. You.* Sweat drips down his face. Our voices are deeper now, less loud. *Claim this, Jed. This is real. This is yours.* His hair is a mess, and he makes no move to fix it. Our voices slowly ebb toward silence. Then we're back in the same room.

Jed has a tremendous amount invested in the "Jed show." Imitation dies slow and hard. Jed has moments like this, when he touches his center and meets a raw expression of himself. But for now, the authentic moments are not getting his full attention.

7

THE PIECE OF SHIT

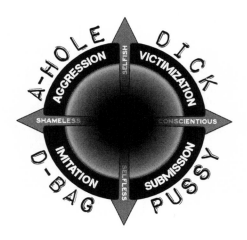

The asshole, the pussy, the douchebag, the dick—can anyone possibly be all those guys every day? Short answer: yes. Long answer: oh, fuck yes. He's the guy who never enters a therapist's office or anywhere else a man must deal with his bullshit honestly. He doesn't allow for a moment of self-doubt or self-reflection. He never considers the possibility that anything lies outside his understanding of life or his interpretation of events.

Here comes the piece of shit.

What's Worse, an Asshole or a Piece of Shit?

While an asshole, a pussy, a douchebag, and a dick exist inside all of us to some degree, the piece of shit is a man whose behavior combines only the worst of all these extremes. He gets the biggest rush by being an abusive asshole, most often to his family. Out in the world, he's often the smarmy douchebag, playing his part in the game. When something doesn't go his way, he's the dickish victim. When he's outmatched, he's a pussy, using submission to manipulate others. We all know this guy. He is many different things depending on the moment, but he's always a piece of shit.

The piece of shit is a slave to his own insecurities. He creates a twisted reality in an attempt to keep fear, shame, and any other uncomfortable sensation out of his awareness. He convinces himself that the self-told stories he relies upon in lieu of reality are true.

So, how is it that this fucker can be an asshole at home, a douchebag at church, a pussy at work, and a dick at the restaurant? It's this simple: he's compartmentalizing, selecting extreme behaviors situationally. He's also dictating the terms for any engagement with him, insisting others meet him out on the perimeter and doing his damnedest to make his bad behavior seem normal. You either interact with him under his extreme conditions, or he won't interact at all.

Brett: The Early Days of Fatherhood

Twins. They cry and eat and do all the things any healthy baby does—it's just doubled. When Brett comes home, there are two laundry baskets on the small kitchen table. In each basket, propped up in the warm clothes, is a baby. The two babies face each other through a kaleidoscope created by the circles of one basket and the squares of the other. Toes and fingers poke through the holes as they reach toward each other. Cynthia, Brett's young wife, is trying her best to keep them entertained while stirring a red sauce and dicing half of a tear-jerking onion.

"Want me to move these things off the table so we can eat?" asks Brett.

"*Things?*" Cynthia asks. "You mean babies? Children? Ben and Sophie?"

"I meant the things they're sitting in. Want me to move them?" As Cynthia leans in for a kiss, he reaches for a handful of tit.

"Sure, if you want. I need to run and get some formula before we eat.

We're completely out. I was waiting for you to get home. I just need a break. I'm at the end of my rope here. Do you need anything?"

"How did we run out?" He doesn't even wait for a response. "Yeah, actually, I need a few things too. I'll get the formula."

Cynthia needs a break, but apparently that's not happening. She releases the elastic on a small expandable file, sorts through the coupons, and hands Brett their WIC voucher. "Please get some extra tubs of wipes. We go through them fast." He snaps the voucher from her and leaves.

As he's driving, he's angry that Cynthia ran out of baby formula. *I give her a hundred bucks a month for groceries—and I had to put gas in her car this week!*

The twins are four months old, and this is the first time Brett is picking up formula. He drives past the grocery store and goes to Walmart instead, where he can also pick up some gear for his fishing trip with his brother Garrett and a few of their friends.

Sticker shock. Brett can't believe how much the formula costs. He confirms that the voucher is good for four cans and gets exactly four, nothing extra. *If she's nursing, why do we need this damn formula?* Together with the formula and some supplies for his fishing trip, he heads to the cashier. He purposefully forgets the wipes.

He hears a familiar voice: "Brett! Hey, man." Chad was in Brett's class at San Jose State. They were in a few labs together. "Hey. I didn't realize that you lived on this side of town." They walk to the cashier together and wait in the same line. Brett is ahead of Chad. "How's Cynthia? We still talk about you, man—getting married to Cynthia before we even graduated. Brett, man, you two were the shit."

Holding his gut tight, Brett looks around to see if there are any other people he might know. "She's great, man. The job at the lab is great." Like a douchebag, Brett pours it on; he starts flat-out lying. "Check this out," he says, gesturing at the fishing gear. "We're taking the twins out for their first fishing trip this weekend. We're excited. Looking forward to having the kids away from the city and noise. It'll be a nice break for Cynthia, too." Not one goddamn truth in any of that.

"Cool. Damn, you two were great. Now there's four of you? Congratulations. That's great. Look at me, man, I got nothing like you got. I'm just here getting shit to hook up a DVD player and a TiVo. You're on your way. Good for you, man."

The cashier announces the total.

Brett looks at the voucher in his hand. Brett sees Chad looking, pockets the voucher, and pays the full amount. The thought of being seen using that damn thing is unbearable. The embarrassment isn't worth a few bucks—or a few hundred bucks. On his way out of Walmart with his fishing supplies and a few days' worth of formula, he crumples the WIC voucher in disgust, tossing it on the wet ground.

By the time he gets home, it's raining, and the covered parking at their complex is full. He parks in the open lot and moves the fishing supplies to the trunk. *I give her a hundred bucks a month for groceries, I had to put gas in her car this week, I had to pay cash for that damn formula, and I have to park in the rain.* The victimized dick.

When he walks in with the formula, the twins have been moved, the table is set, and the apartment smells great. For the moment, the twins are quiet as Cynthia rocks them while nursing. Instead of waiting for her, Brett grabs a plate, serves himself spaghetti with homemade marinara, and sits down in front of the TV in the small apartment living room, with his back to the family Chad congratulated him for having.

Brett, the Everyday Piece of Shit

It's fifteen years later. Brett pulls his brand-new Lexus into the driveway at precisely 5:35 p.m. Seeing his perfect oversized lawn and the two perfectly parallel rows of red rocket crepe myrtles, Brett feels a brief moment of satisfaction. The trees remind him of the time he spent volunteering for his church in Texas and Louisiana after the hurricanes. He's careful not to park too close to the scratched, dented, and kid-destroyed minivan he bought for Cynthia eleven years ago. As he's walking back from the mailbox and across the lawn, he notices his son's bicycle, a scooter, lacrosse gear, and those goddamn Airsoft BBs strewn about. Brett shakes his head in disgust. *Goddammit.*

Brett gives the living room a quick once-over on his way to the kitchen. He glances at the framed family picture above the fireplace. "House of Our Lord," he reads to himself. There are shoes everywhere. A pile of laundry has been dumped onto his recliner, waiting to be folded and put away. His son, Ben, sits at the center of the pile with his iPad. *I work so they can sit around, apparently.*

"Hey, champ," Brett says as he sorts through the bills that he alone is allowed to open. Ben winces inwardly at the sound of his dad's voice. "You and your buddies left the lacrosse goal on the front lawn again." Brett snatches Ben's iPad out of his hands. "Why don't you gather your stuff up? I don't pay the gardener to put your stuff away."

Brett sees all the matching backpacks at the bottom of the stairs. His daughter's whole damn dance team must be upstairs. He feels another rush of resentment, this time for his wife. *She has no job, and she can't even organize the house. What the fuck does she do all day? Watch Judge Judy and play Candy Crush? There hasn't been a single night this week that Ben hasn't been glued to that iPad. Whatever happened to the chore chart? Why doesn't anyone fucking listen to me?*

His rage, wholly concealed—or so he thinks—feels good. His anger is righteous. He feels a sweet anticipation rising in himself as he makes his way further into the house, actively searching for evidence to validate his anger and resentment. In the kitchen, Cynthia is grating cheese. He gives her a perfunctory peck on the cheek, then sighs as he notices the cheap taco shells on the counter. *All the money I give her, and I'll be damned, she's obviously wasted it on something stupid. Those taco shells are for shit.*

As Brett's judgment fills the room, Cynthia turns to the refrigerator for lettuce. She tries to divert his attention by asking about his day, but his ringing phone interrupts her.

"Hey, big brother. What's up?" Brett snaps his fingers, motioning for her to be quiet. "It's taco night. Shame you aren't here; I'd heat you up a homemade tortilla." The conversation continues. Finally: "Sounds good. Got the whole family here, just about to sit down to a family dinner. I'll call you tomorrow to confirm."

"It's probably a good thing Garrett can't come by," Brett observes instantly after hanging up. "If he didn't break his neck falling over the backpacks, he'd choke to death on these crappy taco shells. It's a sinking ship around here."

As dinner is served, Brett asks Ben if he's been practicing basketball or just "playing with his lacrosse stick." Across from him, the boy shifts in his seat and doesn't raise his eyes. Ben is ashamed, but not for himself. He's just taking it again. Cynthia knows, Brett knows, and that's the fucking point. "You've got to be able to dribble with your left hand, son," Brett says levelly. "That kid humiliated you in the last game. Do you want that to happen again?"

"No, Dad," Ben mumbles.

"That's right." With that, Brett reaches over the table and forcefully ruffles Ben's hair. "Garrett and his boys chartered the boat again this weekend. They're going to leave from Half Moon Bay. I'll probably have to take Friday off and head down early that day or late Thursday. Ben, be tough out there on the court this weekend."

Sophie, his daughter, bounds out of her room and down the stairs with her gaggle of friends; each of them stops at the table and hugs Cynthia.

"Bye, Mom."

"Bye-bye, Mom."

"Love you, Sophie's Mom."

"You said I could borrow your earrings for the dance, *riiight*, Sophie's Mom?"

"No, I get to borrow them, right, Cynthia?"

"Of course. Of course. Be safe, girls. Text me when y'all get home so I don't have to call the Pleasanton po-po again. You know how they love it when I call them to find you girls."

Without even a hint of acknowledging Brett, they all file quickly past the end of the table where he is seated. Sophie never invites her friends to stay for dinner when her father is home. It's their "family time." Convenient excuse. Since starting high school, she's distanced herself from her dad. Her friends from school and church understand, and they follow her lead.

Sophie and Ben are digging taco night, pausing between bites to tell Cynthia that it's their favorite, "the best."

Brett is irked by their enthusiasm, their laziness, and the expensive braces they're both wearing, which weren't covered by dental insurance, as he likes to remind the kids. When Sophie reaches for a third taco shell, Brett gently takes the plate from her hand and sets it at the edge of the table. Brett's resentment has found another outlet. "Trust me, sweetheart," he says, "you don't want to be the fat girl on the dance team." Sophie slumps back in her chair, devastated by another fat remark from her father. Brett is the only overweight person in the family.

Cynthia looks directly at Sophie and makes fast eye contact. She also nudges Ben with her foot. Cynthia and the kids have routines for checking in when trouble is brewing. The check-in is subtle but firm—very firm. It's calming and comforting. It's something they rely on. The check-in is a way for Cynthia to connect with the kids and to protect them from unwarranted and unwelcome bullshit from Brett.

"She's not fat, Brett," Cynthia says.

"I didn't say she was fat, Cynthia. I said she doesn't want to *get* fat." He examines his wife, noting the color rising on her pale cheeks. It excites him more than seeing her naked. He turns to Sophie, tilting his head. "Sophie, did I say you were fat?"

Cynthia watches their daughter carefully. Sophie and Cynthia have a deal—a bittersweet deal. They know how to deescalate these situations. Sophie hates to betray her mom, but they know the routine. They do it all the time. "No," Sophie mumbles softly, feeling a blast of bitterness as her twin brother polishes off his fourth taco.

"Well, then," Brett says, "please pass the beans."

Throughout the evening, Brett drops subtle but incisive digs at Cynthia and the kids:

"Didn't have time to go to the grocery store?" he says, looking in the refrigerator for dessert.

"Getting a little old to be calling your mother 'Mommy,' aren't you, darling?"

"Thought you'd be taller by now, champ."

"CrossFit isn't gonna help your sister with her dating prospects, Cyn. Being born a decade later would've helped." (Cynthia is fifteen months older than her sister.)

He digs at Cynthia's intelligence: "Online Economics? Is Cal State trying to make it easy?" He mocks her ambition almost daily. She studies when he's asleep to avoid his needling disdain and routine disparagement of her ambitions. "Your résumé sucks. You can barely clean a house—who the hell is going to hire you with a bachelor's in project management? I'm not paying those loans off; you agreed to that. Such a waste."

She worked after the twins were born. *All* her income went toward Brett's student loans.

He doesn't shout. He walks deliberately, closing doors in a way that demonstrates exactly whose house it is. On the surface, he barely seems to get riled, but underneath his calm-enough disposition is seething denigration. He commands the entire household. Outside his home, he paints a different picture for others to see: a soft-spoken scientist within a US federal agency living a humble, quiet, unassuming life with his adoring wife, Cynthia, and their twin children. He works hard, he goes to church with his family, and he's tirelessly polite. To those who don't live with him, Brett could be the Bob Ross of living family portraits, and his work hangs above the mantle. "House of Our Lord" indeed, you piece of shit.

Will the Piece of Shit Sit on My Couch?

The piece of shit can't do introspection. He won't willingly sit on a therapist's couch. Brett and his kind already know everything, lie about everything, fake everything, and pretend to fear nothing. A therapist does scare him, though. It may sound unlikely that a piece of shit would be intimidated by a therapist, but a man like Brett fears confidences, and he fears the truth. He sees truth and confidentiality as a threat. He smells trouble when his victims talk to a teacher, lawyer, doctor, cop, clergyman—and especially to a therapist. He and his twisted façade are very fragile.

If a piece of shit is forced to meet with a therapist, it's typically a shitshow: "I promise to change. I'm listening. Please, give me this one last chance. I'll kill myself if you leave me." In many cases, this is an extended and calculated dick move when the end is inevitable; this way, it's *her* fault for not giving it one last chance. The shitshow becomes a hyper-cringey reality show when she rejects his final pleas: "You lied to me," he cries. "You said we could work on this, and I believed you. I've been trying. It'll get better." (Wait for it...) "We have so much, and I'm trying. You can't do this to us." (Wait for it...) More tears, acting, faking, whatever, and then the finale: "You crazy fucking cunt. I was honest and came to fucking therapy. You wasted my time, you fucking bitch." (No surprise there.) On his way out, the piece of shit tries to have the final word: "You'll never get another fucking penny out of me, ever. Fuck you." (Who didn't see that coming?)

Congratulations, piece of shit. "It'll get better," you say? In that case, go change—but somewhere else, please. Believe me, the world needs pieces of shit like Brett to change, but in the meantime, Cynthia isn't available for your games. Take your fake shit and your insults and get the fuck out, coward. She needs you to get the fuck out of here so the healing can begin, including yours.

I have met a few of these pieces of shit in couples work, but I deal mostly with those who are recovering from the devastation they leave in their wake. Their children suffer. Their partners suffer. When the dynamic is not identified or addressed, POS behavior can carry on as the norm for generations, resulting in violence, abuse, addiction, illness, and loss.

Cynthia's story is critical for all of us to know and understand. In the face of terror and trauma, Cynthia will find a better path. Brett won't. We can change. We must change. It's hard. Change takes fortitude, strategy, and skills, but we have what it takes.

8
CYNTHIA

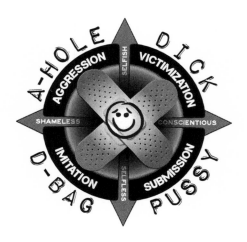

In these early therapy sessions, Cynthia tells her story mostly to herself. She is finally able to hear her own voice, and she is shocked by what she hears. After being an absent and abused character in her own life, she comes alive. She reclaims personhood.

Cynthia's Beginning

In the waiting room, Cynthia sits straight-backed on the edge of her seat, eyes staring into the distance. She startles slightly when I walk in, springs up, and tries to regain her composure.

I fill the silence. "Nice to meet you, Cynthia," I say, extending my hand, which she grips softly. "I'm David. I'm glad you're here."

"Cynthia," she says. "Cynthia," this time louder and clearer. Her smile is big, but it's strained; her eyes are terrified. She makes no sound while following me to my office. I look back several times to make sure she's still there. We sit down. My first impression is that she's not allowed to be here. She's one courageous lady. She's in big trouble.

"I'm, um…I need help with my marriage. My husband, Brett, he's always upset with me. I can't ever seem to make him happy. No matter how hard I try or what I do, he's not happy."

I feel a chill rise up my spine. "Does he know you're here?"

"Heavens, no," she says and stifles a chuckle. "I *can't* be here. I…I love my kids—twins, teenagers. Wow, teenagers. Wow. Time. I've got to find a way to make it better, to make life bearable—for the kids. I'll be alright. I have to help *them*. If I can help the marriage, that will be, um, good for them."

* * *

Cynthia comes in after a month of weekly sessions. "This is how I'm here, okay? I contact you through a portal at my stupid job, one that has protected privacy. My employer pays you directly. I took a job in the service department at the auto mall just so I could get insurance. I have insurance through Brett, but I needed my own so I could come here without him knowing. My entire paycheck is deposited into his account. *His* account. My allowance is unchanged, unless I get paid cash. I borrowed my friend's husband's car to drive here. I do this every week. I leave my car at the church so if my husband checks on me, he'll think I was there or that I met someone there. I even leave my phone in my friend's car. She drives around with my phone, just in case he's stalking me again. I'm afraid that if Brett saw me here or knew where I was, he would lose his shit. My friend even agreed to answer any text messages from him while I'm here. She's the *one* friend who kind of knows. *One*. And she's probably sick of listening to me. That's probably why she's helping me come see you."

She's alive—her presence is louder than her fear. I smile, and she smiles back. "Nice to meet you, Cynthia," I say in acknowledgment. "What else do you want me to know?"

She laughs, not fully recognizing that I'm acknowledging her. "I don't know. I'm trying to figure it out. There are these moments in here and when I'm in class—I'm finishing my undergraduate, which Brett hates—when I feel like...a person. That I exist. I feel it right now. I haven't felt *myself* in...I don't even know. But I know I have to prioritize the kids. I can handle Brett; I just don't want to. Not one more day or one more thing from him. I can't do one more day. I have to, and I will. But. I will for the kids, but it's hard. I'm here for the kids. I don't know how to help them other than by keeping things from getting worse."

"So, you're here to help the kids? We can work with that. For now, I'm curious about you: How do you live your life? How do you do it? I'm curious to know. You've told me about your life, but you've left yourself out of it. How do you manage to keep this going?"

She looks at me. "How do I live? Like a servant, that's how. Empty. This isn't even *me* you're looking at. My sister gave me these boots. This purse was in the lost and found at my friend's work. We live in a four-bedroom house in Pleasanton with a new home theater room and a brand-new leased Lexus in the garage, and I manage this with a weekly allowance of one hundred a week—for everything. Food, clothes, sports, you name it. *That's* how I live. Is that what you wanted to know? I have to feed two teenage kids. Often, they have friends over. And I have to cater to that man-child. And occasionally there's food for me. I do it with *one hundred dollars*. I have to drive the kids and pick up the dry cleaning. I have to pay for their activities or tell them no. If he doesn't like dinner, the next week he won't put money in the savings account I have to use; I'll get gift cards to the grocery store instead. I'm not on the mortgage. I'm not on the car titles or home title. I haven't had a checking account since we got married and he canceled mine. *He* has all that. In fifteen years, I've never had more than three hundred dollars in my account. That's how I live. And that's the easy part. I can manage that."

"Wow," I say, bearing witness. I start to ask a question, but she cuts me off, which is great.

"The hard part now is smiling. And the price for not smiling is unbearable. The servant part is just a process now. I can do that, for the kids. Smiling now, though? It's torture every time. The kids see me not smiling. They didn't always notice. Now they notice, and they've changed. It's different now. I want to smile, and I can't. Not now. He's taken everything from me, and I can't smile, not now."

"Got it. I'm curious: How it is to be sharing this with me? What do you notice? Pause for a minute, and just check in with yourself."

Cynthia is not interested in a break. "I don't want a minute; I want fifteen fucking *years*."

Now she takes a break. She smiles a bit. Cries a bit. Looks out the window.

"I didn't die. I thought about it, you know—fantasies. But I would never do that to my kids. Plus, that would mean Brett had won. Telling you about my life just now, I didn't die either. I'm not crazy, even though he tells me I am. I see that now. He always made me feel crazy when I mention the difficulties with money or refuse sex. He forbids me from even talking to someone at church about it. He literally used those words: 'I forbid you.'" (She says this in character, in a deep voice.) "Can you believe that? He told me to be grateful for the life he provides me and to do my duty as a wife and mother. He said if I ever talked to anyone about my stupid struggles, he'd leave me, and I'd have nothing."

"You're in an emotionally abusive relationship, Cynthia, and it's quite severe. Has anyone else supported you or helped you?"

"I mentioned my friend who covers for me, but other than that? Hell no. I just thought I was here to learn how to get along with Brett better so maybe he wouldn't be such a bastard to our kids, you know? I didn't even know how wrong things were with my own life until I was coming here for a few months. I mean, I knew it was rough, but I see the same look in other women's eyes all the time, the strained smile, the tight jaw. I see it in my mother; I just thought that was what life was. But when I saw him treating my daughter that way, something inside me snapped, my mama bear—that's what they call it, right? I want something better for her. He doesn't get to mess with her about her weight at dinner. He doesn't get to ruin her like he did me. She hates him too, now, and it kills him because she used to love him so much, so he punishes her." Tears run down Cynthia's face.

"You want something better for her," I say, reflecting back what I've just heard.

"Yes, more than anything. What happens to girls, to women in this culture, in the church, everywhere—I see it. I feel it. I've been reading about it. I'm learning about it in school. It's *not* okay." She slouches back into the sofa and cries.

"I'm trapped, though, I'm trapped. I thought it would get better. The kids are older; it had to get better. And then. And then. I was sending myself an email. To me, from me. Got it? Sending myself an email. It was a reminder for something. Brett's phone was on the dresser, and when I hit send, his phone dinged. I thought that was weird, so I did it again—and again, and again. I'm sure I did it forty times before he got out of the shower. And when he got out and heard a ding, he raced over and grabbed the phone. I kept sending myself the same email, a smiling face emoji and an empty message. Just like my life. Just like my life."

"Violation," I say. "Another violation."

"He had hacked into my email and set it up on his phone. Idiot. Sorry. I'm really not this mean. I'm not. He couldn't admit he'd been reading my email. If he did, he'd have to admit that he saw all the times I borrowed twenty bucks from the kids or ten from a neighbor—to eat, or to pick the kids up from school. I've asked for money from strangers just to get home to my house in Pleasanton. I can't even believe I'm telling you this. I can't believe what I'm saying, but it's true. God help me, it's true, I swear."

"Cynthia," I say crisply. "I believe you."

More tears.

Cynthia's Experience with the Piece of Shit

Cynthia's story is as profound, or more profound, than the journey of any of our main archetype characters. Cynthia is not weak; pound for pound, Cynthia can take down the biggest of the assholes. She's bold. Her skills and defenses are as formidable as any of our four archetypes can boast. The force it would take to get herself and her kids to the finish line is more than she knew she had, but she's finding it.

I believed Cynthia (and you should too), but most people believed Brett's lies, his public act—and they continue to believe him. Why? This is important, critically important: Why do most people believe Brett and disbelieve Cynthia? Or to clarify that question, why do we undervalue the experience of a woman like Cynthia and give a piece of shit like Brett the benefit of doubt?

Simply put, Cynthia's story is scary. It requires us to question our own view of the world and confront the unsettling fact that what we thought was true was an awful lie. The details of her story are ugly and horrible, but that's not the issue. We entertain ourselves with horror. We watch horror films and the news. We see horrible things all the time. But when it's someone you know, someone like Cynthia, it's shocking to learn that her husband is a piece of shit and her life with him is hell: *They seemed so great. I'm shocked.* And Brett being a piece of shit is not unique. He is not an outlier. When Cynthia tells her story, it ends a piece of shit's charade and disrupts our reality. For most people, that disruption is uncomfortable, maybe even unacceptable.

Cynthia lives with a perfect storm of extreme behaviors in one man, the worst of the asshole, douchebag, pussy, and dick. She's doing the best she can with the skills she's picked up along the way. Circumstances led her to where she is now, and circumstances have kept her in a bad relationship with the piece of shit. She is resilient; she will rise triumphantly, but not easily. For most of her way along the path to clarity and freedom, she will be destitute and lost. It is an unfair compromise; it is a worthwhile cause.

Cynthia's Living Session

Cynthia enters with energy. She's still afraid. She had Natalie drop her off for this therapy session. They abandoned the minivan at the church parking lot again and left her phone inside the church. They know Brett is a "good church man," so he won't make a scene near the church.

"You want to know more about 'how,' David? You want to know how? I'll tell you how. I plan around it; I work around it. Here you go, this pretty much captures it: My daughter was invited to a dance by a nice boy. She's beautiful and strong. She bought herself a cute dress. It's modest and cute. It's a normal dress that she had to modify. It was all she could afford. She's beautiful. Brett is going to lose his shit. He already has. He tore up her strapless bra. He went through the laundry and tore up her thong underwear and flipped them at her like a rubber band, hitting her in the face. He told her that it's embarrassing that his daughter would even *own* this shit. What if someone saw her? What would they think of him as a father? What about the people at church? Other men? His brother? They'd think *he* had failed." She pauses, breathing hard.

"I replaced the bra and panties. I had a plan. I helped her get ready and got her over to a friend's house before he got home from work on Friday night. I knew if I let Brett have sex with me, he might be asleep when Sophie got home. So I did, and he was out of the picture when our daughter got home from the dance. My daughter got to have a normal experience. This is how, David; this is how. This is my terrible how. This is how I keep Brett from destroying moments in my kids' lives."

She's shaking now, her nervous system unwinding the trauma. She sobs—huge, wailing sobs. "I see what you've done to protect your children," I say, acknowledging the sacrifice.

"I hate him," she yells between sobs. "I hate him, I hate him, I hate him." I'm reminded of something a friend told me: "The system stunts men. It *crushes* women." More months go by, and more heartbreaking stories are brought out into the light, to be made real, to be witnessed, to support the healing process.

"I need to hit him—something, anything," she says right off the bat as she arrives for another session. "I've been hitting myself for so long. I need to hit something else."

We move to the floor, and I stack two couch cushions in front of her. I show her how to bring her fists down together safely and with sound. It's an action that both releases and empowers. "Put whoever or whatever you want into those cushions."

She raises her fists and brings them down with sound. She's sobbing, but she's also smiling, sounding with each blow.

It's hard to describe what it's like to witness the physicality of re-birth—the sounds, the power, the release, the courage. I feel a combination of love, awe, and gratitude. Pride, humility, and grief. This is what we are, this full expression.

She continues: "Do you know the shame I have? Do you know the guilt? Do you know how bad it hurts to have sex when a kiss is as violent as being hit in the face?" She pounds the cushions a dozen more times. "Are you afraid of me? Are you going to shut me down? All men want to do is fuck me or shut me down. And for me to serve them."

Almost Free

"You know what's even worse? I actually feel *sorry* for him. I always have. I saw this more clearly a few weeks back. I see how scared he is, and what do I do? I protect him. What does that make me, David? You should have seen him apologize to the teacher when I stood up for my son at the parent-teacher conference. He has no spine; that's what's so interesting. When he gets upset at home, it scares us—like he's going to crack and explode. He can't handle any resistance. Managing, just managing. We manage him because he feels so fragile. He abuses us; we take care of him. We protect him. How is that the role of the wife and children? We protect a frightening man who wants to hurt us. He wants to scare me. He's hurt us, and he can do it again, and we protect his image out in the world. People think he's nice because we *lie*. We lie for him. We just keep on lying for him. We keep his act going because we're afraid of what might happen if we don't. How can I pity and protect a man that I fear? Why do I let him get away with it? He scares my kids. He scares my kids, David. He scares my kids, and I protect him. Me, I protect *him*. And dammit, the kids protect him, too. He hurts us; we protect him."

Cynthia is breathless, silent. After hearing herself say all this, she is still.

"Women are taught to play this role, Cynthia. Now, though, you *see* it. When you see it clearly, things change. When you feel the pain of playing this role, as you've been doing so bravely these past months, you're working your way out of it. Back to you. Back to yourself, your center. This is what we've been doing. I imagine you don't play along anymore to the same extent that you used to."

"You know what, I don't. You know who doesn't either? My daughter. He was about to shove her hand away from a second helping, and you know what she did? She filled her plate anyway. 'You're not the boss of my food, *Dad*'—she said that to him. We had talked about it; I told her I would back her play. You know what he did? He grabbed his plate and left the dinner table in a childish huff, turned, and said, 'You are a bunch of ingrates.' It was ridiculous. Nobody would believe me if I told them. I was scared. So were the kids; I could feel them panic. But it was also funny somehow. We're less afraid now, though. He's pathetic. In his absence, dinner was very pleasant. It makes me wonder about every woman I see. Now I silently ask them, *Are you protecting your husband, too?* Like we need to help these men pretend they're strong. And for what? So they don't freak out? So we can feel safe and pretend we have strong husbands? What a joke. I've been playing along for so long. The church, same thing. I only go when I want to now. That kills him, but he has less power over me now. He goes by himself. To explain my absence, he's been telling people I've got some strange illness. I have people calling me, asking about my health. His lies, his façade again. He's ridiculous. I'm married to a ridiculous man. But I see it now." Her jaw tenses, and her fists get tight. She pounds them on the sofa, one fist beside each thigh. "I—*thwap*—see—*thwap*—it— *thwap*—now—*thwap!* And I'm getting out somehow. I'm getting out somehow. We're getting out."

PART 3
TRACE

9

TRIGGER: THE T IN TRACE

*You may want the world—partners, politicians, bosses, global warming, whatever—to be different so you won't **feel** triggered. There are things that genuinely need to change in the external world. But believing that the way to avoid being triggered is for a partner to be more considerate, or for new ice to form in Antarctica, does not address the core problem.*

TRACE changes the relationship you have with your triggers.

TRACE: Trigger, Reaction, Awareness, Curiosity, Experiment

We've met the asshole, the pussy, the douchebag, the dick, and the piece of shit. These guys spin out in predictable, destructive patterns, learning nothing along the way. They just keep doubling down, doing the shit they always do, then doing it again tomorrow. That's what all of us do, to some extent—until we learn how to engage with other possibilities.

Let's say you're a total fucking dick at work. Now what? Knowing your inclination toward selfishness and the way you blame and fault others is a start. When you're triggered and all that dickishness is about to take over, you can deal with it in a different way. TRACE is a framework to guide and support you in doing things differently. It's a practice of self-awareness, a method of change, and a framework for an engaged, empowered, dynamic life. Here we go:

TRIGGER
REACTION
AWARENESS
CURIOSITY
EXPERIMENTATION

Most people are stuck in the TR of TRACE: **trigger**, **reaction**, repeat. You can see this clearly with Jonah, George, Jed, Eric, and Brett. When you endlessly repeat the **trigger (T)** and **reaction (R)** cycle of TRACE, you end up out on the perimeter, acting like an asshole, a pussy, a douchebag, a dick...or even a piece of shit.

The ACE in TRACE is the solution; it's how you engage with your process in the moment, through the chaos and triggers of life. When you bring **awareness (A)** and **curiosity (C)** to your **reaction**, things begin to shift, and you can start **experimenting (E)** with new behaviors. The ACE in TRACE is how you break out of habituated trigger-reaction cycles.

[TRIGGER WARNING] Triggers Aren't Excuses

In common parlance, being "triggered" is nothing more than a cliché, an excuse to avoid taking responsibility for your own reactions, or to receive special treatment from others. As in, "You know damn well that triggers me, so you better not do it." Or, in another form of the same nonsense, "I'm triggered now, so you can't blame me for whatever the fuck I do next." Well, that cliché is ridiculous. Hopefully you're not a cliché in your own life.

Don't get me wrong. There are things that genuinely need to change about the external world, and navigating the world is stressful and generally annoying. Triggers will happen. I acknowledge that triggers are real and that people are being sincere when they talk about being triggered. I'm empathetic. I am. There is time and space for frustrations and complaints. Go ahead, bitch and moan to a friend, let it out, but then own your own shit. Stop the fucking blame game, shame game, excuse game, and bullshit game. Own it. You are the one having the experience, regardless of what triggered you.

Being "triggered" may explain what led to a bad reaction, but it doesn't excuse shitty behavior.

Triggers Are Information

We are constantly processing information. Unless you're in a vegetative state, it's more or less impossible to avoid new information. When that information feels personal—when it links to our basic needs, survival instincts, and past trauma—we are prompted to react. These links can be positive or negative, but we tend to associate triggers with information that is exclusively negative. That is simply not accurate. We also have reactions to positive, good things.

Familiar smells can be triggers. Freshly mowed grass! Mom's bread! (The baking craze we are experiencing in the USA right now could be called aromatherapy.) A familiar song can trigger a very specific and positive reaction. There are reasons people stream the oldies and the classics. They bring back good times and good memories. We sign up for triggers that remind us of good and familiar things.

But whether positive or negative, we need the information triggers provide us. Messengers bring valuable information, so we should always welcome the messenger, right? We don't usually welcome negative triggers, but a trigger is a messenger delivering important information about *you*. Shooting the messenger because he brings unsettling news is a shortsighted move—no more messages for you. You don't want to be out of the loop when it comes to yourself. When you were a child, you couldn't maturely process these messages, so you did the best you could. As a grown man who could really use these messages, the cost of shooting or ignoring the messenger is high.

Triggers can be challenging:

- *Feeling triggered sucks—it's physically and emotionally uncomfortable.*
- *You don't get to choose what triggers you—it just happens.*
- *The world will trigger you no matter what—the world is just triggering.*
- *It's "unmanly" to be triggered—isn't that right, you pussy?*
- *The people you rely on the most can trigger you the most.*
- *You were probably never taught how to deal with triggers.*

George, the pussy, knows damn well he's not in *actual* danger when Kayla asks him to be more assertive, but a part of him experiences danger. That fearful part—and its way of reacting—wins every time. Rationality holds limited sway when you're triggered. *It's not supposed to be this way, dammit. I'm a man. I'm the master of my own ship. I chart my own course.* Well, you're not the master. You don't chart shit. Sorry. When you're triggered, the reasons *why* you're doing this, or *why* you should stop, lose relevance—you are beholden to your *how*. Your *how* runs the show. When you're triggered, you're dominated by the way you've responded to triggers in the past—reflexively, habitually, without even knowing it. Because it feels natural and inevitable, you may assume this response is who you are, but it's not *you*. It's your brilliant, strong, stubborn—and in all probability, outdated—*how*.

Whether we're assholes, douchebags, pussies, or dicks, we too often resign ourselves to being led around by our reactions to the external world or letting others make choices for us that determine our state. But living like this, without control, is not the only option. When we process triggers as information and *feel* that information, we can make the difficult things meaningful. When we can use challenging information and experiences to learn about ourselves, to grow, to take responsibility, and to choose our responses, we are in the process of becoming our best selves.

TRACE is how we change our relationship with triggers.

Bad triggers suck, but knowing how to deal with triggers empowers us. I want you to have this relationship with your triggers, to appreciate them for the information they are. Not only is it more interesting and meaningful than being trapped in a cycle of blind reaction, it heals your old wounds and minimizes the wounds you may inflict upon others.

Trigger-Happy

We live in a world with other people who are all reacting to their own triggers. Our triggers coexist with theirs. When the people around you respond to their triggers, you may feel the consequences. You may even fly off the handle because of their reaction and continue a chain reaction of triggers. That's just life intersecting. Information is exchanged among the living.

It's our nature to react or respond quickly rather than considering our own actions thoughtfully. We try to outrun triggers, but they're faster than us. We feel the impact of information, get triggered, and immediately discharge, often with a judgmental thought or comment. We rarely seek to understand before acting, and we judge others without seeing or knowing their triggers. We barely—and often only accidentally—see our own triggers.

We've seen Jonah, George, Jed, and Eric being set off by external events. For example, Eric sees Annie, his girlfriend, talking to another fella at a party and goes full victim mode on her. But we are just as easily triggered by *internal* experiences: the recollection of a painful breakup, looping fear over a risky financial decision or an imagined catastrophe, or the relived memory of a contentious interaction. These internal triggers can be stirred up by our own thoughts, and they produce predictable physical sensations: a sharp pain or tightness in the chest, unsettled guts, an old shoulder injury that resurfaces, or a headache. Our imaginations are powerful. We can, and do, trigger ourselves all the time by believing our own thoughts.

In her abusive marriage to Brett, Cynthia is constantly being triggered, but she's never been taught that triggers are information—to her, from her, about her situation. At first, she thinks that the way to make herself and her children feel safer is to make Brett happy, to submissively meet him on *his* terms. She blames herself for not being happy with her apparently happy life. She's been distanced from herself by a culture that taught her to be a *good* woman, to smile and go along with the program. In learning to listen to what her triggers are trying to tell her, her life changes; her reality changes. She begins to live her life firsthand, based on her own experience—from the inside out, instead of from the outside in.

For Every Action, There Is a "Fuck This"

Responses to triggers are based on history, temperament, and circumstances, but they all have the same goal: to stop uncomfortable feelings. I trip and fall; my friend laughs at me (trigger); I feel unbearable shame; I stand up; I push my friend down (reaction). My friend stops laughing, we're both distracted from my shame, and I feel a little better. This happened to me when my friend and I were about four years old, but this process probably begins around the age of two. Endless variations on this theme play out for all of us. I ask Lauren to dance; she says no; she turns around and dances with Joe Yannotti instead; I don't like what I'm feeling; I pretend I'm as cool and calm as Joe; I leave the dance; I walk home alone, in search of a way to soothe my feelings. We were all twelve. Since the age of twelve, I've hated dances—shocker. High school dances, dancing at weddings, any dancing—I'm a wallflower at best. To this day, I avoid dancing. This pattern started when Lauren said no to me and yes to Joe Yannotti. My priority was to feel better, and leaving the dance did make me feel better. From then on, I've just avoided asking anyone to dance. Disappointment avoided. Problem solved. Sorta.

Traffic is a tangible example of a trigger. Who likes traffic? Who looks forward to being in it? Creeping along the freeway, you're probably mildly triggered. Annoyed. Sitting with all of the suckers, going nowhere. There's usually a bit of tension, a few loud sighs, restlessness, slight irritation.

Hitting traffic when you have an important meeting, though, may be more of a trigger. Body temperature rises; heart rate increases. You may unconsciously grip the steering wheel and mutter curses at other drivers.

Add to this mix hunger, a shitty night's sleep, bickering with your partner earlier that morning, and the guy in a Prius with the stupid "visualize whirled peas" bumper sticker in front of you letting everyone in, and *bam*, road rage! Stress hormones flood the nervous system; muscles grip painfully. You sweat through your clothes. More rage! Fight-or-flight survival fears activate. You pass people on the on-ramp, swear loudly, shoot the finger at cars with children in them, and obsess over possible worst-case scenarios.

We tend to think of our response to triggers as strictly emotional, but this understates the force of them. Information changes your physiology. Stress hormones prep the body for a fight-or-flight response by delivering energy-supplying glucose to your largest muscle groups. Cortisol, critical to coping with stress, floods your system. Your breathing gets shallow, your body temperature rises, and you begin to perspire. At the same time, your heart is thumping. Your shoulders, neck, and jaw tense. Your body is ready for action.

During this fight response, your thinking mind, the one that usually keeps your aggressive tendencies in check, becomes more agitated, less clear. In this moment, what you really need is for your mind to stay calm, but your mind wants to *fuck something up*. As your mind becomes muddled and agitated, it interprets events in skewed, unhelpful, reactive ways, often strengthening the trigger and the reaction. In this physical condition, assholery seems really damn inviting. *Fuck it—and fuck you! Ah, that feels so much better now.* All of these basic—and rather primitive—reactions are evidence of the human animal taking over. This is our survival wiring coming into play.

While there are some commonalities in how our bodies react to triggers, the severity and duration of what we experience when triggered is unique. If you're hungry or tired, for example, the trigger may affect you more deeply. The same holds true if you have trauma in your system, which we all do to varying degrees. You are more vulnerable to triggers if you're already emotionally raw. If you've faced oppression because of your race, gender, sexuality, or zip code, you've been exposed to ongoing triggers. The degree to which you're triggered depends on your overall history and your innate temperament. In short, triggers are subjective and based on many factors.

The Trigger Trap

When you're triggered to the point of terror, raw survival instincts take over completely. You have little, if any, conscious control over your experience. You lose logic and agency, even the ability to see. You freak the fuck out—and there's nothing funny about it. Your nervous system responds as though your life were at stake, and you will do anything, absolutely anything, to stop the terror.

In normal conditions, our lives are not in danger on a moment-to-moment basis, but our brains are still wired to respond to primal threat. Rival clans no longer stalk us. Droughts won't cause a plague. Minor infections are treated. But we still react as if our lives are on the line, as though real, palpable, fatal danger were just around the corner.

Barry Glassner, leading sociologist and author of *The Culture of Fear*, says that "most Americans are living in the safest place at the safest time in human history." In contemporary life, you may have to contend with irate bosses, professional and personal rivals, micro- and macro-aggressions, and your monthly bills. These can be daunting matters—I don't want to sell them short. But they are, for the most part, manageable. But just try telling your nervous system that! Forged over millions of years, the human nervous system hasn't yet settled into the reality of these relatively safe times.

Rick Hanson, best-selling author and renowned psychologist, frames it like this: "As we evolved over millions of years, dodging sticks and chasing carrots, it was a lot more important to notice, react to, and remember sticks than...carrots. That's because—in the tough environments in which our ancestors lived—if they missed out on a carrot, they usually had a shot at another one later on. But if they failed to avoid a stick—a predator, a natural hazard, or aggression from others of their species—WHAM, no more chances to pass on their genes."

"The emotion of fear often works overtime," writes psychologist Tara Brach. "Even when there is no immediate threat, our body may remain tight and on guard, our mind narrowed to focus on what might go wrong. When this happens, fear is no longer functioning to secure our survival. We are caught in the trance of fear and our moment-to-moment experience becomes bound in reactivity. We spend our time and energy defending life rather than living it fully."

Fight or flight, freeze or appease, we are wired to survive. Our survival instincts tell us how to stay alive and get the shit we need. To maximize our chances, we have adapted or been conditioned to interpret our world negatively, seeing threats everywhere. We are much more likely to mistake a coiled rope for a snake than to mistake a coiled snake for a rope. Obviously, reacting to a perceived danger and being wrong is not that big a deal. Misjudging real danger and being wrong? *That* is a problem. Better safe than sorry. Our reactions to negative things are stronger or more convincing for good reasons. This is our negativity bias.

When something sucks, we avoid it. We avoid confrontations. We avoid family gatherings. We avoid all kinds of shit that we know will trigger us. But if everything we do is based on avoiding what triggers us, we're *trapped* by those triggers, owned by our negativity bias without even knowing it—unless we engage with it.

Your life is going to collide with your fears, and hallelujah for that! These life vs. fear collisions tend to happen when your sense of safety, belonging, and agency are threatened. Said another way, when you're not in complete control, you may get scared. If you don't feel in control, you're triggered. The mind does a wonderful job of reframing these situations where fear and life collide:

- *I just don't worry about my health. The ultimate reframe of a life-or-death concern.*
- *That's just the way I am. The reframe of avoiding responsibility.*
- *I'm not scared to leave my job; I like it okay. The reframe of denial (say hello, pussy).*

We avoid triggers by practicing abstinence—from life. We abstain from candid conversations with our partners. We abstain from looking at the consequences of our drinking. We abstain from introspection. We abstain from holiday parties. We do our best. TRACE helps make our best better, without abstaining from life.

Jonah, George, Jed, and Eric have default behaviors, or go-to reactions, which are largely avoidant. When they feel or sense something that's uncomfortable, they shut it down right away. They spin out. Like these men, we are afraid of overwhelming feelings; we are masters of excuses and justifications. Away from our centers, we have no access to the resources we need to move through—and move past—the triggering situations of life, so we stay stuck. Few of us are willing to admit to our own bullshit. Our fear of these uncomfortable states keeps us from seeing, or maybe even caring about, the truth.

I'll do whatever it takes, every one of us says to life at some point, *as long as you don't ever, ever, frighten me like that again. As long as you never take me back to that dark place.* We cash out what's left of our chips from the game of life and say, *Fuck it, I'm not playing anymore.* Instead of going all-in, we go all-out. Why? Because even though we know loss is inevitable, we don't think we can take another hit. "I'll never love again" is the hyperbolic response to intense heartache. It speaks to the depth of pain and the desire to avoid pain in the future at any price. Fear keeps us from seeing that we will, in all likelihood, be okay. We humans are incredibly resilient creatures. We rebuild when disaster strikes. We come together and help one another. We adapt; we begin anew, time and time again. But individually, we still submit to our fears.

When we face our fears in an authentic way, we almost always feel empowered. This is why therapy works. This is why I've applied TRACE in my practice and in my life. The arduous process of engaging with fear is awful at the beginning, but it's a process that leads to a new, richer life. When the possibility of bad feelings or a negative outcome gets too close, and we defer to our fears, past experiences, and old habits and *react* (the R in TRACE), we're stuck. To change old patterns, we must engage the fear.

We may think we fear the disasters our minds so easily imagine, but what we really fear is how these disasters make us *feel.* We fear extreme states where we're overwhelmed, where we lack control and power, and where our rationality is stripped away. It's not just the event that we fear or dislike—we fear the terror. We fear humiliation. We fear losing our sense of solidity and continuity. We fear acting like assholes, pussies, douchebags, or dicks. We fear shame more often and more intensely than we fear death. We give more power to our fear than we give to our own backs, hearts, and intellect. We succumb to fear and lay ourselves down. In other words, we're pussies. Or we blame like dicks, fight like assholes, or fake it like douchebags—we're all these guys.

There's a better way. Triggers are information. Fear is a gift that must be faced. It's only too terrifying until it isn't. We do everything we can—we'll even be complete fucking assholes—so as *not* to feel fear. Until we can't anymore. Until we must.

REACTION: THE R IN TRACE

"He flies off the handle if the lights are left on in the house; that's just the way he is." Bullshit. That's his unexamined reactive habit. Flying off the handle is something that was modeled to him or something he learned to use to settle himself. How we react to events and information—there's that 'how' again—is essential to not being just another asshole who flies off the handle over a lightbulb.

Life Happens, and Then You React

Along with the joy of day-to-day living, there is the discomfort of living. Life happens; we react—in a way that can range from mild to pants-shitting. The most frequent and intense triggers come from those closest to us: partners, ex-partners, children, parents, close friends, siblings, colleagues—those we rely upon the most. There is an infinite range of triggers, from an annoying co-worker who won't shut up to the loss of a close friend's love and trust. There's the partner who leaves dirty dishes in the sink, and there's the partner who vindictively cancels a vacation at the last minute. There's the trigger when you can't get more than your daily cash limit out of the ATM, and there's the burden of crushing credit card debt or a lost job.

Just as triggers vary in intensity, so do reactions. Some of our instant reactions are extremely positive and welcome, and some reactions shut down our vital organs.

These are some typical reactions to negative triggers:

- *We blame and judge others or ourselves.*
- *We distance ourselves.*
- *We catastrophize and future-trip—our minds often go to worst-case scenarios.*
- *We self-medicate.*
- *We lash out.*

Our *reactions* to our triggers often make situations worse and lead to unwanted outcomes: Jonah shoves his employee and ends up in a lawsuit. Jed spends so damn much money on a Cabo bender he can barely manage to get home. George begs Kayla to make every decision for him. Eric bails, bitches, and blames. This is how our guys react to uncomfortable triggers (information).

Why do these guys keep repeating these cycles when the outcomes are shit? Because it's worked *enough* times, and it's become automatic. A habit. A way to avoid feeling the hard stuff. They get lost in it. Narratives are constructed, identities formed, and other options closed off. This is how assholes, pussies, douchebags, and dicks are made. Eventually, they can't see outside their reactive options and accompanying narratives. This is what it means to live out on the perimeter.

Again, Jonah's problem is not that he is selfish and shameless; his problem is that he lives out on the perimeter where his motivations are *only* selfish and shameless, and his default behavior on the perimeter is aggression. It's become his life, his comfort zone. He's lived there so long, he thinks the perimeter is his center; he feels like it's his true self emerging when he reacts. The same is true for all of our archetypes. This is the trigger-reaction cycle, and it is entrenched.

For men, the most common spun-out response to feeling triggered is to withdraw (*I don't want to talk about it*) and numb out. Remember Eric retreating to his six-pack and porn? There may be short-term relief in this approach, but there is no resolution. Simply pulling away, bailing, or pretending shit never happened rarely resolves the actual situation or the feelings inside of us. This is the cycle we are trying to break—or should be, because these reactions create *more* iterations of the trigger-reaction trap, intensifying in effect over time.

The Short Game

Spinning out can be incredibly seductive because in the short term, it *does* discharge the tension and discomfort. It provides us with a sense of control, and it can move us to a more comfortable, settled place. But there's a cost. When Eric bails on Annie's holiday party and walks down the stairs and out the door, he feels over-the-moon ecstatic. Like the rest of us, he doesn't enjoy feeling awkward or jealous, and like the rest of us, he can't wait to make those feelings go away. He wants relief—now. And he gets relief. But the *how* is everything. The *how* is key. He's learned dickishness and self-victimization, and he's never developed any other strategies. He gets short-term relief, but he pays a hefty price. He tells himself he's a bold truth-teller, but he's actually just a dick refusing to take responsibility for the perpetual trigger-reaction cycle that is his life.

For all our archetypes, and for all of us, these behaviors create some respite in the short term, some settling, some affirmation of a long-cherished narrative. This is what makes bad behavior so alluring. But that relief comes at a price—to others and to ourselves. All of these reactions ultimately engender more reactivity. It's a shitshow. George literally can't get a word out, Eric is stuck in the victim role, Jonah destroys any chances for resolution, and Jed digs himself deeper into despair. Nothing changes, and nothing gets reconciled. Nothing is learned from the experience. Stagnation. Different day, same shit, same cycle. More reactivity, unhappiness, resentment, and serious pain and consequences.

I've used all of these reactive strategies myself. Triggered by a fight with my girlfriend, I was sad and upset. I reacted by going out and getting wasted, and I felt better—amazing, even. But the result of feeling better in the short term wasn't any better in the long run. I woke up hung over, less resourced, and more triggered. I was even *more* upset. I didn't process the trigger or work out anything with my girlfriend; I just numbed myself and made the situation worse. Drunken texts compounded the damage. A true act of dickishness disguised as an act of manliness—because tough men drown their pain with booze, right, men? Bullshit.

Reactions become habitual. Habits become reactive. Shit begets shit. We're not thinking things through before we react. We're not thinking about the long game, the consequences we might face in the future, or the people we will affect. This is why we often get into trouble when we get reactive. Assholes and dicks—but also pussies and douchebags—are born out of consistent reactions that settle us down in the short term but ultimately keep us caught in the same cycle: trigger, reaction. Repeat, repeat, repeat.

The Jed Reaction

Fucking Jed. He blows off our next session. Then a bunch more. He's frightened of the raw emotion that came through him that one afternoon. I'm worried about his destructive, reactive behavior. I reach out to him, and he eventually returns my texts. He's back in his shtick. I nudge him to stay in the process with me, and he tells me how busy he is. Two months later, he comes back in to see me after a weekend bender. He looks haggard. He's angry. He's agitated.

I jump in: "We get lost sometimes, man, swept away in it, and important parts of us end up getting left behind. Let's go find them. Tell me about yourself, Jed—not about your success and conquests, but about *you*. What do you love? I want to know you, the *real* you."

"No, you don't," he says in his sad voice. "Everyone wants the show, the winner, the monthly numbers, the other stuff. No one cares about me. They never did." He looks up. "What, were we supposed to hug now?" he asks dismissively.

So much for that genuine moment. But over the next few weeks, Jed actually shows up for all his appointments, and we move past the bravado stuff.

"My parents loved me, but they *really* loved me playing tennis, and they were always pressuring me to practice. I was good, really good. And it was fun—I was in the paper, won state, got a scholarship. They were super proud of me. That felt good. Here's the thing, though: I never really *loved* tennis like they did, but I stayed with it. I liked winning, so I was confused, I guess."

"So, you liked winning, and the parental pride felt good, so you stayed with it. What did you *want* to do in high school?"

He answers right away: "Just hang out—you know, like a normal kid. Play team sports. I wanted that. Instead, I'm going away to elite tennis camps all summer, tournaments every weekend. Fuck, I just wanted to chill out with my friends. But no, it was always more tennis, more pressure, more, more, more—which, come to think of it, is just how I feel now. I like doing well, but it's always about the next month's numbers. And sure, my CEO takes me out on his boat. We eat like kings, and we party. I like that—you know, the attention I get. And, shit, my parents still talk about me all the time to their friends. But I'm not sure

I even *like* what I do. I mean, our product is cool, but it's just software, a platform. I mean, it's not really changing important shit. Seems like all I've been doing my whole life is what other people want me to do, what I think I'm fucking supposed to do."

"Right," I say. "It doesn't feel like you've gotten to choose."

"Yeah, and you know what, David? This is really fucking embarrassing, but fuck it, right? That's what I'm here for, to humiliate myself. When I do spend an occasional night alone, my mind goes crazy, calls me a fraud, a loser, a failure, even with all my success. And to shut it up, I have a twenty-five-year single malt. Or I call one of Scotty's escorts. Usually both. I mean, shit, I'm *killing it*, and I still can't even have a night in peace. And you know what else? The same shit used to happen after I'd win a tennis tournament. I'd be lying there, thinking about the shots I blew, my father shaking his head in disappointment in the stands when I lost serve. And then I'd have to wake up the next day and sit at breakfast and listen to my parents giving me feedback I didn't ask for. And then more practice, of course—and the whole time, I just wanted to scream the truth."

Scream the truth. The feeling in the room shifts again. Something wants to come out. "Close your eyes, Jed. I want you to see that kitchen, see your parents." He nods. I can feel him there. "They're both yapping about you and tennis, going on and on." His fists clench. Fire is building. "What did this frustrated part of you want to say to them?"

"Shut the fuck up! You don't even fucking know me or give a shit about me! I fucking hate tennis!" In this moment, he's fully here, fully real—and he can feel it, too. "Goddamn, that felt good to say." Then something shifts, and his face grows long, pained.

"What just happened?"

"My parents were so supportive and loving. I'm such a piece of shit for saying anything bad about them, telling them to shut the fuck up. They gave me a good life, came to so many of my matches, and they always cheered me on."

I break the silence: "For most of us, there's a part of us that feels a strong love for and loyalty to our parents. It feels like we're betraying them by saying anything negative about our childhood. I'm all for honoring our parents, who sacrifice so much; we won't forget the good stuff, I promise. But it's very important to say and feel the things that weren't allowed. Remember, this is just a *part* of you that felt so trapped and angry. Other parts of you felt deep gratitude and appreciation for the support they gave you. Make sense?"

"I think so, but man, that battle's still going on. A part of me hates my job, and another part says I'm an ingrate and I should thank God every day for that place. I'm worth something like nine fucking mil on paper now, and I'm *complaining*? It fucks me up, you know, all this shit in my head, all this fighting. I just want to feel some peace and quiet, you know?"

I *do* know. Boy, do I know. "Do both sides make sense to you? I mean, can you see how they're both fighting for something good?"

He nods, wide-eyed. "Holy shit," he says, "I do. One side just wants me to be myself. The other wants me to kick ass, compete, kill it, make Mom and Dad proud. But man, that last part has been killing me. It's time for the 'be myself' guy, but every time he tries to come forward, this loud, critical voice comes roaring in."

"See if you can identify this critical voice, the one who berates you late at night. Or maybe an image of him shows up."

"Oh, I don't need to go find that fucker. He's a real dude. A real voice. Right fucking here. Fucker's been right here. He's this loud, hairy guy wearing tennis whites, the prick. With a voice like a whip that never stops cracking in my ear. He looks like a pissed-off young John McEnroe, who was my dad's favorite player of all time, incidentally."

Holy shit. A John McEnroe in your ear? Now *that's* funny. I remember the tantrums he would throw during matches. I'm smiling now. "I've heard a lot of shit in this room and from that couch, but congratulations, man. Nobody's ever showed up here with a John McEnroe in his head, that's for damn sure."

Jed smiles and nods. He likes to be novel.

"Let's find out more about this guy. Even the most intense and menacing parts of us are, in some way, trying to help. They all have positive intentions, even if they're not obvious at first glance. Let's get to know this guy a little better. Let's be curious about this John McEnroe guy. We can learn more about him and why he's doing what he's doing."

"He's got a racket in his hand, and he looks really intense, but also scared. The racket is an old-school wood racket. I've never even played with one of those. My dad has one in his office, and that asshole John McEnroe in my head, he has one."

"Is John McEnroe scared, or is he scary?"

Jed pauses for a moment; he's uncharacteristically still. He takes a deep breath. "I don't know. John Mac ain't scared. *I'm* scared—scared that I'll fail and be humiliated. That everyone will know I'm a fraud. John Mac says, 'There's no way I'm *ever* going to let that happen, punk.'"

"Wow. So, he's really trying to protect you from *that?*"

"Yeah," Jed says. "But he's fucking killing me."

Our time is almost up. "Jed, this week, notice John McEnroe when he shows up. Visualize him when he's there; acknowledge him. Say, 'Hi, I see you there. I see how you're trying to protect me.'"

"Seriously? For fuck's sake, that is ridiculous. But sure. Absolutely. I can do ridiculous."

"Cool. Remember, he's working hard because if he doesn't, he thinks the result will be humiliation. Let him know you see what he's up to. Try to appreciate him for his good intentions. See you in a week, man."

Jed is exhausted, restless, sad, and lonely. His short-term choices— whiskey, escorts, and pushing harder—are destructive. He's trying to escape or outrun his triggers, and he ends up back on the perimeter. In the moment, he finds relief. He drinks, he humps, he hustles. But the triggers get more intense, and so do his reactions. I'm hoping connection with John McEnroe will give him other options and keep him from harm. I hope he can turn a corner. I love Jed, I believe in him, and I'm worried about him.

And John McEnroe coaching a douchebag? That's fucking hysterical.

You're Trying to Tell Yourself Something

It's important to see how you've become conditioned to react automatically to your triggers. Human cultures often normalize questionable or even nonsensical things, like taking off your shoes in the airport security line or saying "bless you" when somebody sneezes. If you're like Jed, and you don't want to let your parents down, what you normalize is ignoring your own sensibilities and playing along with theirs. In Jed's case, this meant playing tennis.

You do this so as not to disappoint. You accept the idea that what this person wants *from* you is more important than what *you* want *for* you. Wow. Once that insanity has been normalized, it creates powerful narratives to justify, compel, and reward the act of giving others what they want, even when you don't want to give it to them. It masterfully manipulates you into leaving yourself behind under the guise of being a "dedicated, hardworking employee," being a "nice boy," or putting the needs of others ahead of your own. There's a time and a place for everything, but if you're habitually ignoring the information (triggers) you're getting from yourself, you're in big fucking trouble. You're moving away from your center and blindly accepting the conditions set by people and institutions. You are being manipulated by others' uncentered, spun-out, perimeter behavior *all the time*, no matter what they call it. You are failing to care for yourself, and that comes with a huge price.

Cynthia is the perfect example of the price you pay for accepting the incessant, irrational conditions set by others. You lose your own life—and not just metaphorically. You are no longer living in your own body in your own way. Cynthia never stopped being alive, but she was no longer living her own life.

As children, we are wired to defer to the external world for cues about what's good and right. This often means ignoring internal cues about our own needs, limits, and conditions. These can include somatic clues: tension, sweating, numbness, frustration, and the like. We learn to ignore what our bodies are telling us and go along with a habit, a prescribed program, or social pressure. Children will sacrifice authenticity for any kind of connection and belonging.

We've all gone to work really sick. We've all said yes in numerous circumstances when it clearly should've been a no. These decisions, made at your own expense, in reaction to expectations or social pressure, can have drastic, sometimes lifelong consequences on your nervous system. Ignore signals from your nervous system, and your mind will eventually filter them out, whether you freely chose to ignore them or felt compelled to do so. Then you walk around unaware that you're missing incredibly important information about your own experience.

We live more and more in the echo chambers of our own minds, unaware that we're missing anything at all. This is a disconnected life, and it leads to endless trigger-reaction cycles out on the perimeter. Your nervous system will not trust you if you are unwilling to honor the information it's conveying to you. Equally (and perhaps unfairly), your nervous system may not trust you if you're *unable* to honor the message.

The way we deal with these messages defines us. If we don't learn how to engage, listen to the information, and respond rather than react, we're not only running on software we never chose to install, we're unable to make choices and evolve.

"I Reject Your Conditions"

We're always dealing with terms and conditions. If you want to drive a car, you must meet some conditions. We're used to it. The asshole, the pussy, the douchebag, and the dick set conditions for interaction with their extreme behavior. Negotiating with, or trying to satisfy, these spun-out men feels unreasonable for a reason—it *is* unreasonable. Their message is clear: *I'm not going to deal calmly or rationally with you or with the situation. I am proceeding only on my extreme terms. I will have the control; you will not.*

There are two options for dealing with unreasonable conditions: accept them or reject them. Once you've advanced that far, you get to choose how to respond. You can respond reasonably, go batshit crazy, or do something in between.

When you spin out, you're in a state of mind that prevents normal perception, behavior, or social interaction, a state that could legitimately be called insane. When two people spin out simultaneously—which I've seen many times working with couples and plenty of times in my own relationships—the insanity is exponential. When I worked with couples, my job was to help them move toward the center, where connection is possible. When two or more people are setting conflicting conditions, there's no room for connection or communication. There is, however, plenty of chaos, drama, and pain.

The condition the dick sets is frustrating. It feels impossible. He is effectively saying: *I am the victim. You are the perpetrator. Accept these terms!* When the dick spins out, he pouts, advertising his victimization. He may default to aggrieved isolation. He is the noble, misunderstood victim. He pouts and sulks some more. He wants you to acknowledge his importance. He wants you to take responsibility for his experience. These are his conditions. You need to make *him* feel better. When he pulls away and mopes in silence, you must grovel out there in the cold, trying to convey how much it sucks for you when he withdraws. You could feel Annie's frustration, right? That's the impossibility of dealing with Eric on his terms.

The pussy wants to control his world *through* you by persuading you to rescue and soothe him, and he sends signals to make that happen. When someone takes care of him, when judging eyes are off him, he is safe, and his world is in order. He submits to his own fear, outsourcing his security to others. Kayla knows this all too well. She would rather just deal with a situation than confront and unwind George's deference, because that kind of scrutiny would send him spiraling into more deference, more submission, and more needy drama. *Okay, George. I'll deal with the contractor. I'll even deal with your job for you.* She'll choose the restaurant. The pussy begs: *Please do this for me now*; the pussy is threatening: *...or it's only going to get worse—and you'll have to do even more for me later.* These are the pussy's outrageous terms. George is trying to change, to stop sending out this S.O.S. for someone to accept his extreme conditions.

The douchebag builds his glittering house on the perimeter and tries to convince you it's made of gold. He wants you to meet him there, way out in Bullshit Valley. He insists that you believe his theatrical display, admire it, compare yourself to it, and validate it. Douchebags like Jed take it even further and add credential requirements. *Brah, if you want to be seen with the Jed-I, you need to dress like me, talk like me, strut like me, and drive a cool-ass buggy like me. Oh, and acknowledge that my strides and rides are always best.*

Finally, there's Jonah, spun way the fuck out in assholery, setting outrageous, unacceptable conditions. Shaylee tried to be reasonable with Jonah. She was patient. She stayed good for her sons. She interrupted his college game day and tried to talk about the boys, but he was having none of it. She took care of herself and the family. She worked with the Montessori preschool board. She cared for the family that Jonah neglected. She found her center. Jonah lost her. He could have done it better. She refused his conditions, and Jonah felt the consequences. Shaylee handled things from a sound, centered foundation. Jonah handled things like an asshole.

The extreme conditions these guys set are all, and I mean *all*, immature bids for control. Unfortunately, rational behavior will not always work when negotiating with them. They've already set the terms for connection, and those terms are irrational. You can't outwit, outrun, or outmaneuver the douchebag in Douchebagland or the dick in Grievanceville. They use extreme behavior to establish an advantage over those they are attempting to control.

Sometimes you're the one out there on the perimeter, acting like a dick, taunting people, daring them to meet your conditions. And sometimes you're the one closer to the center, refusing the dick's taunt. You probably spin out in reaction to one or more of these guys. A real in-your-face asshole will often spin me out to Pussyland, for example, while a real douchebag can instigate my dickishness. This trigger-reaction cycle often recurs in close relationships. You plant yourselves out on the perimeter and volley unreasonable conditions back and forth, making it very difficult to communicate until at least one of you moves toward the center.

When you engage with others on their perimeter terms only, you lose credibility with—and respect for—yourself. Plus, you keep getting played. If a dick knows he can spin you out to win an argument, he'll take this route every time. If a pussy knows from experience that he can rely on you to step up and take care of his shit, he'll approach you in the most submissive posture. The conditions are set by those out on the perimeter, and you're just out there with them, playing along with that go-nowhere game.

Faced with a dick playing the victim, for example, most of us will hem and haw, roll our eyes, and indulge his interpretation. The more reasonable response would be to say, "I hear you saying you've been wronged. I do not accept your version of things. I do not accept those terms. Let's get curious about what's going on here."

Refusing the unwanted or unacceptable conditions set by another person is an act of self-care. This refusal cultivates self-trust. If you don't respond effectively to stop this sort of thing when it happens, you're not fully respecting yourself, and you're less vital in the world as a result. It is harmful and unsustainable to normalize things being done to you that aren't okay with you. By anyone—*anyone*. At any time.

It takes practice and courage to stay centered when others are spun out. Sometimes, it feels impossible. Try to remember that the center is an abstract ideal. In practice, it's more useful to seek progress than perfection. Throughout your life, people will want you to change your standards. These people are trying to lure you away from balanced behavior to get something from you. This should happen only with your informed permission. If you are lost, unable to find your center, you'll be ill at ease, unhappy, and easily manipulated and influenced.

When you're on the perimeter, the conditions you set range from unreasonable to insane. When you're centered, you set conditions that are more balanced, more like your good-natured self. How do you stay closer to your center, especially when your fuckhead neighbor, your ex, the HOA president, your boss, some guy opining on the news, climate change debaters, or your landlord is taunting you from the perimeter? The first step is to have the awareness that you are being lured away from your center on someone else's terms.

11

AWARENESS: THE A IN TRACE

"The range of what we think and do is limited by what we fail to notice. And because we fail to notice that we fail to notice, there is little we can do to change; until we notice how failing to notice shapes our thoughts and deeds."
—R. D. Laing

Pause for a Cause

Awareness is a "pause for a cause," the cause being the situation at hand that could use a new perspective, some fresh eyes. It's the message that goes off in your head, cartoon thought bubble and all, and says: *Hold on! Wait a minute. Slow down. Think. I'm triggered, and the way I'm about to react—that's not the right move.*

Awareness lets you observe how you're thinking, feeling, and responding. Ultimately, it allows you to see the situation from a clearer vantage point. With awareness, you cultivate the ability to witness yourself and halt the automatic reactions. Without awareness, you're at the mercy of your own automatic trigger-reaction cycle. You are also subject to the automatic reactions of the people around you.

When you're triggered, the ability to make a rational, well-thought-out decision, and to think logically, dissipates. The world looks and feels like a very different place, a very dangerous place.

Simply naming what's happening grants you some perspective. With one modest nod to the condition of your nervous system, you can start to settle yourself: *Okay, I'm triggered.* It's that simple. Now you can think more clearly again: *I'm okay. What's the move? First, slow down. My mind is spinning, and that's only making me more anxious. I can do this.*

Identifying what's true in the moment has huge implications. When you're triggered, the air raid siren of your brain is blaring—and by air raid siren, I mean your amygdala. This part of the brain uses about two-thirds of its neurons to look for bad news. It's primed to go negative. Pausing to collect the facts, or the rest of the story, weakens the effect of negativity bias. It gives you new and better options.

Awareness really is simple, and it's crucial. Stop and acknowledge that the trigger just hit: *I'm triggered; triggers are information.* A trigger set you off, you're aware of what's happening, and now you have options. This is how to break through the automatic trigger-reaction cycle. Awareness really is that simple.

Jonah's Awareness

Jonah is not free to roam the planet without consequences. Nobody is. He feels punished, ashamed, and damaged—and lately, he says he deserves to feel this way. Jonah's sessions ebb and flow between the old explosive narrative (*Fuck them!*) and this new implosion (*I fucked everything up*). At first, he started with "fuck them," and for a while, he stuck with it. But as the weeks go by, we linger with the explosions for shorter periods of time before dropping into the inward stuff, the self-blame and shame.

My overall priority with Jonah is to keep him healthy, safe, and generally moving forward. My priority at this stage of our work is to keep the momentum going. It's not my momentum; it's Jonah's. He's practiced trusting me, up to a point, and that got him here. In this room, Jonah is practicing something new. He's practicing acknowledging Shaylee. Sometimes his practice involves talking about his role in his situation. Some days he spends more time in silence, just thinking about it all.

"You said you deserve to feel this way. Tell me more about this word 'deserve,'" I say.

There's no focus to his thoughts. He starts tapping his foot; the tapping accelerates. I watch him. He's looking at his foot as it taps. Still no answer. I break the silence: "You're right where you need to be, Jonah. You're doing great. Tell me more about this word 'deserve.'"

"Yeah, I mean, I deserve it. I did this. I…I…I…Shit. Fuck me." His lower lip quivers. "I deserve this, too. Shaylee, she'd wait up for me, have dinner ready. But, shit, I don't know, she always seemed to want something, and whatever the fuck that was, I just…I don't know. I didn't know what the hell to do or say. When she'd put her hand on my arm, just to touch me or something, I still didn't know what to say. Not knowing made me uncomfortable as hell."

The rocking returns. The grip on his fingers and discolored scars are back. Jonah's grip tells me that something he's saying feels true—and terrifying. Jonah is expanding his capacity to hold uncertainty, complexity, to feel the mess he's avoided for so long. I feel something new coming into existence.

"Shaylee didn't want to be…Fuck. She never said she was depressed, even when she got that prescription. Sometimes she'd call it her Wonder Woman superpower pill. She said that her superpower was to be visible. Ah, fuck. I wasn't even paying attention. She said if she took the pills people would see her—something like that. Whatever was wrong, I made it worse by just ignoring her. And after I had an affair—fuck, affairs—I know she knew about them. Didn't know she knew Megan's name, or her fucking social security number, or whatever the fuck Oprah and Dr. Phil told her to find out. But it was me. I hurt her. I hurt my boys. I hurt the mother of my children. Fuck. David, what the fuck was she? I've told you everything. What *was* she?" he asks, or says, on the verge of tears. "I fucking deserved this."

Jonah was once a complete asshole who never questioned his version of things. Now he's starting to recognize Shaylee and his impact on her. This is another gift of awareness—a humbling and painful gift, but essential for Jonah. He's starting to feel her existence. He's starting to see his own choices and actions differently. He's connecting with the non-asshole parts of himself. Has he recovered from his assholery? Nope. But he's becoming aware of others and of the conflicting parts of himself. He's feeling. Things aren't so black and white anymore. He has no clue what to do with any of this—and for now, that's fine. He has to start somewhere. Any awareness is progress for Jonah.

Be Aware of Your Personal Parts

When you are spun out to the perimeter, know this: it's only a *part* of you that's triggered. It may feel like all of you, but the rest of you doesn't cease to exist when you're triggered. Let's say a fearful part of you has you pussing out on the perimeter. You may feel as though the fear is all there is, and submission is your only option. This isn't true, but it feels really, really true.

With awareness and practice, you can reframe your experience: *A part of me is triggered. It's real fucking big. But it's just a part of me.* Your job is to remember this fact when you're triggered. It's a part of you. It's a part of you. It's a part of you. A part can and will feel like you. Holy shit will it sometimes feel like you in your totality, but it's only a part of you. Why is recognizing this helpful? This simple awareness and reframe gives you some space from the triggered part of you, and it gives your centered self a shot at dealing with the situation. These are good things.

By the same token, when someone close to you is triggered, it's only a part of them that's triggered, but that part has taken over in this moment. You may react by getting triggered yourself: *Where is the person I know and love and rely upon? Oh, shit! Where the hell did she go?* This is a scary, triggering interpretation of events. Here's a better option: *Whoa, a part of her is super pissed right now.* By seeing her as a whole person co-opted by an angry part, you keep yourself more centered, more able to navigate the situation. This is a gift of awareness. You can change the frame of the situation. Seeing the other person in terms of "parts" is a powerful use of awareness.

When I tell you I'm pissed, I may only be describing a mild feeling, but to you, I may have become "the pissed guy." The guy you know and love, he's not there anymore. All that's left is the pissed guy. I threw the statement out there; you dialed it all the way up, even though it's not what I meant. *Holy shit, he's pissed! From the top of his head to his goddamn toes, he's pissed. What if the pissed guy goes full asshole on me?* This is not an exaggeration; it's how our emotions work.

When I wholly identify myself with a single state—in this case, it's "pissed," but it could also be "sad," "afraid," "indifferent"—it's intense and alarming. When I identify myself entirely with an experience I'm having in the presence of someone close to me, they lose their human connection with me; it's as if the person they knew and relied on is gone. If I trigger you, you're likely to relate to me only as "the pissed guy," not as the person I am.

When I say a part of me is pissed, I'm communicating more clearly: *I'm still here. I haven't been possessed by, or transformed into, the pissed guy.* This is calming to others and to me. Just using this language—again, this is an aspect of awareness—provides me with some clarity and confirms that I'm still there. I haven't been completely taken hostage by a pissed part of myself. The logic applies both ways: the next time you hear someone say, "I'm pissed," or when you get flipped off on Highway 1, lighten up. It's just a *part* of them.

As a therapist, I've helped clients form this new habit of parts awareness. "I'm super pissed off at my girlfriend" is met with "Let's hear more from the *part* of you that's pissed off." I've never seen a client as *wholly* or *exclusively* pissed off. My intention is always to help the client build awareness that this feeling or reaction is just a part of him. If he can see it as just a part of him, he'll be less taken over by that part, and this starts his movement back to his center.

When George says a part of him is super nervous, he's gaining clarity and control and offering the same to Kayla. He's not saying *he's* super nervous; that would mean, absurdly, becoming the embodiment of nervousness—plus, he'd be disparaging the mettle and determination it took for him to initiate a difficult conversation. A *part* of him is nervous, but George is much more than that. It's empowering language. It tells you and others: *Hey, I got shit going on, I'm triggered, but I'm here with it. I'm more than this.* This is awareness in real time and in real life; it has a tremendous impact on others.

Be Aware of Your Options

I've said it before, and I'll say it again and again: when someone, anyone, is triggered out on the perimeter and setting unreasonable conditions, you do *not* have to meet them on their terms. With awareness, you can recognize manipulative bullshit. The extreme shitty behavior of the asshole, douchebag, pussy, and dick is triggering. If you're on autopilot, you'll react to these guys in your own habituated ways. You'll take care of the pussy, apologize to the dick to get him to stop moping, defer to the asshole to break the tension, or nod along to the douchebag. Awareness in these moments changes everything: *Wait a minute*, you can say to yourself. *I see what's going on here. This is some perimeter game bullshit.* From this place of awareness, you can decide what you'd like to do. Awareness allows for something more fulfilling than the reactive chain: a deliberate response.

I get it. It seems implausible, downright unrealistic to think you can pause every time and take in the circumstances before you react. I get it. I get it. I got it. You aren't wrong to feel that. But if you've gotten this far, you've become aware that you have options. We all have options. Going in headfirst with your worst option when you're triggered by some perimeter behavior is as automatic as looking left, then taking the first step out onto the road. In the USA, you don't over-process this; you look left, then step forward. But when you only look left, then step forward in Australia, for example—just one simple change—the same automatic reaction could get you hit by a goddamn bus. At some point, and possibly at most points, there are adverse consequences for our default reactions.

There's a better way. First, be aware of the simple facts, like which way traffic travels. Then calm yourself down and choose your response with the best information you can gather. Awareness is your alert mechanism, your alarm in the trigger-reaction cycle. After all, triggers are just information; they can be destructive, beneficial, or benign, depending on how you engage with them.

Jed Breaks Through, but Not Out

"John McEnroe is there all the fucking time." This is the first thing Jed says as he sits down for another session. We've been working with this part of him for a while now. "He's there when I wake up, pushing me to get to the gym. He's there at work, pushing me to push my team. He's there when I'm with friends at the bar and I end up ordering another round of shots. It's funny; I notice that Scotty gets him fired up. Johnny Mac's always pushing me. He keeps me focused when I'm tired; he keeps pushing me in my workouts. When I acknowledge him for trying to help me, he relaxes a bit, which is cool."

"Great awareness, man," I say. "So, when you acknowledge him, something happens—he relaxes. Let's be curious here. See if there's more this guy wants you to know."

"Man, so much pressure, always pressure. In my family you either made an A or you fucked up. You either won the match or you'd done something wrong. It was all about achievement."

"How was that for you, when you lost the match or made less than an A?"

"Sucked *so* bad. I remember the look on my parents' faces. It was just...disappointment. And man, it was such a shitty feeling. I had let them down, and I felt like the worst kid in the world. I wish they'd have yelled at me—even slapping me would have been something. Anything would've been better than Mom's tight-lipped smile, telling me I'd do better next time, and Dad giving me more feedback on my backhand, some shit like that. It was the worst!"

"Does it make sense to you why McEnroe is so committed to his job?"

"Yeah, I mean, when I slip up and things don't go well, I feel that way all over again, and shit, man, I can't describe it; it's so fucking painful. It's shitty. It's just so damn shitty. John fucking McEnroe is just trying to keep me from experiencing that—I get it."

"Right, so see if you can feel the kid right now, the one who feels so shitty. The one McEnroe is trying to keep from being a disappointment. Maybe we can help him."

Something shifts suddenly. Jed rubs his eyes and looks around the room. "Nah, man, no need to revisit the past. The past is the past. Let sleeping dogs lie, you know what I'm saying? I'm good, David, I'm good. I think I got what I needed. I'll keep an eye on Johnny Mac, maybe come back and see you in a month or so."

Jed's back in character. This is the posturing Jed that I've been think-ing of as the Jed-I, the polished, confident, shiny, avoidant-as-shit guy.

"Here's what I just noticed, Jed: we were connecting with McEnroe and this kid he's trying to protect, then your 'I'm all good' guy came in strong. Did you catch that?"

"Yeah, that's cool, but I've got a life to live, and that stuff brings me *way* down, so I'm good. Besides, Johnny Mac is why I've made it as far as I have. I'm super focused, and I work hard. I need that drive to keep my edge in the dog-eat-dog."

"So, there's some fear that you might lose your edge, your focus, and your work ethic if we help that kid feel better. I get that. But in my experience, that's not what happens."

"It's all good. Thanks for your help, really, but I got this now."

Jed is afraid that if he heals this internal rift and changes the formula, he'll fail at his job and lose what he's achieved. In truth, a great deal often changes when we heal. When we're no longer replaying the same old logic, we may no longer have the same priorities or goals. In Jed's case, old routines and habits served him well. I understand his fear of losing his "edge." But things are changing, whether he likes it or not.

Jed comes in every couple of weeks, and we work with these different parts of him. We get to know the "party" part that just wants to feel good and the way it rebels against Johnny Mac. He feels some moments of freedom, but he won't let us connect with the hurt kid for more than a moment before the "it's all good" guy shoos us away and closes the door. Jed keeps coming back and engaging, though.

At the same time, he keeps partying harder and harder, doubling down on glorious mayhem and taunting Jed McKenna's Maya. I'm worried about him, but I can't stop him. We talk about Scotty, who I call out as an unhealthy friend and hanger-on who encourages the glory-seeking, raging partier in Jed. He refuses to take this in. "Scotty's my boy," he says. "Scotty hooks me up." I try to contract with him to stay off the blow for a week between sessions. Nothing. He'll let me into his inner world up to a point, but he won't introspectively engage with his external behaviors and choices.

12
CURIOSITY: THE C IN TRACE

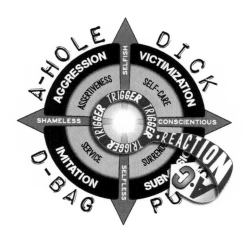

"Curiosity...is a lust of the mind."
—*Thomas Hobbes*

Jonah's Christmas Eve Reaction

"Jonah, can you help me?" Shaylee asks. "Maria, one of the teachers at the Montessori school, doesn't have anywhere to go tomorrow. I just found out, and I invited her to join the boys and us for Christmas. Can you please run and get a few things so we can have a stocking for her? I have some gifts we can wrap. Let's try to make her feel included when she comes over."

It's 9:30 p.m. on Christmas Eve. Not many options for shopping. Jonah and Shaylee decide to get creative. Jonah heads out to find an open store and buy some stocking stuffers.

Across town, there's another father who wants to do something for his daughter this Christmas. Things have been tough for this fella. He doesn't have a damn thing to give his daughter. He too heads out on Christmas Eve to find an open store and get some stocking stuffers. He's desperate. He's sad. He's also hungry. He'll do anything. Anything. He's trembling with shame and fear when he arrives at Walgreens. The shame is overwhelming. He collects cosmetics, a magazine, a stocking, a hairbrush, and some gummy candy that looks like Santa. He'll do anything for the possibility of one better day—or even one moment. He's overcome by the triggers of the holiday season.

The desperate fella opts for the five-finger discount. He bolts out of Walgreens, setting off the alarm. Jonah is walking in as the desperate man runs out. Jonah's reaction is immediate, without any thought whatsoever: he turns and chases the guy. Jonah's cowboy boots are like thunder coming up behind the man. The desperate man is scared and disoriented. He falls, and shoplifted gifts spill onto the sidewalk. Blood drips from the man's head onto lipstick and gummy Santas.

Shamelessly, Jonah stands over the desperate fella and says, "I think it would be a good idea if you stayed right there."

Police and an ambulance arrive before Jonah has finished his shopping. The police take a report from Jonah, who explains truthfully that he never touched the desperate fella, that he just stood over him and suggested he stay put. Jonah goes home to his house in Piedmont. The other fella doesn't go home. The shoplifter has warrants out, so he's not going home. His daughter gets nothing for Christmas—not even a dad.

Merry Christmas.

Chasing down shoplifters is something even store employees and owners don't do. Who the hell does this as a citizen or a shopper? Without thinking, Jonah did. He is many months into his process with me when this story is revealed. By the time he retells this story to me, he is deep in messes with lawsuits, his divorce, and his business partners.

Initially, he repeats the story with a shit ton of bravado, as if to say,

That's how I roll, fuckers. But that macho bullshit doesn't last. For Jonah, this isn't a story about right or wrong. It's not about vigilante justice, shoplifting, or poverty. It's just one example of the many reactionary moments that Jonah revisits with sincere curiosity.

Jonah often comes back to this story as an example of his automatic reactions. He describes it as something he experienced instantly, like a passenger on a ride, action without a thought process. It becomes a marker in his life, but only after he takes the time to consider what really happened to him.

"I took off after a shoplifter with nothing but my fists and these cowboy boots," he recalls in a later session. "It was over a fucking pack of gummy Santas. I probably ruined some kid's Christmas over a fucking pack of gummy Santas. I reacted, and that dude split his head open— over a fucking pack of gummy Santas. Why the fuck do I keep doing this shit? Why do I react like this?"

Now he's curious. Now he asks why. *Why do I do the shit that I do?*

There's Something Better Than the Shit You Think You Know

Curiosity entertains the radical idea that there are things unknown to us. Imagine that; things exist completely outside of our knowledge. Admitting the existence of other possibilities, or unknowns, can be especially difficult for men. Take an asshole, for example, stubbornly convinced as hell that others are misinformed and equally convinced about how perfectly *he* is informed: *You're a dumbfuck, I am not a dumbfuck.* When he's triggered, he doesn't question himself. He just reacts, with absolute conviction that what he's doing is exactly the right thing. He skips reflection. He blames. He justifies whatever it is he's doing or about to do. The blame and shame game is also a dick move.

Curiosity allows us to be interested in our own experience. Awareness brings a pause and some perspective, but curiosity is the deeper study. Watching Annie laugh with "Bradley Cooper," here's what curiosity might've looked like for Eric, the dick: *Well, this fucking sucks. This stings. Why am I so out of my fucking mind with jealousy and self-pity right now? What's the story I'm telling myself? What's here, dammit? Something is sure here, because I'm losing my shit.*

From this place of attentiveness, a thing unknown to us can be revealed. Curiosity is the lure that catches new knowledge, and knowledge is power. "Curiosity is, in great and generous minds, the first passion and the last," Samuel Johnson remarked.

For many men in this pumped-up and conditioned civilization, curiosity means weakness; it's scary and dangerous. It means entertaining a horrific possibility: *Maybe I don't know what the fuck is going on. Maybe there's something I'm missing. Maybe my story of what's happening is not actually what's happening.*

Imagine being called on in science class and answering with, "I don't know, but I sure am *curious* about the speed of light." No points for you. Maybe a few chuckles from your classmates and a disappointed look from your teacher. "It's a miracle," a curious character named Albert Einstein is credited with saying, "that curiosity survives formal education."

Knowing, on the other hand, is valued. If you know, you exude confidence. Knowing gets you good grades, and, later, the hot-shit job. We want to be right more than we want to know the truth. And from what I've seen, especially in new clients, we *choose* to be right more than we *choose* to acknowledge the truth. The distinction I'm making is that we actively and deliberately shit on the truth when dogma, or already "knowing" something, serves our needs. And we'll keep doing that until we can't get away with shitting on the truth one more time.

I learned early on—and I bet you did, too—to posture even if I didn't know the answers. If I didn't *know*, I must be a complete fuckin' dumbass. I've laughed at jokes I patently didn't get. After all, curiosity suggests ignorance, and ignorance means stupidity...or does it?

It's true that in many instances, we need to know. Measure twice, cut once, right? But in relationships, outright knowing (or thinking we know) suffocates. How do you like it when someone "knows" some-thing about you? *You're being selfish. You're lazy. You, my friend, are a dick. You ruined everything! You should set some boundaries. You have no idea what you're talking about. Here's what you should say to her next time. You suck.* We humans don't like it when anyone presumes to know something about us or about a situation that involves us. We particularly don't need other people to tell us that we suck, *what* we suck, or what we *should* suck. We're so quick to assess blame when hard feelings are involved, but in reality, things are *always* more com-plex, and they're rarely any single person's fault. Curiosity allows us to be in intense situations without repressing, aggressing, fizzling out, numbing, appeasing, or pulling away. It allows us to respond without blaming, judging, or attacking. Curiosity keeps the experiment going. It makes connection possible.

A man who clings to the altar of "I know who I am" may feel a sense of security, but it's false, and clinging to falsity removes the common ground for growth or deep connection with others. A man isolated in his own interpretation of events has crushed his natural curiosity. This man thinks he knows who he is, who others are, what should happen in national politics, you name it. The shit he knows is endless. Just ask his knowing face and listen and watch as the shit he knows comes spewing out. In this vise grip of certainty, with no space for anything new, life is neutered. It is stagnant and dull. It's like watching the same season of a favorite show again and again, or watching the same pun-dits make the same arguments on the same media platforms. If you keep too tight a grip on "knowing" who you are, you may become an outdated rerun of yourself.

Existing in a state of not-knowing can be intense at first, but damn, it's interesting. Endlessly exciting. And if you want a big, rich life—and I'm not talking about money here—it's impossible to avoid. It requires a temporary uprooting, and this means being at the mercy of the winds for a time. But it's through such a process that we learn to trust and come to see that we are more than we thought. This world is vast, mysterious, wondrous, and meaningful. Curiosity is the key to this discovery.

Women love when you're curious about them. Genuine curiosity, my female friends assure me, is one of the biggest turn-ons. When you turn your curious attention on someone, they get to come out in an authentic way; they reveal themselves. This builds trust, connection, and desire.

When people enter my practice for the first time, they are rarely curious about what is happening inside of them—they just want to *feel* different. Better. In general, they are anxious or depressed and full of grievances against themselves, others, or something in the external world. They've tried everything they know, and they've been unsuccessful. They feel as if they've failed because they can't do it on their own, and they reluctantly end up sitting with a therapist. I see it differently. I see them as ready to launch.

Much of the beginning of therapy is teaching them to be curious, and I do this by being curious myself. It's interesting how this rich, complex, fascinating person in front of me is put together, only he or she doesn't see it. Not yet. They're too busy wanting themselves or others to be different—both losing propositions. Once they learn to be curious, exciting things start to happen. They can begin to move away from their quiet desperation and toward a new relationship with life.

Use Your Words

Most of us can wax poetic about the things that rev our engines: sports, fitness, politics, stock markets, music, movies, cars. When our interest is piqued, we learn the technical terminology as well as the slang. Lacking the training or conditioning to be passionate about ourselves—a topic that should thrill and engross us—we lack the specific, telling language to describe it: *I feel fucked. I feel like hell. I feel like a bucket of fucking shit.* It gets the point across...but *what* point? Is it any wonder that we struggle to navigate our inner world when the language that surrounds it is so vague and muddied, generalized to the point of obscurity? Even when we do attempt to express how we're feeling—happy, sad, angry, horny—the available words seldom provide an apt description of what we're actually experiencing inside.

When you're triggered, a variety of things can happen: your body temperature rises; tightness shows up in your chest, gut, shoulders, or throat. You may feel nausea or a knot in your stomach. Your senses get sharper—although some people disassociate, and their senses get duller. Subtle sensations manifest in the body. Posture changes. Tone, inflection, rhythm, and volume of voice shift. Within the knot in the stomach, there can be a churning or a gripping. It can be solid or hollow. It can be still or moving. The emotional tone of the knot can be one of longing, fear, anger, or disgust. Use clear language to more fully describe your experience; this will help you feel better. It will help you respond better. We can and should describe our inner experience passionately, with nuance, and without reservation.

By cultivating awareness and curiosity, you can acquire a richer language for your internal experience. When you describe it, you are valuing it, which settles your nervous system. Plus, you're able to express yourself with more distinction, individualism, and complexity.

Learning to describe your experience with greater refinement and acuteness also builds connection with others. Those close to you can feel what's happening inside of you—you're not fooling anyone. When your kids ask how you're doing and you say "okay" and look away, they know you're anything but "okay," which makes them nervous. If you're aware of what you're feeling, and you're candid and precise about expressing it, everyone feels safer, more settled, and less alienated from you.

We're always scanning for congruence—consistency and harmony—between people's words and behavior. People who are congruent are trusted. They demonstrate a realness that encourages others to be more real as well, which is something everyone wants, whether they know it or not. Everyone is tired of the pretend game—even, deep down, the douchebag. When a person shares in a way that's clearly real, it resonates as "true" inside of us; in turn, we feel more connected. Conversely, the greater the felt incongruence, the less safe we feel. We can tell when someone is disingenuous and trying to manipulate us. It makes us uncomfortable. And the guy who says he's "fine" while he's clenching his jaw and pacing and muttering curses? He makes us real fucking nervous. He's *not* fine, and we know it. And his dishonesty makes him seem unpredictable, which triggers "danger ahead" in our survival systems.

As for the guy who's being unnaturally nice and trying too hard to be friends with us and everyone else at the party, he makes us uncomfortable and defensive, too, but on a more intellectual level. The overly slick douchebag leaves us feeling solicited, and we can't help but wonder if he's about to pitch his latest multi-level marketing scheme. You can get fucked *over* by somebody without necessarily getting fucked *up* by them; that's danger, too.

Looking back, you'll see that none of the outrageous archetype characters are congruent. Not. At. All. They never shared the experiences they were actually having; hell, they didn't even *know* anything about the experiences they were actually having. They only shared their ongoing, unyielding, *incurious* narratives. At no point did they let others know what was really going on—that would be too vulnerable, too terrifying. Instead, they hoped everyone would believe their bullshit as much as they did.

Confirmation Bias

Confirmation bias is our ingrained tendency to seek out, interpret, favor, and recall information in a way that confirms our preexisting beliefs, while giving much less consideration to alternatives—and by much less, I mean virtually none. We have a tendency to affirm and validate our beliefs. Eric thought Annie was flirting at the party. Triggered by Annie's innocuous conversation with a colleague, Eric slipped on his confirmation goggles and saw a flirty laugh, slutty body language, and a solicitous smile.

Let's talk about grievances. Maybe your partner is messy, leaving clothes and half-empty cups of coffee around the house, and that bothers you. What do you think you focus on when you walk in the door? The tidy living room—or the dirty dishes in the kitchen sink? Exactly. You're looking to confirm your bias, so you fixate on the dishes in the sink and dismiss the clean living room. Plus, you're likely to forget about the days when you came home and the whole place was immaculate, with delicious food cooking on the stove.

It's human nature. We want to confirm our own story more than we want to know the truth. We see reality with tunnel vision. We're blinded by our own filters and have a tremendously difficult time seeing anything else—especially someone else's point of view.

To varying degrees, we each live in our own personal bubble. It's a cliché, but a hard-earned one. Eric relentlessly maintains and finds justification within his bubble. If Annie is *not* in fact flirting with her tall, handsome co-worker, it means that Eric is feeling insecure in his relationship and in himself and that he's imagining things—literally seeing something that isn't there. He'll have none of this unflattering version of events, and I mean *none*, even if this is the plain truth of the situation. His pride would never allow it. What's more, he's in deep denial over how much Annie matters to him, how much he needs her, and how afraid he is of being betrayed. He can't see himself or the situation as they are. Our systems work overtime to keep unflattering and painful truths away. Where does that leave Eric? Hunkered down in his bubble, sticking to his reactive and biased version of things to avoid facing unpleasant realities. It leaves him being a complete dick.

The truth fucks with our contrived inner world in ways that tend to trigger us, so we deny it, even to ourselves. Only when we learn to be honest about ourselves and with ourselves can we build an inner world that can handle the truth without triggering us. This entails putting on the awareness and curiosity goggles and seeing beyond our filtered version of things.

This is why awareness and curiosity are so important. If you don't take a look inside, negativity bias and confirmation bias will rule you without you even knowing it. Negativity bias will steer you toward the worst, most catastrophic perception. Then confirmation bias will make sure you selectively gather evidence that corroborates that perception while rejecting contradictory evidence. When these biases go unchecked, we get stuck repeating bad choices and excluding better options.

Curious Fucking George

"Hey, there's something that's really been...Well, I've been thinking about it a lot. Never told anyone about this. But you told me to be curious and stuff. I was thinking...I've never told Kayla about this, and...maybe we went a bit too far with our work here. Because, well, I've really been thinking about this a lot."

"What have you been chewing on, George?"

"Yeah, well, before I met Kayla I was living in Berkeley in this apartment. The lady who owned it was really nice. She took great care of the place, and she really liked me. We'd fix something now and then or just hang out. When she came by, she'd sit with me and talk. Well..."

Even when telling a story about himself, George has a familiar nervousness. "What was...?" I start, but George interrupts before I can ask a question.

"Jean. She's great. It was easy hanging out with her. I was just a tenant who took better care of my place than those kids from UC Berkeley. She cut my rent once because I helped her after the spring semester. These students trashed the place. Well, she...she came by a few times, and after she and I fixed whatever we had to fix, we would watch the

Cal games. Just chilling out. I liked it, ya know. This one time though, we were laughing, and she just said, 'You know what, George? You're one hell of a guy.' She was laughing. Me, too. I told her I wasn't really, and she bet me a dollar that I was. I took the bet. She…she put my hand on her breast. I was a man alright. She won the dollar."

"Holy shit, George. That's a pretty big smile you got on your face. I never knew you were a gambler."

"Yeah. It was fun. She proved it alright. She won the bet. We ended up having the fastest sex of my life. It was kind of embarrassing. She said it was perfect. She just kept doing more and more and I was…well, I barely moved, really. It was fast. She was fun. That was fun. I remember her saying that it was fun and she loved it. She said, 'Perfect. Thank you. You're better at this than you are at gambling.'"

"Did you keep seeing her?"

"Yeah. Yeah. I think that's why I keep thinking about it. The next time Cal played, she came over. I wanted her to; I just didn't dare ask. Normally, I don't pay much attention to football. Damn. Never had anything like that. She…she was great, Jean. So great. I still see her from time to time. We don't talk about that season though. Sounds made-up, right?"

"Are you curious about why these memories are coming up now?"

"Oh, you have no idea. I can't seem to shake the thoughts. It's not her or those afternoons. It was always daytimes except for one night game. That was a memorable football season, though. Now I'm not even sure what made me want to tell you that. It's just something that I've been thinking about. I never told Kayla about it. It happened before I met Kayla. Maybe I shouldn't be thinking about it, but I've been thinking about it a lot lately." He's smiling this whole time.

Now I'm smiling, too. "I'm glad you told me, George. Let's stay right here and be curious. I trust this memory is coming up for a reason. How do you feel dropping back into that time with Jean? What was there for you?"

George is quiet for a moment. "You know, I was just being me, taking the time to help out. I like that about me, that I do stuff like that, and Jean, she absolutely loved that about me. It was a good thing I was doing, and I wasn't expecting anything in return—certainly not the, uh...the sex. But that happened, and it was fun, really fun, and we had a thing that just worked. She'd come by, I'd help her out, and it was simple—that's it, simple. I wasn't worried about what Jean was thinking." He pauses, tapping his fingers on the cushions. "That's it, dammit. I was just being me. Jean, she appreciated the way I was just being myself. I was free from the constant worrying that I feel with Kayla. I miss that. I want that. I want that with Kayla. I'm a good guy. I'm a good guy, David, and she, Kayla, she's hard, um, she...dang it, sometimes I just wish things were different."

Curiosity Informs You

At our best, we are curious creatures. We put the pieces together. We seek to understand our environment. We entertain ourselves with puzzles and riddles. But all too often, we aren't the focus of our own curiosity. Perimeter behavior, with its agenda to manipulate and enroll, works to separate us away from our natural curiosity. A company wants us to buy the shit they're selling; they want us to be curious about what they're slinging, but not about ourselves. A politician wants our votes, not the complexity of our hearts and minds. A douchebag wants us to believe his act is legit. A pussy wants us to take care of him. None of our guys want us to be who we really are; they want us to be what *they* need. They want what they want from us, period. We are objects in the games they play. Until we're aware. Until we're curious. Until we put the pieces together and see our participation in a game we didn't even know we were playing.

The asshole aggresses, the douchebag imitates, the pussy submits, and the dick plays the victim, and all of this in service of enrolling us in their perimeter world. These unwinnable games suck the soul out of us. Consider Jonah's wife, Shaylee, Eric's girlfriend, Annie, and Brett's wife, Cynthia. They've all tried very hard to make it work with these guys spun out on the perimeter. All of them are waking up out of that perimeter game. They see that it's unwinnable. Think about your own life: Have you ever apologized to a dick for your so-called offenses to the point where he stopped playing the victim? Have you ever sheltered a pussy until he started taking responsibility for himself? Have you ever catered to an asshole with such love and patience that he became kind and considerate and gave up his aggression? Have you ever indulged a douchebag to the point where he sought out his authentic self and let go of his bullshit? No. They only want more of the same concessions, and it's never enough.

Many have tried to save a partner and be the one that finally reforms their beautiful, tragic soul. Do you really want to help? Keep your center, then. Refuse bullshit perimeter conditions from immature partners. Insist on better terms of interaction. Be willing to let them exist on the perimeter without you. This is tough, I know.

Curiosity breaks us out of the blind cycles that run our lives. At work. At home. Anywhere. Everywhere. When you feel the pull from someone trying to claim you, when you feel yourself wanting to move out there, away from your own center, you must get curious. You must be interested in the ways you are affected by the behavior of our four archetypes. You must be curious about the ways you are *available* to be hooked into a douchebag's shtick, or a pussy's plea. This information will help you choose a response instead of quick-snapping a reaction. Be curious or be manipulated.

13
EXPERIMENT: THE E IN TRACE

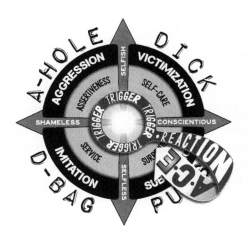

"It's not an experiment if you know it's going to work."
—Jeff Bezos

Try It; Maybe You'll Like It

An experiment is "a procedure carried out to support, refute, or validate a hypothesis. Experiments provide insight into cause-and-effect by demonstrating what outcome occurs when a particular factor is manipulated." Thanks, Wikipedia.

Experimenting is taking awareness and curiosity live. It's about finally taking all the stuff I've been going on about and putting it into practice.

We've been experimenting our entire lives. Very young children conduct rudimentary experiments to teach themselves about the world and how things work, whether it's sticking disgusting things in their mouths or running away to see if someone follows. Teenagers experiment with their bodies, relationships, sex, drugs, attitudes, clothes, friends, and everything else. Adults test out cars, college majors, veganism, yoga, bourbon. It's natural. We're always trying things, seeing how they make us feel, and deciding whether or not we like them enough to adopt them into our lives.

I'm talking about experimenting with yourself, and within your relationships, in a very deliberate way, one aimed at pushing your edges—expanding your options for living your life. You may not be a complete and total asshole, pussy, douchebag, or dick, but you can certainly relate to a few of their tendencies and see a part of yourself in their behavior. Chances are that these behaviors have been going on for a good long time by now. If you're interested in understanding yourself or breaking out of some painful patterns, perhaps it's time for some experimenting.

When we experiment with new shows, clothes, or vacation spots, these are not deeply personal experiments. ACE takes a more intimate approach to experimentation because the subject you're learning about is *you*. Experimenting with a new show is dull by comparison. You matter, you beautiful, stubborn bastard. Try doing something new and meaningful that scares you a bit. Take a risk. See how you respond. There's a deep drive within each of us to understand and discover, to have new experiences, to explore new territory. We don't often make ourselves the primary focus, but we should.

Every Part Is Trying to Help

One of the keys to living a life of authenticity, wonder, and solidity is recognizing that the internal narratives spurring our behavior always have positive intentions—even the voices in our heads that we dismiss. Parts of us are often in conflict with one another, but they're all trying to help.

The judge in your mind calling you "Fatty" really thinks that life would be better if you were thinner. Whether this is actually true or not is outside its jurisdiction. *Fuck you, Judge,* says another part of you, who's eating some key lime pie. You can probably see where this is going; it's an episode of *The Sopranos* in your own mind: *Fuck me? Fuck you! And now I'm gonna ride your fat ass all night long. Tomorrow, too.* Hate the lazy part of you and tell it as much? *Fuck you! Now we're definitely not going to the gym. Let's surf the 'net for hours, bitch.* It's difficult to remember that these voices, these instigators, came into being as intelligent adaptations to situations you've found yourself in—or represent real and valid fears of what *might* happen. But they're obstinate jerks, these devils on our shoulders. Or are they?

Remember that couple you've known for years? You can't understand why they stay together when all they seem to do is bicker and yell and battle and talk shit about each other. In your own mind, you're hosting opposing voices that are something like that couple. How do you find resolution? With awareness and curiosity. Understand that both sides are fighting for something that, to them, is positive—and that they have your well-being at heart. The judge, the drinker, the critic, they're all sticking to some story: *If you would just...then we'd be happy, and I wouldn't ride your ass anymore.* Other voices counter, and it goes back and forth. And as bestselling author Dan Siegel puts it, "If you have a fight with yourself, who can win?"

For years, I couldn't stand the pussy in me. I still feel the echoes of self-hatred, remembering what came down upon me from the bullies of my youth. I haven't forgotten that being a sensitive kid made me a target. At times, the pussy in me kept me from getting my ass kicked by older boys in the neighborhood—and that's a serious, solid benefit. If I showed up harmless and eager to please, I could often escape harm. If I can appreciate that boy, that part of me, he can quiet down a bit and allow me to be more assertive. Likewise, the douchebag in me originally emerged to help me fit in and feel less awkward. If I give credit where credit's due, he'll settle down, too.

This attitude toward your internal world is crucial. It's an attitude that assumes the best: If a part of me is scared, I can deepen my breath and engage the fear. *Hey, super-scared guy. I feel you in there. I'm right here with you. I want to get to know you. I trust that there's something you need me to know.* This is what George and I work on in our sessions. This helps settle his nervous system. This sort of experiment is one I cannot recommend highly enough. In short, learn to understand how your own John McEnroe is trying to help you, and appreciate him for it.

Jed on His Bicycle

Jed experiments with every trend or craze that comes along. He's a douchebag, and that's what douchebags do: they consume, they copy shit, and they imitate. Jed followed the men in Lycra into the prestigious Sandhill Road Triathlon Club. For years, he's gone for Saturday and mid-week rides with these guys.

A month ago, he stopped riding with the club. No more networking and high-fives. No more "masters of the universe" circle jerks. Now he only rides his bike alone.

Today is another weekday ride for Jed. He leaves SoMa and heads across the bridge and up to the peak of the Marin Headlands. This is his happy place. No monthly numbers. No Scotty. No cell phone, just an old iPod that can't ring. Today, Jed is riding a seventy-mile loop along the Pacific Ocean ranges.

Going out, Jed feels something new—an easeful joy. A genuine smile. There's a peaceful rhythm in this aloneness. The voices in his head are quiet. He pedals to the beat. Even when he's climbing, he rarely gets up off the saddle. He's steady, riding away from San Francisco and away from his life. Jed feels good. He's enjoying the climbs and descents through the headlands and up to Mount Tamalpais.

It doesn't matter where he is or how long the ride is; halfway out is halfway in. At the midpoint his experience begins to change. He thinks of what he has to do when he gets back. He feels the shell he has become and the costumes he wears, and he hurts. He's not just the sole rider; he's the soulless rider. He rides alone because here, on these roads, on this bike, with ridiculous oversized blade sunglasses covering his face, he cries. He cries a lot—and he cries alone—on the loop back to his enviable life. These rides are his sanctuary. When he's retracing his way back through Tiburon and Sausalito, the tears roll across his face and dry in his hair and ears.

As he crosses the Golden Gate Bridge, he tries to shake it off. Like a douchebag, he pretends again that if he can wipe these tears away, he can just wipe the feelings away. *Enough of this. There's shit to do now.* Change is happening. It's slow, and it's against a mountain of resistance, but finally, it's not too much for Jed. He can face these climbs, and he can face life and all its challenges. He just refuses to know it. Not now. Not yet.

He's not experimenting with expensive Italian bicycles, steep inclines, or heartbeats per minute. He is experimenting with his heart, his head, his plan, and those goddamn tears. Alone, he dares to try it. It's new. Jed is giving it a go. Fuck yeah, Jed. About goddamn time. Baby steps, bro.

George After Six Months

"So, what are you afraid would happen if you interacted with Kayla from this stronger place, like you've been doing with me these last five months?"

"Oh, I don't know. I want to, but she'd be, um…" George pauses. "I don't know how'd she be. I'm still afraid she'd be disappointed. I actually don't know what she would do. I think she'd be hurt or upset, and I'm afraid of that."

"Name the split, George."

"One part of me wants to speak up to her, to be more myself, you know. I also just want to go along with things the way they've been. I also know Kayla wants to hear from me."

"Often, parts of us are caught in the past. They aren't aware that things are different now. It's our job to help these parts see they're not stuck in the same situation as before. That's what we've been doing these last few months—helping you feel connected to the kid who played tic-tac-toe on the couch, the younger version of you. It's important that this part of you feels safer in the world. He'll feel safer in the world if you two are connected. This way, you'll know you're okay even if Kayla or anyone else out there is critical or rejecting.

"When others—usually parents, siblings, friends—are frustrated with or don't like a part of you, it hurts like hell, so you end up not liking that part of you either. You associate that part of you with hurt. You try to change it, but it never works. The conflict stays unresolved and sows resentment until you figure something out."

We continue to experiment: I ask him for something, and his job is to say no. These experiments are designed to help George work with his triggers and give him some new, positive examples of assertiveness.

"George, can I borrow ten thousand dollars?"

"George, will you come over and wash my car later?"

"George, will you jump up and down and cluck like a frickin' chicken?"

With each of these questions, I ask George to be curious about what happens inside of him when he tries to say no. "My throat gets so tight," he says, "it's like the words can't come out. It's even hard to breathe. This happens with Kayla, too, and I feel so embarrassed." We stay curious.

"George, what are you most afraid would happen in this moment if you said no?"

George pauses for a moment. "That you'd be mad at me."

"Then what would happen?"

"You wouldn't want to meet with me anymore." His eyes go down to the floor. A pause follows his comment. He takes a few breaths and regroups.

"Kind of amazing, right? This part is really trying hard to keep you from being rejected, so much so that it literally won't let you speak. I really want to honor that. You've got damn good reasons to back up that fear. We all have a deep need to belong, and we're willing to sacrifice a great deal to minimize the risk of disconnect from those close to us. That being said, let's experiment here and be playful. I'm not going anywhere, I promise. Let's say no together."

"No, no, no, no," we say, a little louder each time. I drop off after a few moments, but he continues—as I hoped he would—getting louder and louder. Pretty soon, he's smiling.

I repeat the questions I asked earlier, and this time, each no is clear and smooth.

Then we stand across from one another, and I walk toward him with my arms out. I'm Frankenstein. It looks ridiculous. When I'm at arm's reach, he pushes me away. It's important to learn to embody your personal space, so I often incorporate physical exercises into my work. At first, this is terrifying for George, and his pushes are apologetic and without any force.

"I'm so afraid you'll push me back, and..." He pauses. "Wait, that's the kid again. He's scared about pushback," he says enthusiastically.

"Great awareness. Actually, I love feeling your no. It's clear, and it helps *my* nervous system feel safer with you. That's the magic. We feel better with people we can trust to say no when they mean no, and yes when they mean yes. It keeps things clear and honest. When we try to take care of one another by saying yes when we don't mean it, resentment builds, and things get shaky. You see this with Kayla. She doesn't want your yes, she wants *you*!"

"I just go along with what Kayla wants. Sometimes I don't want to, and I get annoyed, but of course I never say anything to her."

"Exactly. There's so much fear about upsetting those close to us. We all feel this, and for good reason. We're careful because we're so important to one another. The irony is that when we stop being honest to protect the relationship, we're actually wrecking the very thing we're trying to preserve. The way we try to protect the precious thing kills the thing."

George nods, taking this in. "I love her so much, and I'm so careful with her, with you, with everyone, but I don't want to be. I'm so tired of myself. I'm tired of being scared *all the fucking time.*"

Whoa. George said "fucking." This is good. "How the fuck do you really *want* to be—with Kayla, in the world? If there were no fear of consequences, how would you show up?"

"I actually don't even know," George says, somewhere between laughing and crying.

"I don't believe you, George." I let that sink in. "You never saw a racquetball court until you were asked to play in an intramural league in college. Now, how do you show up on the racquetball court?"

He smiles, devilishly. "Ruthlessly."

Now we're talking. I give George assertiveness exercises to try between sessions. These include walking quickly and passing people on the sidewalk and shaking hands more firmly.

* * *

"What are you passionate about, George?" We've been working together for six months, and it's time to broaden George's work beyond Kayla.

"I don't know, really."

"What did you love as a kid?"

George blushes and says, "RC cars. The kids in my neighborhood used to call me RC George. They would try to run them over with their bicycles, but I was too damn good."

I love feeling George the badass. I loved radio-controlled cars when I was a kid too, and I tell him so. We proceed to geek out for the next ten minutes about RC10s and Ultimas, two RC cars we both loved. Turns out George still has his old RC cars at his mom's.

"Have her send them to you," I say.

"Kayla already thinks I'm too much like a kid. She'd make fun of me, and I'd feel too embarrassed."

"Why not have *one* of them sent out? Just see if you're interested, and then bring it to our next session."

George reluctantly agrees.

A few weeks pass, and he shows up for his session with a sheepish look on his face and an RC10 in hand. "Still works," he says, smiling.

"Wanna take it out for a spin?" I ask.

"Really?"

We've never been outside of my office together. "Absolutely."

We walk to a parking lot, and George tears it up. He can really corner that thing! He's an excellent driver, and I tell him so. He nods knowingly, and this makes me smile.

"How did Kayla respond to the RC cars, man?"

He smiles and stops the car. He hands me the controls. "If you can drive this better than her, I'll give you the fucking car."

Holy shit. "No, thanks. No way, man. Let's grab some tea and go inside."

"That's Not Going to Work for Me"

Here is one of my favorite experiments; it's one I've taught to hundreds of clients and students. Say it aloud: *That's not going to work for me.* I love that line. This statement is real and clear. It does not apologize. This specific experiment is focused on dealing with other people: the partners, strangers, acquaintances, or pieces of shit you meet every day.

Saying no is particularly difficult for pussies, and by pussies I mean all of us. Too many believe that saying no is rude and inappropriate. Unfortunately, many of us believe that our internal no isn't enough, or isn't valid, or that it requires a winning explanation. Bullshit. It's enough. It *is* the explanation.

This doesn't mean that saying no or saying that something "won't work for you" requires no communication at all. It may require a lot of communication, or a simple no may be just enough. Read the room or the situation. The point is to recognize what's true and authentic for yourself and honor it. Making your no clear takes practice and some experimentation.

You don't have to meet others out on the perimeter. You don't have to be spun out to the perimeter by others' demands or behavior. Hold your center. *I do not accept your conditions* is another succinct communication when we're being expected to meet someone on their terms. A refusal to take part in insane and impossible scenarios is an experiment I highly recommend.

Cynthia had to reject a metric shit ton of conditions to regain her balance. Finding clarity on what she was rejecting was a difficult journey. Knowing what to say—and when—was a learned process for her. There are appropriate times to reject others' conditions, and clear and practiced communication can work in those situations.

Experiment with these expressions and your own versions:

- *That's not going to work for me.*
- *I do not accept your conditions.*
- *We may have some common ground; come back with a better proposal.*
- *Those conditions are yours only—not mine.*
- *I am not negotiating on these terms.*
- *I am not meeting you on the perimeter.*
- *You are spun out and not actually a victim.*
- *It's a no from me. (Classic. Thanks, American Idol.)*
- *I can wait until you're more centered, so for now, no.*

Know your goddamn no.

PART 4

THE CENTERED MAN

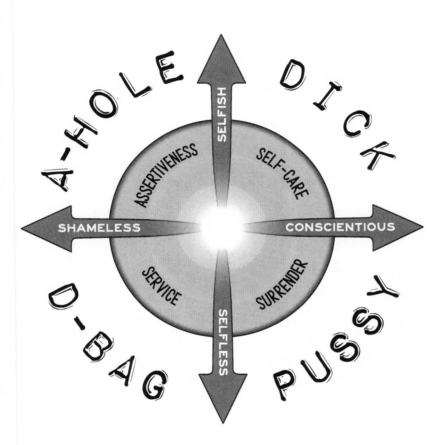

14
THE INNER CIRCLE

Many men and women exude the qualities of assertion, surrender, self-care, and service. They surrender and find truth that benefits the world. They serve simply by being themselves and sharing. Some have started large, transformative organizations, while others work completely under the radar. Some teach in classrooms. Whatever this magic is that wakes up inside of us when we do our work, it expresses itself differently in everyone.

Every Given Sunday

Jed wakes up on Sunday with the granddaddy of hangovers. Being swole ain't helping this headache. But he rallies, and forty-five minutes later, he's getting out of an Uber car at an assisted-living community. He covers his sleeve tattoo. He wears socks. He walks into the rec room with two minutes to spare, having missed lunch with Grandpa Hank and his "lady friends." He has a box of Cranberry Bliss bars under one arm and a stash of twenties in his pocket to tip the caretakers.

Seeing his grandpa weekly is Jed's most non-negotiable priority. Even in the obnoxious hell of his own douchebaggery, he rarely skips a visit, unless he's off on a bender in Cabo, of course.

* * *

On Sunday morning, George gets up early to make Kayla breakfast with grapefruit. By 9:00 a.m., he's on his second banana-guava smoothie of the day. He turns up the stereo in his car, rolls down the windows, drives exactly five miles an hour over the speed limit, and sings along to AC/DC.

He's grinning from ear to ear as he parks at the Y, and he's still grinning as he goes through an old-school calisthenics routine that would make Jack LaLanne smile from his grave. He's grinning even more as he confidently pummels his opponent on the racquetball court and ups his rank in the U30 advanced league.

He's all wit and charisma as he casually chats with his opponent of the week over lunch at his favorite Berkeley deli. Normally, the loser buys the winner a sandwich. This is a new opponent. George beats the guy and still buys him lunch.

* * *

Eric strolls alone into the Mission District. He doesn't tell many people this, but he volunteers as a Big Brother. In addition to the standard meetings and obligations, he meets up most Sundays with his kid Gabe to kick a ball around, shoot the shit, eat pizza, and write. He never misses Gabe's soccer games. Gabe is Salvadoran, thirteen, sharp, independent, and fast.

On this particular Sunday, they sit in the workshop room in the back of Dave Eggers's store, 826 Valencia. Gabe listens intently as Eric talks to him about a favorite topic: microlending in Latin America. In turn, Eric listens intently as Gabe talks about girls, gang-lore, and a bad eighth-grade teacher. Apparently, Gabe has the world's worst teacher.

By the time Eric gets home that night, he's feeling relieved. He's tired. Calm. He's hopeful about his own future. He doesn't even check the news.

* * *

My labels for Jonah, George, Jed, and Eric are not the entirety of the person. A douchebag isn't a douchebag all day, every day. Maybe pussy behavior is George's default when he's pressured. Assholery could surface in Jonah after three drinks or a canceled contract. Eric's dick-ishness might go along with fatigue or a big trigger. At their core, these men are good, and they're all working their way back to their good, centered selves.

The Center: Assertiveness, Surrender, Service, and Self-Care

Each of these archetypal men is overcommitted to his view, his orientation, and his experience. It doesn't have to be that way, nor should it be. We're all more complex than that. Some days we're selfish to an extreme, sometimes just a *bit* selfish, and at other times very selfless. When we are lost in extreme behavior, and we need a way back from the edge, it helps to picture our model.

Moving in from the perimeter to the center, you'll find a spectrum of behaviors that are less and less influenced by the self and care motivations that are overwhelming at the perimeter. For each quadrant, there is a healthy, balanced, *centered* version of the unhealthy, spun-out, perimeter behavior. As we move toward the center, the asshole's aggression becomes assertiveness, the pussy's submission becomes surrender, the douchebag's imitation becomes service, and the dick's self-victimization becomes self-care. From the perimeter, the path to healthy change is to move back toward the center.

It's easy, of course, to say, *Move to the center, dummy,* but what does that even look like? What does it mean? Well, it sure as shit doesn't mean instantly becoming an enlightened bodhisattva; in fact, it often doesn't look like anything other than a change in mindset and focus. Despite the simplicity of our model, don't expect your path back to center to look like anybody else's path. There's no one-size-fits-all formula. Life isn't simple, people aren't simple, and a model is an abstraction. In real life, successfully reaching the center through TRACE takes purpose, creativity, and practice.

The path from the perimeter to the center requires experimentation. It isn't necessarily linear or direct, and it may involve testing strategies and skills that are found in other archetype quadrants. For example, if you realize you're being an insufferable dick today, you'll naturally see that you could perhaps be a bit more considerate and a bit less rigid. Picture where you are on the model: the northeast quadrant, on the selfish end of the self axis and the conscientious end of the care axis. Nudge your behavior in the selfless direction by doing something for someone else. Hell, for starters, try just seeing a situation from another person's point of view. Experiment with the care axis by abandoning some of the fucks you normally carry around and go care-free for the rest of the day. If that feels impossible, try temporarily replacing your normal focus with something different, like finding gratitude for the things you normally find annoying. Roll with it, or at least roll differently, for God's sake.

Self-Care: Better Than Self-Victimization

"Take care." I grew up in the South. "Take care" is the way many folks said goodbye. As a clinician, I often say "Take care of yourself" to clients walking out at the end of a session, but it turns out some people are not so good at this. Why? Because if you've never learned to listen to and process information, you *can't* take good care of yourself. Do our guys have any idea how to take care of themselves? Hell no. They have been completely mis-attuned to what was going on inside them. Their reactive minds stopped taking in new information a long time ago.

Eric, our poster boy for dickish self-victimization, suffers from an *excess* of what it takes to engage in healthy self-care: conscientious self-focus. He proves that there can be too much of a good thing—a problem, you'll notice, that all of our archetypes share.

I've spent some time not "taking care" myself. In my twenties, I tried to make a career in the corporate world. Accounting. Tech. Sales. Real estate development. My back hurt, I drank too much, I was depressed, but still I pressed on with my agenda. I had a firm idea about who I was and what I was going to do, and I wasn't going to listen to the feedback. Fuck my back, my hangovers, my depression.

Miserable, I finally sat in front of a psychotherapist and hashed it out. I hated myself for not fitting into this world. And it wasn't for lack of trying; I had tried again and again. I just wasn't listening to myself—the corporate path was not for me. Once I let go of my douchey business-man dream (painful as that was), and found my path in psychology, I felt what it was like to truly "take care."

Learning how to take care of yourself begins with listening internally. TRACE teaches us how to build this habit. When you have a rigid idea of who you are, who you're supposed to be, who others are, and what the world is, you're not listening to and responding to your actual experience. You're living in a fucking fantasy land. Most of us don't know how to take care of ourselves, but we damn sure hear plenty of opinions telling us how to do it.

When we first met Jed, our symbol of "care-less" abandonment of the self, he relied completely on the external world. He postured and manipulated, and even with everything he had accumulated, he felt empty and alone. He could take care of his tan and his muscles and a huge sales team, but at night, he couldn't find a moment of peace for Jed; he turned to booze and escorts to soothe him.

Many of us rely on unhealthy things to feel better. It rarely works out. We need healthy connection with others and healthy habits built into our lives. Taking shitty care of ourselves is a kind of avoidance; it's how we remain stuck in a rut—often willfully. By staying under-resourced, hung over, or in some other state of dulled-out desperation, we are left to rely on those same old fortified habits and narratives. The TRACE method is a way to establish healthy connections and habits, but it demands resources. It requires energy and attention.

Jonah Slides

Jonah sits down, puts his quart-size mason jar of black coffee on the side table, and grabs a tissue out of the box. He's smiling, but he's quivering. He shrugs. "I got nothing, Dave. I got nothing." His smile is sagging. "There's nothing to say. I got nothing." The smile fades completely. Obviously, he has *something*. His voice fades: "Nothing."

This larger-than-life asshole is hurt. He wouldn't look out of place sitting in an emergency room. So far, he appears to want nothing but silence. I'm cool with that. He's fine just being seen. I have nothing to add. Jonah is present. This is strength. This is pain. I can feel him. He begins to cry. I don't ask what happened. I don't know what hurt him or shamed him.

"You know, I can't seem to do anything right, but Shaylee gets things right with the kids. We have them in this Montessori preschool thing over there with all those fancy families in Piedmont. It's funny, you know, people move there to put their kids in public school, but we still have this pissing contest to get our kids into these private pre-schools. Twenty fucking thousand dollars a fucking year for preschool. Well, the director of the preschool is some sort of a pussy..." (This is Jonah's go-to insult; I don't think he knows what it really means.) "Anyway, the teachers were pissed. And if things aren't going right in preschool, then a kid can't go to kindergarten or college, or get a job as an adult. So, this is where the shit starts, right? Apparently, this is a big goddamn deal."

I'm listening. *Where the hell is this going?*

Jonah continues. "We had to have a family meeting with the faculty and shit, at the Montessori House Preschool of Piedmont or whatever the fuck it is. I went. Trying to be better at this co-parenting thing. And it didn't work out. I called that pussy director a fucking asshole. And I grabbed his little pussy arm when I called him that. There were families there. His girlfriend. Kids. All of it."

My first thought is that he's exaggerating. "Hang on—you grabbed a preschool director by the arm, in front of all the families, and called him a fucking asshole?"

"Yep. Then the board members of the preschool asked me to leave, and the director yelled, 'That man called me a fucking asshole! That man called me a fucking asshole!'" Jonah described the rest of that night—walking from Piedmont to Berkeley, and eventually getting his truck and heading to the city.

"I was out of control," Jonah continues. "Something just snapped. I couldn't believe what I'd done. I knew this was something that my family would feel. He *is* a fucking asshole." Jonah stops. A cold stop. "Well, not really. He's just a guy running our preschool. He's done a lot for my family, and I didn't even know. I had no idea. But he isn't an asshole, and I knew that. I know he's not. I hurt him. I hurt my kids. I think I hurt my wife. Nobody should've got hurt. I hurt a lot of people. This shit has to stop at some point. I'm getting tired, David. I can't keep doing this shit. I think I hurt that guy."

Jonah is moving fast. He's regretful. He's sad, but he's moving along with his story, not interested in processing anything just yet. "The next day I got a call..." Jonah collapses into the couch. "The school called... David, fuck this shit. Fuck this. Fuck these cocksuckers. Maybe I didn't hurt them *enough*."

I don't respond with words. I model a posture that will give him some breath. I exaggerate my own breath, enough for him to see it and hear it.

Jonah follows suit and sits back up. "Those fucking assholes, those cocksucking fucking assholes. Some fucking pansy parents said they wanted my son kicked out of the school. He's a little kid. Zack didn't do anything. They said I was a monster and that their kids weren't safe in a fucking Montessori preschool with my son. Those self-righteous fucks even said that *Zack* was a monster. He's just a little kid."

Jonah can barely talk.

I get up from my seat, hand Jonah a dry tissue. He takes the tissue, then reaches for his black coffee.

"How's your chest?" I ask.

"It's numb. I can't feel it. Don't worry, I won't have another heart attack. My chest is fine right now." (Jonah already experienced one unscheduled heart attack on the street in San Francisco. I have to ask.)

"David, I'm not a nice guy. I'm not a good guy. But I can't. I can't. I can't hurt the kids. I know I do sometimes, but I *can't*. Fuck. Fuck. I can't. But those fucking assholes can't do this to my son. They can't. I will fuck them up forever. They can't do this."

"Jonah, your son is going to be okay. He's not a monster, and he won't hurt anyone. You know that. I'm sorry they said that about your kid. Let's go back to that moment. How were you doing, sitting there with those parents, with Shaylee nearby? How was Jonah?"

"Bad. I was hung over, on no sleep, taking shit care of myself—I know we talked about fucking self-care, but I suck at it, I fucking hate it—and shit, man, I didn't want to be there, but I was trying, goddammit, I was trying to show up for my kids." (More tears, followed by a nose-blowing heard by people in the street.) "But I was so on edge, man, I just…I just spun the fuck out."

Jonah breaks. He feels the impact of his actions. He feels the consequences. The shamelessness that's kept him oblivious is crumbling. He cries for his sons. He misses his marriage.

A line from a Bukowski novel enters my mind: "I can see the beauty in this now-calm man surrounded by disasters."

After this session, he slowly starts to take better care of himself. I ask him to check in with me between sessions about exercise, food, sleep—the basics—and about his drinking, and he does. Over time, he learns to listen to what his body needs. He's slowly ending his war with himself.

Even though Jonah is making progress in our sessions, old habits linger. Something triggers Jonah, and he goes straight to his default reaction: blind aggression. Jonah knows he's embraced that instinctive response; he's going to need more practice to eliminate it. He knows self-care is key. He can do it. He will.

Assertiveness: Better Than Aggression

"Fight as if you are right; listen as if you are wrong," says organizational theorist Karl E. Weick. Assertive men express feelings, thoughts, beliefs, and opinions strongly, and they do so in an open manner that doesn't violate or dismiss the rights of others. The pussy, douchebag, and dick each lack the essential recipe for assertiveness: care-free self-focus. The asshole? Yeah. Too much of a good thing.

Being assertive means you're willing to hold your position fairly, without attacking others and without diminishing your stance. You don't give your own power away to appease (like George), nor do you take another's power away to control (like Jonah).

In our work together, George first practiced being assertive in small ways: he firmed his grip when shaking hands, passed people on the sidewalk and freeway, and said no to me during practice sessions. I've always found it best to start with small experiments. This way, you teach your sensitive nervous system that it's beneficial to be assertive. Assertiveness, like a muscle and like muscle memory, is built over time through repeated acts of awareness, curiosity, and experimentation.

At first glance, Eric and Jed might seem assertive. Any dick can take an inflexible position, and any douchebag can push his shtick. Both, however, are completely closed off and dismissive of others, and that makes them dickishly passive-aggressive or douchily evasive, not assertive. Real assertiveness is being strong and curious, maintaining a broad perspective, and being vulnerable. Assertiveness is *genuine* power. "To know oneself, one should assert oneself," as Albert Camus said.

Assertiveness gives us choices. With assertiveness, a man can enter into the challenges of new situations, confident and relaxed, knowing he is looking out for himself and can get what's fair from others. He can contribute, take action, speak out, or walk away. This man knows he can respond skillfully to triggers rather than react without a plan.

While some men say, "Don't rock the boat," the assertive man knows when to rock the boat and when to stop. He uses honesty as a guiding tenet. If there's an issue with colleagues, relationships, money, or whatever (and there always is), he'll address it *now*. He knows that festering issues root resentment. Assertiveness becomes a natural skill. It is a skill that keeps things from getting stagnant; it gets shit done.

So, how do you learn to be assertive? Get curious about what happens to you in the moment when you need to bring your opinion or position forward. What happens in your body? In your closest relationships, what needs to be said? In times of fear and doubt, get to know yourself. When there's resistance to life changes, ACE the moment. Allow the resistance to reveal your fear to you, then interpret that information thoughtfully. My resistance to writing this book, for example, is rooted in my fear of public humiliation. A book about what? Assholes and pussies? Who would conceive of such a thing? How fucking vulgar!

Unfortunately, too many men are taught to be aggressive if someone "disrespects" them. "Don't take any shit," and that kind of bravado. What a bunch of angsty horseshit. If others can easily spin you out, you're never really free, and you're not truly powerful. Especially if you spin out over insignificant things, like someone not liking your act or someone hurting your feelings. That's the fragile man masquerading as a tough guy. I'm not buying the cover-up. Assertive men can walk away from bullshit.

Assertiveness is the willingness and courage to enter the fray—not with guns blazing, not cringing with your tail between your legs, not looking to manipulate or guilt someone with threats. Assertiveness respects. It's self-respect: you speak your truth, you talk your talk and walk your walk. It respects others: it allows them to be who they are, to talk *their* talk and walk *their* walk.

George's Assertiveness, Finally

After eight months of working together on a weekly basis, George comes in looking pleased with himself. "I said something. I can't believe I did. Kayla was getting on me about being so passive, and I said, 'Anytime I *do* suggest something, I feel like you just snort or shoot it down, so maybe if you weren't so dismissive, I'd say more.' And she was shocked. And she sat there staring at me—and my 'scared guy.' I was terrified. And then she actually said, 'I'm sorry.' I couldn't believe it."

"How'd that feel?"

"Scary, but good, real good...Oh, man. I was feeling so much. But she didn't need to apologize. It was all I could do not to apologize to *her*." George is answering differently than he did eight, six, or even two months ago.

"Does it make sense to you that you'd have fears?"

"For sure. I don't usually hold my ground or ask for anything like that."

"How is it telling me about this?"

"It's fun, actually, and interesting." George is blushing. Something big is coming. "We, umm...We even had great sex. It was different. Better. She even said so. I felt like...I don't know, like I was a bit of the racquetball guy. I wasn't so worried about her. I could actually let myself go a little bit. It was fun, really fun."

I'm grinning big. I can't help myself. It feels great seeing him in this moment, and I tell him so. I prepare to say more, but I'm interrupted.

"The kitchen," George mutters.

"The kitchen?"

"Thank you. Yeah. Not for the kitchen. But yeah...we did it in the kitchen."

"The kitchen," I say, nodding, smiling.

Surrender: Better than Submission

We surrender often, so this concept shouldn't be new to you. When it's cold outside, we surrender to the elements and find a coat. When we're ill, we surrender to the chills and fever. We surrender to our need for food when hungry, water when thirsty, rest when tired. When it comes to nature, we respond to most limits and circumstances quite gracefully. If it is too damn cold, we surrender to that. When you're thirsty, your body isn't "wrong" or "bad"—it's telling you what you need. It's just a fact. You don't resist or rationalize it away; you just drink something.

But when it comes to our emotional needs and limits? *We shall never surrender, and never admit defeat!* This is the battle cry when men conflate healthy surrender with cringey submission and decide to write off everything that isn't obstinate resistance as a failure of manhood— pussying out. Bullshit. Surrendering doesn't make you a pussy, or weak, or a loser, or any of that shit. That's not what it is. Not at all.

Surrender is accepting reality.

Surrender is authentic.

Surrender is owning your shit.

We've all heard that the truth will set you free, but it's not truth itself that frees you, it's your relationship to the truth. *Surrendering* to the truth will set you free. Surrender is the first step in finding out what's real, knowing that you *don't* know, that you don't have the answers. Let's rid ourselves of the ridiculous notion that "I don't know" is a pussy's response. If *not* knowing is the authentic truth, surrender to that fact.

Some confusion in distinguishing between surrender and submission is understandable. After all, the same basic motivation that leads to surrender—namely, selfless conscientiousness—is what overwhelms the submissive pussy. The dick, asshole, and douchebag, on the other hand, are ruled by motivations that drive them to fight against reality, a fight they can't win. Their path back to center will involve learning to surrender.

Surrender is not giving up or quitting before the situation requires it. It's an interest in, and a respect for, the truth of the situation. The clarity and confidence that comes from accepting that truth can give rise to other healthy, adaptive skills, like assertiveness. For example, it can be terrifying to run out of money, but surrendering to the fact that you're scared allows you to distinguish your fear from the other facts, which you're then able to deal with effectively, each in turn, rather than running or hiding from them.

The shit hits the fan in a variety of ways. That's life. As humans, our first response to emotional pain, discomfort, and uncertainty is to resist them. But as the psychiatrist Carl Jung famously said, "What we resist not only persists, but will grow in size."

I'm not saying surrendering is simple, especially in relationships. It's sometimes easier to label another person "wrong" than to listen to them, hear what they're actually saying, and deal with reality. Instead of surrendering, we too often lay this kind of shit on people:

- *Don't take it that way.*
- *You're crazy.*
- *What's wrong with you?*
- *Are you still caught up in that fight we had last week?*
- *Why don't you just change?*
- *Hand wave/eye roll/exasperated sigh*

This rejection or dismissal of someone else's feelings is cruel, and it's a mindfuck. We all want to be seen and accepted in what we're feeling. This applies to everyone—and I mean *everyone*. If I'm upset and you tell me that "there's no reason to be upset," what the fuck can I do with that? Instead of wanting others to be different, surrender to your own experience and to the situation at hand. Accept it. If you're triggered by someone's big emotions, ACE your experience.

Without surrender, shit builds up, and distance creeps in. Unproductive fights happen. Or things get suppressed, nothing is ever resolved, and the connection weakens. Oh, and sex goes bye-bye. I've seen hundreds of couples, and the number one sex-killer is unprocessed resentment.

But I can't just surrender, you may be thinking, because:

- *If I surrender, I'll look weak.*
- *If I surrender, I'll seem stupid.*
- *If I surrender, I'm a pussy.*
- *If I surrender, I'm _____.*

Nope. If you surrender, life will get a great deal easier. As Byron Katie famously said, "When I argue with reality I lose—but only 100% of the time." When the alternative is another pointless argument with yourself, surrendering to the facts is the better choice.

Over and over again, I've heard some version of this from clients: *If I surrender to the way things are, it means accepting that they'll always be this way.* This is one of the biggest, most consistent misunderstandings I've seen over the years. Surrendering isn't a fatalistic excuse for complacency; it doesn't mean resigning yourself to a shitty world situation. Surrendering means acknowledging, and feeling the impact of, the facts and the truth. *Submitting* to something means being subjected to it; *surrendering* to something means truly seeing and accepting it. Once you see it, you can change it. You can't change what you deny exists.

For our dick Eric, who is used to feeling the familiar weight of his narrative, surrender is an added weight—the weight of the *whole truth*. His loneliness, his anger with and fear of women, the wrongness of his job, and his growing disappointment and dissatisfaction with his life are all part of this narrative—*his* narrative, *his* views, *his* interpretation, *his* bullshit. He believes it wholeheartedly, and he is mostly half full of shit.

Surrender is a deep letting in of the actual truth, and letting in the truth often means feeling emotions we don't want. Thus far, Eric has remained on the perimeter, where he can feel the familiar emotions that he prefers, acting like a dick, playing a victim in bondage. As much as Eric hates his life, he still refuses to surrender to the whole truth and set himself free.

Eric Actually Surrenders

After spending a couple of weeks exploring his shocking experience of betrayal, Eric announces, "Feeling better, man. Thanks. I can breathe again after all this time—it's like a weight off my chest. I'm ready to move on. I think I'm done with therapy for a while."

This guy is not done. *Holy fucking shit* is he not done. Something is off here; I can feel it in my bones. I want him to get this right. It's time to go beyond his version of the story, the one where he casts himself as the innocent victim. Dicks do this. We all do this. It's not good for anybody.

"I've heard you talk about how good you felt when you were with her, how you were shopping for a ring, but you've never actually told me about the relationship. You've never told me about *her*—not one thing about her, other than her cheating."

"What's there to tell? She broke my fucking heart, man, with my friend. What the fuck?"

This is touchy, but it's essential. Nervously, I press on. "Part of your narrative is that you were blindsided, and you've lived your life since then unable to trust anybody or anything. We need to know *how* you were blindsided. I want us to understand your role in this disaster."

"*My* role?" he hisses. "I loved her. I fucking loved her. That was my role, that was my crime, and this is fucking bullshit."

"This is important, and it's uncomfortable for me, too, and I wouldn't be bringing this painful idea up if I wasn't committed to you healing this and moving on. We have another round here."

"I just told you I want to stop coming. Is this some kind of tactic to keep the money flowing in?"

My heart is thundering in my chest, but by this point, I love this guy, and I'm not going to let him leave with his bullshit dick narrative intact.

"You're a smart guy, Eric, and if you leave here now, your past will still own your ass. You weren't seeing what was going on around you; you were missing signs; you were so trapped in your own head that you weren't able to take in what was going on with her. We have to understand *how* that happened."

"What the fuck are you talking about?"

"You were lost in your *idea* of her, how great you felt when you were around her, and you lost *her* somehow. You were disconnected from Jodee the college girl, the complex human being, and from all the shit she had going on. You weren't taking in new information. You were living your story of being in love, but you weren't actually in a relationship."

He gets up to leave. *Dammit. I'm losing him.*

I stand up. "You two rarely went out alone anymore, and never sober. You rarely had sex, except when she was drunk. You were seeing less of her because she was busy. You started going to bed at different times. When she tried talking to you about her struggles, you minimized it or told her it was all good and not to worry. She even tried to break up with you a few times, but you pleaded for her to stay and promised to change, yet you never did."

Eric looks at me. I haven't seen him like this before. His eyes shift to the upper left. He remembers. His eyes widen—really wide, scared wide. He sits down heavily on the sofa, rubbing his face.

"How did you know that? I never said anything about that. I had forgotten about...all of that."

"Eric, the omissions from your story are also part of your story."

"Yeah. Obviously, you were paying attention."

"You lose the person to the *idea* of the person. You disconnect from the relationship when it's in trouble and you don't know what to do, and from there you move into a fantasy about the relationship."

* * *

Eric skips the next session, giving me exactly twenty-four hours' notice so he won't be charged. But he comes to his appointment the following week.

"Well, David, just when it couldn't get any worse," he leads in, "it turns out she felt sorry for me. I called Will, an old roommate from the college days. He's the only guy from that group who also came to SF. We got together over some beers at the Glen Park Station. It was the writer in me kicking in. I wanted to know what happened. The true story. Will was actually pretty cool about it all. We had a few beers down there at the Station and talked shit for hours.

"Jodee was afraid of what would happen if she broke up with me, like I'd go off the rails or something. Plus, she liked living in the house with all of our friends. She didn't want to get kicked out, and she didn't want me to get kicked out, so she...she made it work. Oh, and she was in love with the other guy, not me. He was in love with her, like, madly in love. They're married with kids now. They all felt terrible when I disappeared, so that's something—the bastards. But you know what? It was good talking to Will. I mean, damn, it was hard, but I had buried it so deep. No one knew what to do, no one wanted to break up the band, so they just, you know, kept it quiet. We were always so drunk and stoned back then. Man, how did I not see it? It's funny, that's the kind of person I can't stand—the ones with their heads so far up their asses that they can't see what's right in front of their fucking faces—and lo and behold, that was me, David. That was me."

When you surrender to the whole truth and all of its consequences and implications, even when it's brutal, there's a relief, a strange satisfaction. We work with the curious part of Eric, the part that falls crazy in love, the angry part that feels victimized, the part that feels so stupid for missing the cues, the part that feels bad about disconnecting from Jodee and others. This is the work—connecting with all the parts of ourselves.

Eric centers a lot of his ongoing work around a phrase that he repeats: "Leave no one behind." While many of my clients have taken that phrase with them from our work, Eric has his own twist on it; he revisits his own self-told stories as an investigative writer.

"I never wanted to admit it, what happened. I never wanted it to be true," Eric says three months later. "I tried to erase it from my mind, to move on. I drove that same car to another school that summer. *Clean fucking slate*, that's what I told myself. *Starting over*. But it was always there. I registered for classes, moved into my own place. That didn't work out so well either. Shit, you know what? I've always lived alone since then, man. Makes sense now that I understand, now that I see..."

He pauses and looks thoughtfully around my office. "Annie wanted to move in together once. I freaked out, but I never put the pieces together. I wish I'd faced this earlier. Maybe things could have worked out with her. God, I owe her an apology, and not just her, either— others. When she would smile at another guy, I would fly off the handle. Shit. I was making a fool of myself, but I never saw it. I never saw *her*, either—just my fear. I thought...Oh, man, I thought I was just being 'real,' 'honest,' 'authentic,' some bullshit like that. What was I really, David? Who am I now?"

I don't want to rush in with an answer. He has to find one for himself, over time. We all have to make sense of our pasts and make meaning from our choices. It's a way we move forward in our lives.

Protective strategies shield us from painful experiences, but they don't heal us. When you're hurt—and we all get hurt—you instinctively move to protect yourself from further hurt. Blame and self-victimization are two ways of protecting yourself. But to *heal* these emotional wounds, you have to surrender. You have to come into relationship with your pain. TRACE is a healing process, not a protective one. It aims to engage directly with the parts of you that hold on to pain and trauma. When you're healed, there's no need for protection, just as there's no need for a cast once a broken bone is healed. When you protect yourself without healing yourself, you are on a one-way road to rigidity and reactivity. Higher walls. Less connection. Tragedy. Dick Country.

* * *

Eric has been using all of his vitality and creativity to protect himself, and it's time for him to experiment. This is a vital step for dicks. Instead of resisting, whining, and complaining, he needs to do something meaningful and creative with that energy. I begin to nudge him on this front.

"Goddammit," he says. "I really want to be a writer. I'm tired of editing someone else's crap, but when I try to write I get so fixated on what I *don't* like that I never finish anything."

"A thousand words," I say. "Every week. You bring it in and read it aloud in here. Deal?"

Each week, we begin the session with his story. I start to look forward to them. He's an excellent writer—snarky, insightful, profane, and provocative. My kind of guy. We spend time each session talking about this experiment. At first, he's awkward and fearful of my judgment, and we TRACE these fears back and connect with the parts we meet there. After a few months, he's submitting short stories and news articles to online providers. He's beginning to have fun again as a writer. He even gets back to working on his manuscript.

* * *

Eric has more to talk about now. More to live for. And he's becoming a more interesting person. Before, he was closed off in his own self-affirming bubble, fueled by confirmation and negativity bias. With support, he was able to surrender to the reality of his life, to face his fears, feel his pain, and heal, and with this, things shifted. *We have to see how full of shit we are.* I've often said that to clients over the years… when they were ready.

Eric's experience felt absolute to him. But it was all just a brilliant attempt to protect himself—to feel safe, powerful, and unique. He had been spun out for so long that he believed it was the objective truth of life. This is a trap—and it's a bear trap, not a mousetrap. When we're struggling, it's up to us to find the courage to examine our own stories. Otherwise, we'll go to the grave with our tired, dull narratives unchecked and unchanged—and that's a sad thing indeed.

Jed in the Wild Again

Jed scrambles again on Sunday morning, but finally, he makes it to see his grandfather. He goes through his normal routine with the nurses and staff. He visits with his grandpa's friends. He's present—but not fully. His grandpa convinces him to stick around a bit longer and join him for a ride. Reluctantly, Jed climbs in the passenger side and buckles up.

"What the hell is wrong with you, Jedediah? You think I don't notice that things aren't right? I ain't sitting in this place because I've lost my mind completely. I ain't fucking stupid or blind; I just can't do as much as I used to. It hurts to open a can of Pepsi, but I can still do it. I can still be your grandpa and I can still see bullshit. What's going on?"

"Gramps, I know. I'm busy. Just busy. Preoccupied and busy."

"Right. Okay. I'll just turn this car around and you can go back to the office, then. You can get all your work done. Bullshit, Jed. Bullshit. Just bullshit.

"You get here late. Your face is a wreck. You tell the same damn stories and say the same damn things. Every week you tell me the same shit. You used to hang out with that Mandy girl, and she would even come over to the house. Now, you show up here alone telling the same stories about these places and work. Who the hell are you now?

"Remember, I used to pick you up from school and go to your matches and drive you when your folks were busy. We used to talk about skipping class and homework and friends. Or you would talk to me about your tennis coaches. Remember that? Now, you just say the same shit over and over, and you can't wait to leave. What the hell is going on?"

"I don't know," Jed finally answers. "Just busy. Things change, you know." A part of Jed is relieved to be talking with his grandpa, but a part of him is terrified.

"You changed." Grandpa Hank is on a roll. He's been hoping to have this conversation for quite some time. "C'mon, son. What's going on? I know you cover up those ridiculous tattoos when you come see me. I know you have friends you don't bring around. I know when you're off doing all that fast-living stuff that you kids like. I can tell when you're hung over. But I also know that there's more to you than that.

"You used to like taking a day off from work and planting a garden at the neighbors' with me. We used to do that every spring together. We even did that stuff when you moved back here for this job you have. Shit, when you were really little, you would even wear my boots and hat and just be funny for the neighbors while we planted a row of potatoes. I thought you liked that stuff. We planted gardens for them sumbitches that didn't even deserve a garden."

"Yeah, well, Gramps, not a lot of people growing gardens in San Francisco. The times they are a changed." The part of Jed that's scared—terrified, really—is getting more uncomfortable. He's preparing deflections and an exit.

But Grandpa Hank is wise, and his patience is just about gone. "No,

Jed. I miss you. There is a lot I can't care about. Time ain't something I can give a damn about. I'm almost out of time. San Francisco might be another something I don't give a damn about. Your vacations. Your jobs. Your cars. All your bullshit. I love *you*, Jed. Where the hell did you go?"

Service: Better Than Imitation

It's easy to see that the world needs people to look out for each other and to serve one another. The opportunities to fulfill the wants and needs of others are nearly limitless. Not everybody has what it takes, however, to engage in a non-transactional act of service—an act without a reward, whether immediate or in the afterlife. To have what it takes to *freely* serve is to be in the quadrant occupied by the douchebag, both selfless and oblivious to the haters or the naysayers.

The true douchebag, of course, is so detached from himself and the feedback of others that he has no concept of serving anything but his imaginary persona. Those with similar, but less extreme, motivations are self-aware enough to know that they have something unique to offer a cause and are careful enough to choose a worthy cause, all while still not giving a fuck how their choices look to other people. Their talent, and their comfort zone, is to serve without reservation. A douchebag who successfully finds his way back from the perimeter to the center will stop *imitating* others and start *serving* them.

Engaging in service does not come naturally to the asshole, the pussy, or the dick. A dick can't stand giving up the spotlight, and he's too preoccupied with the long odds of ever making a difference, all things considered, to serve any cause effectively. A pussy is too preoccupied as well, not by his own interests, of course, but by the interests of all the others out there who demand his attention, or who he might disturb by standing for a specific cause. An asshole only serves himself, so any alliance with a cause will fall apart as soon as there's nothing in it for him. Men in these other quadrants have a lot to learn from service.

For people with the tendency to get wrapped up in their own concerns and interests, their world can start to feel very small. As their world gets closer to a population of one, their personal problems will start to feel very, very big. Maybe too big to handle, or too big to solve. Well, that's just horseshit—an illusion created by living in an artificially limited, self-focused world. Service is a way to keep our shrinking world in check—it's a window to the vast, real world of options and solutions, reminding us that the size and severity of our problems is relative. Service, by its nature, creates human connection that many of us are desperately missing. It assures us that we are not alone in our own problems; we're actually in damn good company.

This is the paradoxical magic of service: setting your own worries and selfish bullshit aside, and working instead to solve somebody else's problem, can make you not just pleased with yourself for a minute or two, but deeply satisfied, more capable of joy and personal fulfillment than ever before. You leave the experience of service a changed man who sees a larger world of possibilities. Becoming that kind of man makes life better for everybody.

A man who has developed the skills to serve others is an effective and beloved friend, father, brother, son, and husband. Service is also becoming more and more essential to material success, as technological advancement creates and expands service industries, and many jobs take on a component of service that demands teamwork, loyalty, passionate teachers, and empathetic helpers.

Like any of the centered behaviors, the motivations behind service can be indulged too much. When that happens, you get douchebaggery and imitation—replacing your core identity with your chosen cause. Centered service is not giving it all away and ignoring yourself. Do *not* give it all away. You don't get a cookie for giving up nor for giving your *self* up. Service is the common-sense organization of your priorities. It's a trade. It's a deal. And it's a very good deal if you do it well.

Jed Hits Bottom and Pushes Off

Jed is in a panic. He's talking before he even sits down. "Fuck, David. Scotty and I got arrested in Miami. I got a DUI and had a crashed Bentley impounded. And all we did was stupid fucking shit. I was so messed up. They found coke and molly in the car. And Scotty, of course, that shitbird, made up some shit story and put the whole goddamn mess on my shoulders. He said he had priors. Ain't that something? Fucking priors. Did I really take the fall for that guy? Thought I knew that fuck. Apparently, he's not who I thought he was, that piece of shit. Of course, again, I had to bail everyone's ass out. Goddammit. I was in fucking jail, and they took the boat. I spent two days thinking someone died or fell overboard or something. Thank God that turned out to not be true.

"I was already getting into deep shit at work. I've got to figure something out. Fuck, David. I could lose my job. You can't have an officer crashing Bentleys and facing cocaine charges in Florida. Fuck. I just keep pushing it. Fuck. *Now* what have I done?"

I see fear and terror in Jed's face. "We're going to sort this out. We'll get through this. There's another side, and we'll get there. What are you noticing right now?"

"I notice that I'm about to lose my fucking shit. That's what I notice."

"What else?" I ask.

"I'm just…I'm just…I'm just fucking broken. I'm done. I'm broken."

"What does 'broken' mean?"

"This goddamn Scotty got me into a mess again. I didn't go see my Grandpa this week; I couldn't face him. What have I done now? I couldn't see my Grandpa after that mess, not after what he said the last time I saw him."

"Jed, I want you to stay in this and talk to me, but I'm going to ask that you slow down and try and finish your thoughts. I know you don't like it when I ask you to breathe or pause or do hippy shit. But I'm going to ask you to pause and breathe and do hippy shit anyways. You cool with that?"

My intent here is to get Jed to feel what he's saying. I want him to set his flailing act aside. The douchebag and therapy—not a perfect match. And Jed, in this moment, is a case in point: his entire life centers around not showing up as his true, authentic self, with his true, authentic feelings. In his own twisted logic, he can't tell the difference between what's real and what's the shtick. Jed is in a huge mess, but he's still on the stage. I want Jed to show up for real. That is my intent in slowing him down and asking him to acknowledge what he's feeling now, in this room.

"Yeah. No problem." Jed pauses. When he resumes, he's slower and more deliberate. "My grandpa cares about me. He's the one guy, that old man. He's the only one. He's interested in me, you know? Shit. I could really have used a talk with him, but I didn't go. I can't talk. That's broken as shit. That's me. That's what I mean by broken: I can't do good things because I'm so deep in bad things. I'm broken. I'm so sorry, Grandpa. I'm so sorry."

Jed went to Miami and got popped for all kinds of risky and illicit nonsense. He's about to lose his job and possibly his equity. He's in deep shit. But he's crying because he let his grandfather down.

For the next month, we process. Jed asks to meet multiple times a week. We deal with the arrest, the parties, the betrayal, and his strategy for keeping his job and his equity. There's no pomp. No strut. The douchebaggery is not as appealing when it isn't working. There are layers of regret, guilt, and shame. What we do during this time is simple: we're curious. *How did it come to this?* We explore his party part and what it was trying to prove—or avoid. We dissect the system: Scotty (that fuckhead), the women, the relationships, the cocaine and booze, the money, the rep, and the scenes. We explore it together.

We come back to the competitive kid that McEnroe was *coaching* and trying to protect from feeling like a disappointment. We revisit shame. There's always shame; it's at the core of every person I've ever worked with. At *my* core, too. Shame is a powerful part of us; it makes us feel that we are—that *I* am—inherently bad and deserving of bad things.

"Can you understand the importance of the kid who never got seen and supported for who he *really* was?"

"David, look, I get it. We have to deal with this. And there's this part of me that this kid represents. I fucking get it. Or this part of me that is that kid. I get it. But I just don't get why this matters now. I'm not being a dick or being harsh on your trade or anything. I honor what you do, really. I'm just asking, really, who cares?"

Before I can answer the question, Jed continues. "Okay. Maybe that was a bit much. Seriously though. Who cares? I'm in deep shit here, and you're helping me clean this up. Just knowing that you're in my corner a few times a week is helping me day to day. But the kid thing, the Johnny Mac thing feels like a distraction here."

"Well, for one, I care. That was your question, right? Who cares? The answer is that *I* care. That's one person. And Grandpa Hank. And based on your question, I think you care."

"Yeah, fine. I was sorta prepared for that. Sorta." Jed is more relaxed. He shifts a few times, moving from one side of the couch to the other, and continues. "Even though I don't really get it all, I used to think of that kid and feel sad. I even practiced telling you about that kid." Jed pauses to laugh—at himself. "I practiced it in case I ever had to explain this Johnny Mac thing to you or anyone else again. Can you believe that shit? I practiced answering that question and telling this sad story about this kid and John McEnroe: 'I just want him to be happy, to be a kid, but this maniac Mac is in my ear.' Whatever. I thought I figured it out."

"Of course you practiced explaining that," I answer quickly. "That's awesome. Can you get the relevance of that kid's ride with this high-strung life coach of yours, this Mac guy? Can you be curious about how that shaped so much of your life?"

"You know, I spent my whole life being the family mascot. I was the team mascot. I tried being the company mascot. And then I tried being the mascot on this lifestyle of fucking bullshit. Mac coached me to win, at any cost. To be the fucking man. To never see that disappointed look on my mom's face. Here is what kills me: I did win. I won so damn many times and in so many ways, and they were happy, coach was happy, the investors are happy, at the same time I was also lost. I was winning, but I also felt like I was losing. So, yeah, okay, this other part of me got pushed to play along."

"Exactly. And this kid, or your true self that he represents, wants to speak up now that you're connecting to him. What do you want to know about him? Or maybe you have something you want to say to him."

He tries to laugh it off. He really has practiced his answer to these questions. He laughs at himself again as he realizes his practiced act isn't going to work. He takes a deep breath and smiles.

"My grandpa looked sad when he asked me, 'Where did you go?' This was just before the week that it all went to hell in Miami. You know, for most of my life, as soon as Gramps started to show a little bit of heart, he'd start talking about something else. Getting too close would always trigger a diversion of some kind. He'd change the subject if he thought he'd be caught looking sentimental. You know what I'm saying? Like, he couldn't really show me that he was sad or anything, even when he was very sad. I think that's why him talking to me so directly was so...I don't know, hurtful. Or powerful, or something.

"Anyways, right after that, Grandpa says, 'Jedediah, I was in the Navy, and I saw some crazy shit. I saw all kinds of tattoos—sailors and anchors and tits and "Mom," and all that stuff. I tell you what, though, I never saw a tattoo like yours. It looks like a monkey fucking a sprocket or whatever the hell that is on your arm.' I told him it was steampunk, and we laughed so hard he almost crashed his Buick."

"You and your grandpa have a lot in common, I see."

"The point is, I didn't think Gramps had seen my tattoos, but he had. Even though I tried to hide them. Anyways, I was talking about that kid. Went a bit off the path there."

"You're doing great, Jed."

"I want to say one thing to that kid. One thing. I want to say to him, 'I will show up for real, kid. I will chill the fuck out.' So, two things, I guess."

"Nice. Nice, man. Now what is *he* trying to say? What is it that this kid wants, really? Don't worry about what John McEnroe wants, or your grandpa. What does *he* want?"

"He just wants to be a kid."

"Right. Can you let him do that, finally? Without pushing him aside to be a mascot for the world, or the party champion, or to be John McEnroe's protégé?"

"For sure. Yeah. I think I'm getting this. That's it, though? That? All this, and you just want me to acknowledge that the kid wants to be a kid? That's it?"

This is a good time to just say it straight. "I don't just want you to tell me that the kid wants to be a kid. You're going to acknowledge the kid by staying connected to yourself instead of getting lost in something outside of you. You can be *you*. Got it?"

Jed gets it, at last. He's still afraid no one will like him if he's just himself, and he's afraid he'll fail. As we progress in our work and process, he inches closer and closer to authenticity. We clarify what douchebaggery really is, and how imitation creeps in and gets extreme.

"McEnroe or the party guy might want to come in. If they do, just notice them. Make a point to check in with yourself and be aware of what triggers you or draws you away from what you need. If you start to give a shit about the mascot stuff, be aware of that, get curious, then move back toward your center. Let yourself be real in your world. No more bullshit. This will take some practice."

"Will do. And D, thanks, man. This feels like it's the start of something." With that, he gives me a bro hug.

Jed looks relieved. Nobody would ever choose to be in as much trouble as he's found himself in lately. He wanted to stop the carousel of douchebaggery, but he couldn't, and he didn't, and eventually, the ride came to a tragic end. In truth, he always wanted this, but now he can admit it.

* * *

Jed comes in consistently for more than a year. We use TRACE to work with the kid and with other parts of him as well. He stops doing cocaine and very rarely goes out until the wee hours anymore. He reconnects with his old friends and makes amends. He starts playing the guitar again. We work in depth with the part of him that feels really guilty about what happened in Miami.

Jed shares with me a plan of traveling the world, something his parents would deem indulgent and wasteful. We work with the part of him that wants to travel and be free. We also work with the responsible part of him that wants to stay put, earn more money, hold on to the prestige that comes with his position, and make his parents happy. We make a plan for him to continue beyond our therapy. He joins another group to further his process.

When his company shares vest—which makes his responsible part happy—Jed leaves his job, rents out his place, and plans a trip to Australia. He has no timeline. "I'm going to let that kid play, man. He's made me curious about stuff again. I'm up for whatever he wants to do. No pressure, no responsibilities. I'll swim with sharks and crocodiles or something. Maybe waltz around with simpler swag, who knows? But I'm going."

THEIR NEXT CHAPTER

The characters in Be Less Dickish *are adaptations of real people, real experiences, and real stories. We all interact with these characters every day. They are the men and women you know, and they are you and me.*

A rewarding part of therapy and TRACE is looking back, smiling, laughing, and appreciating ourselves and our lives.

All of Us Are Jonah, George, Jed, and Eric

You may have found yourself cringing at Jonah, George, Jed, and Eric's hurtful behavior. While they may have been repulsive to you in the beginning, I imagine you found them more relatable as you got to know them better. You began to recognize the specific (and rather poignant) causes of their reactionary behavior. They became—or so

I hope—more human. More familiar. They went through trials, and they survived the consequences of their own choices. They changed for the better. It turns out that their extreme reactions were strategies they used to survive and adapt. They acted—as all of us do—on tendencies that they picked up along the way. In these men and in every asshole, pussy, douchebag, and dick, there is also goodness. The degree of goodness may vary, but the core is generally good. People are good. We just spin out, away from our centers, too far and too often. Hopefully, we find our way back.

With each of my clients, there is a process for winding down our work together. The process varies. I prefer that it not be abrupt. In many cases, my clients continue their process in groups where they interact with people who've had similar experiences.

Almost always, there is some reflection about where we've been together. It is their journey, their adventure, but I always enjoy reviewing and debriefing with them.

Steaks, Cigars, and Grandpa's Buick

Jed is fashionably late to the accountability group's spring party. He's handing out Folsom Prison cigars he picked up while crossing the Central Valley in his grandfather's Buick Roadmaster. Gone are the obnoxious strut and the sizing-you-up gaze. He still overdresses. That hasn't changed, and it accurately reflects his real personality.

Eric is tossing horseshoes with a local publisher. His laugh can be heard across the yard. He laughs even more when he sees Jed. "Oh, man. Been a while, Jed. God, I still owe you one for that scene I caused at your douchey-as-hell holiday party."

"No. No. I owe *you* one. Seriously. Here, have a heater." They each fire up them big ol' cigars.

George is absolutely owning the outdoor kitchen—one of his many surprising talents. Blood Orange IPA in one hand, spatula in the other, he flips burgers and pineapple rings with celebrity chef expertise. Jonah's older sons are working the grill with George, cooking and serving Jonah's favorite porterhouse steaks. George is a griller, but Jonah's sons prefer to cook steaks on seasoned cast iron and in a hot-as-hell oven; Jonah taught the boys to "cook steaks the right way, goddammit." They look like mini-Jonahs, they work like big Jonahs, and they play like court jesters as they shuttle steaks for the guests.

The party is steady. The buffet is large. The steaks are hot.

George turns the grill over to the boys. He introduces Kayla to a few people and asks for one of Jed's cigars. The party stays at a level volume as people catch up and check in with each other.

Jonah Needs George; George Needs Jonah

Jonah and his youngest son try to keep an RC car from crashing into guests, the horses, or the pool. Clearly, Jonah has spent no time playing video games or driving RC cars. His patience is...on display. But just as Jonah is about to put an end to this bullshit and denounce RC cars with one of his crude and vulgar rants, he catches himself. He stops, and a smile spreads across his face. "Old habits die hard," he says to no one and everyone, but mostly to himself. "Hey, Super-Z. C'mon, buddy. It's okay, let's focus here...What's our rule about secrets, lil' Z-Man? The secrets rule. Remember that one?"

In a six-year-old child's cadence, Zack repeats, "Don't tell Mom what we got her for Mother's Day, but tell Mom and Dad *everything* else."

"Tell Mom what else?"

"Everything else, Dad. You always ask that."

"Exactly. Exactly. One more thing, though: don't tell your brothers I can't drive this goddamn car. I have no idea how to do this. You know, sometimes even a strong old dad needs a bit of help. Remember when we couldn't find the cereal you like, and we had to ask that kid with the blue vest to help us? Remember that? We gotta ask for some help here, Z-Man."

With a new approach, Jonah helps his son in a way his father could never help Jonah, chipping away at the violence, addiction, and reactive behaviors that have haunted the men in his family for too goddamn long. Here's a man who's been through his own gates of hell and survived. Jonah holds out his scarred hand and takes his son's smooth hand. He picks up the RC car he can't operate, and they look for help. "Remember, Z, don't tell the big boys I can't drive a shitty little car. We got this. Deal?"

The boy smiles. "Dad?"

"What's up, Super-Z? You see someone who can help us?"

"You say a lot of bad words. You're funny, Dad."

"How's it goin', bro?" Jonah hears a deep, awkward voice behind him and turns around to find George, chest puffed out and hand stiffly extended. Jonah gives him a stiff nod in return and fiercely shakes his hand. "Wassup, bitch?" George says. Then they're both laughing and hugging. "What, you weren't buying that as the new me? How about a chest bump?" There follows the most awkward attempt at a chest bump in the history of chest bumps, and they laugh even harder.

George nods his head to the music and tells Jonah that he hopes Kayla is having a good time, even though she's pretty damn pregnant at this point. "You know," says George, leaning in a little closer, smirking, "she didn't want to come…but I insisted."

"Nice work, George. Congrats, you giant stud." Jonah is genuinely happy for his friend.

This guy. This George guy. He is loved. He would do anything for anybody, for any reason. The relaxed version of George is damn refreshing for everyone around him.

Jonah's black T-shirt is smeared with a dollop of what George confirms—with some relief—is ketchup, not blood. "Yeah, fuck you," Jonah says, pushing George lovingly on the shoulder. "I went to therapy, and yeah, I got my shit together, which I needed to do." The smile never leaves his face, and the vibes from people around him suggest that he isn't so scary anymore, but still, Jonah is a presence. It's probably best not to cross this guy.

"Yeah, remember how you scared me when you came to the bank? I thought you needed anger management or something. That's why *I* gave *you* David Coates's name and number. Remember that?" With occasional embellishments, George repeats this story every time the men see each other.

"Well, George, you were too damn nice. And that's why *I* gave *you* David's number." Jonah repeats variations of this anecdote every time the two men see each other. This version is closer to the truth.

"You know what, though, Mr. Banker Man George," Jonah says, "I still have to ACE my shit all the time. I can't be slippin', as my sons say. I'm still scared, especially for my kids, but I think we're going to be okay." He takes a step toward George. "Hey, man. Can I ask you for something?" His face is serious.

George is prepared to drive an RC car. "Yeah. Sure."

"I'm doing well lately, not drinking or anything. But I'm not sticking to this meeting schedule thing, the program stuff. You know how I am, right? But if the alcoholism and asshole-ism are about to kick my fucking ass again, would you mind being on my short list of people I can call? Anyway, it's cool, you know. Just…"

Have you ever met a powerful man? Real power, surging power. Stand with a scarred, long-haired man who methodically aligned his support team, quit drinking on his father's birthday, owns it, and lives to ask that question while holding his child's hand in his.

"For all my life, Jonah. For all my life. Yes." George answers without any hesitation.

Each of them nods. Enough said about that. They have both crawled back from some dark places. They understand that they might need each other. They understand that they can help each other.

The Asshole's Gift

When he's *our* guy, the asshole is *the* guy. When he's on watch, his conviction makes others feel safe, free to be themselves. He is armor for those of us who don't have the same mental or physical stature.

What the hell do we gain by being selfish and shameless? A hell of a lot. Being an aggressive, extreme asshole is obviously problematic, but being driven sometimes to do things your own way, for yourself, without crippling concern for everyone's opinions…that's a damn good thing. More of that, please.

A world full of assholes? Oh, hell no. Nobody wants that. A world without any self-interested singlemindedness, however, would be equally awful. Assertive men are leaders, defenders, and protectors with the focused vision to drive innovation and progress. In entrepreneurs, assertiveness is the backbone of invention and leadership.

You can be selfish and shameless without being threatening and aggressive. You can be the tough guy on the pitch or on the gridiron. Being unflappable at work may be an opportunistic way to get ahead, but let that shit go at the end of the game. Putting up a tough front has a place, but it sure as hell isn't appropriate everywhere.

A balanced, fair, and assertive life is the adventure that others want to enjoy. With humility, you will enjoy the company on this ride.

The Pussy's Gift

Being selfless and having an acute awareness of others is a heavy burden. It takes immense strength to give more than you get, which is what pussies often do. The opposite of "like a pussy" is *not* "like a man." Fuck that. The ubiquitous "man up" bullshit has got to end. If anything, we need to "man *in*." "Manning *in*" requires us to own our shit, surrendering to reality not with disgust, but with boldness. This includes our vulnerability. We have to quit propagating the idea that a real man is a solid, unmovable thing.

The gift of this orientation is the profound generosity to make the experience of others a priority and to do so sincerely. A centered man in this quadrant, one who surrenders to reality in a reasonable way instead of reflexively submitting to everything, is able to make choices with concern for others and for the facts. He is humble, not debased; he is adaptable, not passive-aggressive. He is a peacemaker, a real peacemaker, with a gift for harmonizing perspectives and finding the common ground. We certainly need more of that. We need people who engage with reality, and who contribute, without asking for power or pity.

We are capable of getting along with others because we use tools from the pussy's quadrant—we have learned to see the world from other perspectives, to find common ground when disagreements arise, and to meet the needs of others while keeping things fair for everybody. Without selfless and conscientious people, humanity would be isolated and hopeless. Selfless and conscientious men make a place at life's table for everybody; we need more of that!

Eric Beats Jed

Jed has gifts for us, too—and not just those Folsom Prison cigars. "What is *up*, dude?" he asks, approaching Eric again at the party. "Did you see that woman I walked in with? Man, so fucking hot." Jed starts laughing as Eric rolls his eyes—both of them arrived alone. "I can't even get a date these days. I thought my Grandpa's big sexy car would be a babe-catching buggy; that's not working out at all."

"Jed, you're the motherfuckin' *man*," Eric says sarcastically. "I thought you went walkabout in Australia. I heard you walked away from the game and now you're killing it in this whole self-discovery deal. You're the next Tony Robbins. You should start a podcast. Think of all the money you could make if that took off."

Jed's eyes get big for a moment. "Fucking genius," he says. "I could call it *The Douchebag Diaries.* No, hang on. We're kicking the douchebags out, right? We gotta do this. Let's do this. You're a writer. You can help me with this. C'mon. How about *The Douchebag Dystopia?*"

"No, Jed. *We* are not doing this. Plus, I don't recommend using titles or words that could offend anyone."

"Hey, man, how's that kid doing, the one you would write with in the city?" Jed asks.

"Gabe? I love that kid," Eric responds. "I catch up with him from time to time, but not as much as I used to. But yeah, remember 826 Valencia over there in your hipster neighborhood? Eggers threw us out of the store for stealing the pirate treasures."

"That's awesome. It's about time you broke some laws and got arrested. We need more mischief, not less. Thanks for doing your part." Jed says. "Maybe you have some empathy for the rest of us outlaws now."

Laughter is their shared medicine, or therapy. They both need it. They both need each other. The douchebag needs to reach and figure out how to care for his real self, finally. And the dick needs to figure out how not to make everything about himself. These dudes have a lot to offer each other.

Eric has a *real* deadline—not an excuse to leave the party, not an arbitrary deadline. He's under contract now, typical of the many ways the universe starts working in our favor when we open up to it. His work is interesting, finally. And he's interested, finally. He's less dickish, finally. But he sets the deadline aside and stays at the ranch to beat Jed's ass in a game of horseshoes. Take that, John McEnroe. Your guy just lost to a dick.

The Douchebag's Gift

Lighten the fuck up. Don't take everything so seriously—especially not yourself. Laughing at life and letting others laugh with you is the fun and rowdy gift of the service-oriented man. Thanks, Jed.

There is deep and abiding satisfaction in serving others. At his extreme, the douchebag destroys his authentic self. When centered, men in this orientation make the world go 'round. They embody loyalty. They give, they serve, they work. They show up on time and they do it for years and decades. They are the foundation of companies, agencies, and large forces. Most importantly, selfless people who serve others are the foundation and infrastructure of families and relationships. We rely on the folks that look out for us, and they do so without a lot of drama and worries. They arrive for the fight with all their guts and conviction, always in your corner. Oh, fuck yes! We like that.

And goddamn, have a little fun, for hell's sake. This is the orientation for good times. These dudes use creativity to their advantage. They experiment, explore, and discover new and cool shit about the world and themselves—which is a huge gift to us. Their shamelessness illuminates and supports what matters to them. They bring richness and joy into the lives that are lucky enough to warrant their attention. When they are centered, they are not dependent upon the approval of others. At ease, they don't get swept up in the hype, bullshit, gallery comments, and fear. A selfless and shameless man is a free man. To a free man, life is a process of self-discovery and service to worthy causes.

Their loyalty means selfless dedication and commitment. They see that you need something; they get a charge out of doing it for you, or with you. We rely on the work and service of others every day. Hard-working, dedicated people don't make excuses or worry too much. We are blessed to have service-oriented people around us. When someone is selflessly dedicated to a good cause, others will be loyal.

When we are genuinely grateful, we can enjoy the service we receive. Being helpful is a liberating and happy state.

Unchain yourself from what you, or others, *think* you are supposed to be, and get busy being authentic and helpful. Just do it—do it for the other guy, do it for her, do it for the family, do it for the cause. Do it shamelessly and joyfully. Thanks in advance! I am grateful for who you are, and what you do. More of that too, please.

The Dick's Gift

You are a unique individual, and you're also part of something larger; both you and the larger system matter. And here's the gift of the dick: *he gets it.* He knows he matters and also that systems matter; and he cares for himself and others accordingly. When a dick is committed to his own personal mission, talents, and responsibilities, good things happen.

There are a lot of good dudes who can see the complexities of our big, huge world without losing their individuality. A man with a deep appreciation for both his own self-interest and the importance of human relationships can readily gain practical insights into society—insights that motivate the world to change for the better. A selfish and con-scientious man reminds us that individuals matter, and he shows us how communities are getting that right or wrong. He speaks truth to power. He cares about being seen and heard for who he really is. He will not be left behind; he will not be lost in the crowd.

Great movements in human history have been sparked, and even led, by caring individuals with a selfish sense of personal destiny.

There's a source of keen intelligence inside of you, in your gut, that just *knows.* The dick's intuition—when he is not being a spun-out, pet-ulant, whining, and victimized pain in the ass—is awesome. When a selfish and conscientious man is operating from his center and taking good care of himself, his wisdom is accessible.

Think about your mom, or your friends' moms. Moms know things.

They know shit about you before *you* know it. I'm not suggesting that moms have superpowers. I am suggesting that some self-care and self-knowledge goes a long way in understanding how the world, or a family, works. A man who cares for himself and is aware of others can have a similar intuition and make his environment a better place.

It comes down to this: dicks care.

This book is called *Be Less Dickish*. Why? Because its central message is that when you're not being a dick, you are cooler and greater than when you *are* being a dick. And because when you take care of yourself, the world (specifically *your* world) is pleasant. Being less assholish, or less of a pussy or douchebag, is equally rewarding.

We want to be part of a good man's life. I want you to be that good man. I want you to love that good man. I want him to love you. I'm talking about *love*, knuckleheads. Jesus was talking about love. The Beatles said that love is all you need. Let go of control and let life and love touch you. Being an untouchable dick? That's yesterday's dull-ass game.

Cynthia Arrives

Cynthia arrives at the ranch in her shiny, black King Ranch F-250. Of everyone, she had the longest drive to get here. Is that a metaphor? Yes. And no. When she opens the door of her truck, Cody Jinks blares louder than the party music. She is wearing the same boots her sister gave her years ago. The leather has been repaired. She's attached to these boots and their new "souls." Cynthia steps up to the counter and taps her new rings to get the two boys' attention.

"Sorry, ma'am. My big brother wasn't paying attention. How can *I* help you?"

"Right. This ain't my first rodeo, boys. How did you two end up behind the counter?"

"Well, our dad made us do it. Well, he *asked* us to do it. Well, he said if we did it, we could meet, you know, *people*."

"Meet girls?" Cynthia knows boys are never as clever as they think.

"How do you like...well, I mean, we can get you, uh...steaks, or if you want a steak or something, how would you, um, like that?"

"Well done. That's a compliment, boys. But I would *also* like a petite steak well done. A princess steak, well done."

The boys take one of the prepared steaks and put it back in the oven to cook it some more.

"Thanks. Hey, I think I know—the smiles and the eyes give it away— but tell me anyways: Who's your dad?"

"The guy with the tall hat. The one wearing the awesome sunglasses with glitter and guns. The one with the little kid. He still can't drive that RC car worth a damn. That guy. Here's your plate, ma'am."

"I knew it. You're *Jonah's* boys. I didn't even need to ask. Nice to finally meet you. I've known Jonah most of my life; you look just like him," she says with a smile, taking the plate.

She joins a small gathering. Within the group, there are four guys she knows well. Four guys we all know well. "Glad you guys made it here." She pauses for a moment. She has the attention of the group. "Most men don't make it," she says. "Most don't. And what a goddamn shame that is."

Be Less Dickish

TRACE, the archetype model, and the description of these four guys living out on the perimeter are all rolled into one book for a simple purpose: to invite you to get on with a real and fulfilling life. You are cordially invited to get on with the show. Get busy living.

Let's not spin out into hurtful assholes, oblivious douchebags, self-righteous dicks, or meek pussies. Let's not be spun out *by* them, either. Stop trying to force life into submission, or kowtow to it, or shit on it, or con it. Stop playing the victim. So much more is possible. I'm not telling you anything you don't already know; I'm just trying to nudge you toward *living* this knowledge. Not tomorrow, not next year, not when you have two hundred thousand dollars in Bitcoin. Now.

A centered man is a steady man. Other people will be fickle—they may not like your social media posts, they may show up late in your hour of need, they may lie to you, or they may forget you altogether—but you can be steady for yourself, regardless. When you have *you*, other people get to be the fallible, disappointing human beings they sometimes are, and you can cut them some slack. And trust me when I say this: they will love you all the more for it and be better friends and partners as a result. It's what they've always wanted from you—to be accepted.

You will find that steady, centered version of you by mastering TRACE. On our life's journey, we've all left cherished parts of ourselves behind and carried other parts too far. TRACE is an opportunity to explore, experiment, and choose the right parts for the road we're on today.

We don't have to be triggered into aggression, submission, imitation, or victimhood; we can do better, and we must do better, for ourselves and for others. It takes work and practice. It takes intention. It takes the cultivation of assertion, surrender, self-care, and service. Now that you have a method for returning to your good, centered self, I invite you to be less dickish. I dare you.

AFTERWORD

by David Coates

I started this project ten years ago. Ten. But me and the asshole, the pussy, the dick, and the douchebag go way, way back. I've got the scars to prove it. I bet you do too.

Profanity fascinates me. When wielded well, it cuts through the niceties and the bullshit. I also love the right word used in the right context. There are times when "asshole" is the perfect—perhaps the only—word to describe a guy, and so arose the question: Why is this guy an asshole, and not a dick or a bastard?

As a clinician, I regularly heard "pussy," "dick," "asshole," and "douchebag" from my clients. I paid attention. I stayed curious. I was fascinated by the intuitive but somewhat undefined distinctions between them. I wanted to make the words meaningful and useful in helping men. So I began researching and writing.

I pulled friends together to discuss the subtle differences between these labels: Is ghosting, for example, a dick move, or an asshole move? Is this guy being a pussy, or a bitch? How is a fucker different from a prick? I would read a short anecdote and ask friends, "So, what would you call this guy, and why?" It was powerful for all involved, and it was useful. These discussions helped us to understand men better. Shit got real. We also laughed hysterically.

In the beginning, there were sixteen kinds of guys. Besides the archetypes you've read about, there was a douche (yes, there was a douche *and* a douchebag), a fucker, a dickwad, a dickhead, a nerd, a jerk, a prick, a bitch, an asshat, a dork, a jackass, and a shithead. These characters were eventually simplified, consolidated, or eliminated.

In the years I was writing *Be Less Dickish*, Corey Kilpack was a client in my psychotherapy practice. He inspired me and challenged me, and he wrote to me from his own gates of hell. Writing for himself and to a few trusted friends was the way he moved through his therapy process and his life. It was an expression of his inner world, past and present. His style was authentic and raw—packed with profanity and not bound by grammar rules or punctuation. It was chaotic, but coherent at the same time, unlike anything I had read before. Pure guts, in both senses of the word. I was moved. I was enthralled. I love him. I trust him, and I trust his bold process.

* * *

In early 2019, I thought *Be Less Dickish* was nearly complete. In reality, the book was stuck. I needed help. The model was not fully developed, and the damned thing lacked clarity and a solid story arc. I found myself thinking about Corey. It had been four years since our work together ended, and we had kept occasional contact through email. His writing style fit perfectly with what I had started. He and his wife Kellee printed out my bloated manuscript and read it aloud to each other on a road trip, and they not only got what I was trying to do, they saw what it needed to become.

"So, what's the difference between a dick and an asshole?" Corey asked after finishing his first read-through. I gave an answer, but it wasn't convincing. His point was well made. "This all has to be definable and defensible," he said. "As it is right now, you're going to get killed if you put this out there." He was right. When writing about men, especially men in the wild and men unhinged, it has to be solid. Structure is not my strength. I like possibility and exploration.

Corey brought the ground game. He extracted and developed the detailed model, and he made the dialogue more personal. Characters and concepts were developed and brought to huge, real life. We argued, we laughed, and we cut. We were devastated to chop some of the characters. We loved those guys.

"You know, Dave," Corey said, "you were watching me all of those years, but I was also watching you." Whoa. Right. Our clinical work was about him—so obviously, I had my eyes on him—but he was also watching *me*. With this in mind, we dove back into the therapy sessions portrayed in the book, adding Corey's own insight as the client working with me as the therapist.

Kellee Kilpack was intimately involved in the development of the characters in *Be Less Dickish*. She and Corey had been high school sweethearts, but Kellee had one hell of a journey before they reunited and married thirty-one years later. We added the piece of shit. It took some time—and some patience from Kellee and Corey—before I understood his prevalence as a personality type and his place in the perimeter of the model.

Being a psychotherapist was a solo job, and I hadn't realized how isolated I felt at times in that profession. Collaboration was damn hard after so much independent work and writing, but it was right. Partnering has been profound, and it helped complete this book.

Corey and I did it our own way as therapist and client, and we did it our own way as coauthors. This book got the best of both of us. And we had Kellee with us along the way, making sure we got it right.

Nathan Jensen joined the process close to the end of production. He has been a valuable link in the illustration of the archetype model. He made the graphics and worked closely with us to describe the archetype elements.

I hope *Be Less Dickish* shakes you up and gets you curious about yourself. I hope you recognize these characters in the people around you, including partners, parents, children, and all the people you love. Over the course of writing, we guessed the archetypes of friends, family, and public figures. I hope you continue to have fun with the archetype model. I hope you figure out which archetype describes you, particularly when you're triggered.

I hope you are now more interested in your own experience. I hope you move toward your center. I hope you make sense of your own behavior. I hope you laugh.

I hope you use TRACE and ACE your shit.

I hope *Be Less Dickish* makes many days better for many people, and particularly for you.

Thanks for coming on the ride with us.

ACKNOWLEDGMENTS

Kellee Kilpack
Thank you, thank you, thank you.
Thanks for coming to the party. We needed you.

Nathan Jensen
Thank you for the graphics, content, and counsel. Your insight and wisdom clarified the archetype model.

Gestalt Theory and Internal Family Systems
You are the greatest influence on my work as a clinician. Your influence was prominent in my private practice and in the book's therapy sessions.

Robyn Russell, Working Title Editorial
You believed in this batshit crazy idea.

Scot Hill, Brit Estep, Ezra Johnson, Rick Smith, Daniel Rechtschaffen, David Treleaven, Steve Seto, David and Lani Yadegar, Leslie McClurg, Emily Fasten, Britt Barrett, Shereef Bishay, Govinda Bader, Julie Wilson, Kat Conour, Kent Sorsky, Mattie Bamman, Kristen Kearns, Wes Rosacker, David Clausen, David Q. Kelly, Andrew and Elaine Lawry, Barry and Mary Jane Rhein, Jessica Theroux, Emily Drabek, Alex Beard, and Sheldon "is that your shitbox" Kilpack
Thank you.

Made in the USA
Columbia, SC
09 July 2021

41606310R10157